Joseph Conrad's
Heart of Darkness

D1147473

Jos⋯ ⋯⋯⋯d's novella, *Heart of Darkness*, has fascinated critics and readers alik⋯ ⋯⋯⋯g them in highly controversial debate as it deals with fundamental issu⋯ ⋯⋯ and evil, civilisation, race, love and heroism. This classic tale tran⋯ ⋯⋯ boundaries of time and place and has inspired famous film and telev⋯ ⋯tations emphasising the cultural significance and continued relev⋯ book.

T⋯ Conrad's captivating novel offers:

* ⋯le introduction to the text and contexts of *Heart of Darkness*;
* ⋯istory, surveying the many interpretations of the text from publi-⋯⋯e present;
* ⋯ of new essays and reprinted critical essays on *Heart of Darkness*, ⋯att, Linda Dryden, Ruth Nadelhaft, J. Hillis Miller and Peter ⋯roviding a range of perspectives on the novel and extending the ⋯f key critical approaches identified in the survey section;
* ⋯rences between sections of the guide, in order to suggest links ⋯texts, contexts and criticism;
* su⋯⋯ns for further reading.

Part of ⋯⋯utledge Guides to Literature series, this volume is essential reading for all tho⋯ beginning detailed study of *Heart of Darkness* and seeking not only a guide to ⋯ novel, but a way through the wealth of contextual and critical material that surrounds Conrad's text.

D.C.R.A. Goonetilleke is Emeritus Professor of English at the University of Kelaniya, Sri Lanka. He is a well-established and recognized critic of twentieth century and post-colonial literature and his books include *Developing Countries in British Fiction*, *Images of the Raj*, *Joseph Conrad: Beyond Culture* and *Salman Rushdie*.

Routledge Guides to Literature

Editorial Advisory Board: Richard Bradford (University of Ulster at Coleraine), Shirley Chew (University of Leeds), Mick Gidley (University of Leeds), Jan Jedrzejewski (University of Ulster at Coleraine), Ed Larrissy (University of Leeds), Duncan Wu (St. Catherine's College, University of Oxford)

Routledge Guides to Literature offer clear introductions to the most widely studied authors and texts.

Each book engages with texts, contexts and criticism, highlighting the range of critical views and contextual factors that need to be taken into consideration in advanced studies of literary works. The series encourages informed but independent readings of texts by ranging as widely as possible across the contextual and critical issues relevant to the works examined, rather than presenting a single interpretation. Alongside general guides to texts and authors, the series includes 'Sourcebooks', which allow access to reprinted contextual and critical materials as well as annotated extracts of primary text.

Already available:*

Geoffrey Chaucer by Gillian Rudd
Ben Jonson by James Loxley
William Shakespeare's The Merchant of Venice: A Sourcebook edited by S. P. Cerasano
William Shakespeare's King Lear: A Sourcebook edited by Grace Ioppolo
William Shakespeare's Othello: A Sourcebook edited by Andrew Hadfield
William Shakespeare's Macbeth: A Sourcebook edited by Alexander Leggatt
William Shakespeare's Hamlet: A Sourcebook edited by Sean McEvoy
William Shakespeare's Twelfth Night: A Sourcebook edited by Sonia Massai
John Milton by Richard Bradford
John Milton's Paradise Lost: A Sourcebook edited by Margaret Kean
Alexander Pope by Paul Baines
Jonathan Swift's Gulliver's Travels: A Sourcebook edited by Roger D. Lund
Mary Wollstonecraft's A Vindication of the Rights of Woman: A Sourcebook edited by Adriana Craciun
Jane Austen by Robert P. Irvine
Jane Austen's Emma: A Sourcebook edited by Paula Byrne
Jane Austen's Pride and Prejudice: A Sourcebook edited by Robert Morrison
Byron, by Caroline Franklin
Mary Shelley's Frankenstein: A Sourcebook edited by Timothy Morton
The Poems of John Keats: A Sourcebook edited by John Strachan
The Poems of Gerard Manley Hopkins: A Sourcebook Edited by Alice Jenkins
Charles Dickens's David Copperfield: A Sourcebook edited by Richard J. Dunn
Charles Dickens's Bleak House: A Sourcebook edited by Janice M. Allan

* Some titles in this series were first published in the Routledge Literary Sourcebooks series, edited by Duncan Wu, or the Complete Critical Guide to Literature series, edited by Jan Jedrzejewski and Richard Bradford.

Joseph Conrad's
Heart of Darkness

D.C.R.A. Goonetilleke

Routledge
Taylor & Francis Group

LONDON AND NEW YORK

First published 2007
by Routledge
2 Park Square, Milton Park, Abingdon, Oxon OX14 4RN

Simultaneously published in the USA and Canada
by Routledge
270 Madison Ave, New York, NY 10016

Routledge is an imprint of the Taylor & Francis Group, an informa business

© 2007 D.C.R.A. Goonetilleke

Typeset in Sabon and Gill Sans by
RefineCatch Limited, Bungay, Suffolk
Printed and bound in Great Britain by
Antony Rowe Ltd, Chippenham, Wiltshire

British Library Cataloguing in Publication Data
A catalogue record for this book is available from the British Library.

Library of Congress Cataloging in Publication Data
Goonetilleke, D. C. R. A.
Joseph Conrad's heart of darkness / D.C.R.A. Goonetilleke.
    p. cm. — (Routledge guides to literature)
    Includes bibliographical references and index.
    1. Conrad, Joseph, 1857–1924. Heart of darkness. 2. Psychological fiction,
English—History and criticism. 3. Africa—In literature. I. Title.
    PR6005.O4H4766 2007
    823'.912—dc22

                                                            2007011782

ISBN 10: 0–415–35775–6 (hbk)
ISBN 10: 0–415–35776–4 (pbk)
ISBN 10: 0–203–00378–0 (ebk)

ISBN 13: 978–0–415–35775–3 (hbk)
ISBN 13: 978–0–415–35776–0 (pbk)
ISBN 13: 978–0–203–00378–7 (ebk)

Contents

Acknowledgements

The publisher and author would like to thank the following for permission to reprint material under copyright:

From 'Reading for the Plot' by Peter Brooks, copyright © 1984 by Peter Brooks. Used by permission of Alfred A. Knopf, a division of Random House inc.

Ian Watt, '*Heart of Darkness* and Nineteenth-Century Thought', *Partisan Review* 45, No. 1, 1978 reproduced by kind permission of Josephine Watt.

Tropes, Parables and Performatives: Essays on Twentieth Century Literature, J. Hillis Miller, Pearson Education Limited

Every effort has been made to trace and contact copyright holders. The publishers would be pleased to hear from any copyright holders not acknowledged here, so that this acknowledgement page may be amended at the earliest opportunity.

For invaluable assistance in preparing this book, I wish to thank my wife Chinchi, Dr Lakshmi de Silva, L.A. Jayatissa, Librarian of the University of Kelaniya, and Nirmali Amarasiri, Information Resource Coordinator of the American Center Library, Colombo.

Notes and references

Primary text

Unless otherwise stated, all references to the primary text are taken from D.C.R.A. Goonetilleke (ed.), *Heart of Darkness, Joseph Conrad*, Peterborough, Ontario, Canada & New York: Broadview Press, 2nd edition 1999, reprinted 2003.

The initial reference in each part will contain full bibliographic details and all subsequent references will be in parentheses in the body of the text, stating the chapter, page number and part number, e.g (Ch. I, p. 45). The chapter number is provided to help anyone reading an edition of the novel that differs from this one.

Secondary text

References to any secondary material can be found in the footnotes. The first reference will contain full bibliographic details, and each subsequent reference to the same text will contain the author's surname, title and page number.

Footnotes

All footnotes that are not by the author of this volume will identify the source in square brackets, e.g. [Dryden's note].

Cross-referencing

Cross-referencing between sections is a feature of each volume in the Routledge Guides to Literature series. Cross-references appear in brackets and include section titles as well as the relevant page numbers in bold type, e.g (see Texts and contexts, **pp. 00–00**).

Abbreviations

The following abbreviations are used:
G:HD – D.C.R.A. Goonetilleke (ed.), *Heart of Darkness, Joseph Conrad,*

Peterborough, Ontario, Canada & New York: Broadview Press, 2nd edition 1999, reprinted 2003.
  UP – University Press
  NY – New York

Introduction

The story of Marlow travelling upriver in central Africa to find Kurtz, an ivory agent as consumed by the horror of life as he is by physical illness, is an important part of the Western canon. It is the twentieth-century literature classic most widely read by students and general readers. It expresses the essence of the writer. It was a favourite of Conrad; he called it 'my pet Heart of Darkness'.[1]

The novella was begun in December 1898 and completed by early February 1899. Written with extraordinary rapidity, the story developed in the writing. It had an obsessive power on the writer, as it now has on the reader. Yet a comparison of the manuscript with the final version shows careful revision (pp. 59, 242–7).[2] It appeared in the February, March and April issues of *Blackwood's Edinburgh Magazine* in 1899 as *The Heart of Darkness*. It was issued in book form in November 1902 in *Youth and Other Stories* without the article in the title. The presence of 'The' in the title in the magazine version suggests that it operates on the level of a popular, exotic adventure story at a time when the Congo was a sure-fire seller subject.[3] In a letter to Edward Garnett at the time he was writing *Heart of Darkness*, Conrad mentions 'a short story for B'wood which I must get out for the sake of the shekels'.[4] The factors that led to its writing included financial pressures. The absence of the article in the title of the book version intimates a serious narrative with a wide application. The notion of parallel narratives (and infinite interpretations), depending on the capacity of the reader, originates in Nietzsche (see Text and contexts, **p. 14**). He wrote: 'Ultimately, no one can extract from things, books included, more than he already knows. What one has no access to through experience one has no ear for.'[5]

1   Conrad, letter to Elsie Hueffer, 3 December 1902, in *The Collected Letters of Joseph Conrad: Vol.II 1898–1902*, ed. Frederick R. Karl & Laurence Davies, Cambridge: Cambridge UP, 1986, p. 460; *G:HD*, p. 170.
2   D.C.R.A. Goonetilleke (ed.), *Heart of Darkness, Joseph Conrad*, Peterborough, Ontario, Canada & New York: Broadview Press, 2nd edition 1999, reprinted 2003. Unless otherwise stated, all subsequent quotations from this novel are drawn from the same edition. Subsequent references will appear in the body text, taking the form of a chapter title and page number in parentheses.
3   H.M. Stanley's *How I Found Livingstone, Through the Dark Continent, The Congo and the Founding of a Free State* and *In Darkest Africa* sold an aggregate of over one hundred thousand copies in England and, probably, a much larger number in America. See *G:HD*, pp. 206–7.
4   Conrad, letter to Garnett, 18 December 1898, in *Collected Letters II*, p. 132.
5   Friedrich Nietzsche, trans. R.J. Hollingdale, *Ecce Homo: How One Becomes What One Is*, London: Penguin, 1992 edn, p. 40.

This book addresses the literary issues intrinsic to the novella as well as the cultural, political and historical issues that pertained to 1900 and continue to affect us. Imperialism, which is the context and an important part of the themes of *Heart of Darkness*, is arguably the major historical phenomenon that has shaped the modern world. The arguments I set out for the relevance of contexts to the literary study are of utmost relevance to readers today trying to understand a work as complex and controversial as *Heart of Darkness* is. This book brings together a rich array of biographical, literary, cultural and historical contexts and, at the same time, treats coherently of the novella's cruxes – its apparently irreconcilable antagonisms. These have given rise to a diversity of fertile, seemingly inexhaustible discussion, which can be sampled through the inclusion of five essays by other hands and also as encapsulated in the chapter on critical history. The impact of the novella on other media is discussed, especially the films available on videotape/DVD. The fact that *Heart of Darkness* has so engaged the creative energies of a number of contemporary film-makers and that the title has become part of common usage, particularly in news reportage, confirms that Conrad's imagination, fuelled by his age, goes beyond his period to mesh with the concerns and anxieties of ours.

1

Text and contexts

The author

The traditional image of Joseph Conrad, partly encouraged by Conrad himself, was of a 'homo duplex', of dual Polish and English affinities. Later critics have argued for a tri-lingual and tri-cultural identity, stressing the French influences on Conrad. Some of his formative years (1874–78) were spent in Marseilles. France bulked particularly large in Conrad's lifetime as a fount of the arts, whether of painting or letters, and its influence would naturally be felt by a writer such as Conrad with his continental links and knowledge of French. It has long been recognized, for instance, that Conrad's rigorously economical and highly wrought style and his tight and complex construction have antecedents in Flaubert and Maupassant. Detachment or 'objectivity', the essence of Conrad's technique, became important to novelists after Flaubert. However, too strong an emphasis has now been placed on the French influence, while the dual identity and triple identity theses are neat but inadequate. A richer understanding would result if attention is called to the importance of Conrad's sea-going experiences from 1874 to 1893, almost the whole of his working life, which, taking off from France, brought him into contact with the Caribbean, South-East Asia, Australia and Africa, and instilled a sense of respect for other cultures and an awareness that ways of life other than the European were as right as the European. In his 1895 'Author's Note' to *Almayer's Folly* (the manuscript he was working on during his Congo journey), he countered the censure that his tales were 'decivilized' because of their portrayal of 'strange people' and 'far-off countries'. In an ironic, comic tone, making no apology for depicting 'honest cannibals', Conrad concludes:

> I am content to sympathize with common mortals, no matter where they live; in houses or in tents, in the streets under a fog, or in the forests behind the dark line of dismal mangroves that fringe the vast solitude of the sea.[1]

---

1   Conrad, 'Author's Note', in *Almayer's Folly and Tales of Unrest*, London: Dent, 1947 edn, p. viii. ∎

These non-European cultures too exerted a strong influence on him and contributed significantly to fashioning his sensibility. I would suggest that Conrad possesses a multiple identity that is the result of the influence of all the cultures he encountered. Indeed, his is a more complex version of the 'identity at once partial and plural'[2] which Salman Rushdie saw as characteristic of the immigrant. Such a personality, in the 'real world' – in society as well as in personal and even domestic relations – may experience alienation, self-consciousness and strains, as Conrad did in his adopted country, England, where he married an English wife, Jessie George. But it is also an artistically enabling experience, which permits access to many worlds. While he was from one perspective déraciné, rootless or uprooted, from another Conrad was many-rooted, drawing sustenance from several cultures. He was a migrant writer long before the term became fashionable, and arguably one of the first of that kind.

Conrad's life has been, roughly, divided into three phases – as a Pole (1857–73), as a seaman (1874–93) and as a writer (1894–1924). In 1795, Poland was partitioned among three neighbouring powers, Russia, Austria-Hungary and Prussia (Germany), and disappeared as a nation till 1918, a period of 123 years that included almost the whole of Conrad's life. He was born in the Ukraine, a part of Poland annexed by Russia, said to be the worst of the oppressors. He was the only child of Ewa (née Bobrowska) and Apollo Korzeniowski. Nationalism was a prominent part of Conrad's class (the gentry, the most important section of Polish society, which, with the landed nobility, formed the sole ruling class, the *szlachta*) and family tradition. The Korzeniowskis were 'Reds' or 'activists', while the Bobrowskis were generally 'Whites' or 'appeasers'. In 1861, Apollo was arrested for anti-Russian activity and exiled, with Ewa and Conrad, to Vologda, 300 miles north-east of Moscow. The parents suffered hardship, illness and finally death because of their political ideals. Conrad's uncle, Stefan Bobrowski, one of the leaders of the January 1863 uprising, also sacrificed his life. His uncle and guardian, Tadeusz Bobrowski, was also dedicated to duty, but favoured compromise. The roots of Conrad's extraordinarily humane and critical responses to various imperial systems and realities can be traced, in part, to his Polish origins. It was not only his political heritage that is important; his paternal literary heritage, like V.S. Naipaul's, is equally so. Apollo knew four languages, English, French, German and Russian, in addition to his mother tongue, and was a poet, playwright and translator (he translated Shakespeare and Dickens). That he was a translator is important because this exposure of Conrad as a child to his father's habit of seeking for precise words and making fine adjustments between cultures, may have sensitized him to the possibilities and limits of language. Conrad's reading of Shakespeare and the great Polish Romantic poets, Adam Mickiewicz (1798–1855), Julius Slowacki (1809–49) and Sygmunt Krasinski (1812–59), the most powerful of his Polish literary influences, would have seeped into him and contributed to the sonority of his prose and the poetic side of his novelistic talent. Almost certainly, it would have sharpened his sense of the moral and public

2   Rushdie, 'Imaginary Homelands' (1982), in *Imaginary Homelands: Essays in Criticism 1981–91*, London & Delhi: Granta & Penguin India, 1991, p. 15.

function of art. The mythical significance of his father's name – Apollo was the Greek god of poetry – would have not been lost on the son.

The link between the restless literary mind and the sea, first celebrated in England by the Romantics, and the role of books (by the age of thirteen, Conrad recalls, he was 'addicted' to 'map-gazing'), probably motivated Conrad to go to sea in 1874 – his chosen avenue of escape from service in the Russian army. He sailed on French imperial business in the French Mercantile Service out of Marseilles, where he also engaged in conspiratorial conversations – and, perhaps, activities – in support of the Carlists in Spain. In 1878 he joined the British Merchant Service. The British Service gave the feckless orphan abroad a sort of niche, inculcated a work ethic and provided valuable experiences which he later transmuted into fiction. But as 'a Polish nobleman, cased in British tar',[3] there was a wide gulf between him and his fellow seamen. But while the Service could not satisfy his cultural needs, his choice of Marlow as a narrator is a tribute to the Service. These formative years, then, gave Conrad knowledge of a variety of imperial systems and sea adventures at first-hand.

During this period, when Conrad was in search of employment, the possibility arose of working in Africa. He may have accepted the job in the absence of a better alternative, though it was more remunerative than a command at sea. Moreover, his boyhood enthusiasm for Africa (as an instance of the 'faraway') is likely to have been rekindled by the current interest (and greed) excited by Africa, and fanned by Henry Morton Stanley's sensational exploits in discovering, in 1871, David Livingstone and, then, in February 1889, Emin Pasha (see *G:HD*, pp. 182–208). Recommended by various shipping agents, Conrad met Albert Thys, the director of the Société Anonyme Belge pour le Commerce du Haut-Congo (SAB), but Thys was dilatory in offering him a post. Marguerite (whom Conrad addressed as 'aunt'), the well-connected widow of his recently deceased distant relative, Aleksander Poradowski, intervened on his behalf (see Text and contexts, **p. 18**). But it was the killing by local tribesmen of Johannes Freiesleben, the Danish master of the steamship *Florida*, which precipitated Conrad's appointment as his successor. On 10 May 1890, he left Brussels for the Congo.

Conrad reached Matadi on 13 June. Like Marlow, he started off his journey with high expectations, not ideal, but reasonable. Yet setbacks soon led to a process of disillusionment. He had understood that he was to command a river steamer for the duration of his three-year contract. In Kinshasa on 2 August, he found that the steamer he was to command was disabled and he was assigned as second-in-command to a Captain L.R. Koch. The commercial agent at the Stanley Falls station, Georges Antoine Klein (see Text and contexts, **p. 35**), was suffering from dysentery. The *Roi des Belges* arrived on 1 September, by which time Koch had also taken ill. Camille Delcommune, the Acting Manager of the Company, appointed Conrad to take over the command of the steamer until Koch had recovered. When the steamer arrived in Bangala on 15 September, Koch was back at the helm. So much for Conrad's later claim of having commanded a steamer. Klein died on board on 21 September. Conrad was at Kinshasa when the exploratory exped-

---

3   Conrad, letter to Karol Zogorski, 22 May 1890, in *The Collected Letters of Joseph Conrad: Vol. I 1861–1897*, ed. Karl & Davies, Cambridge: Cambridge UP, 1983, p. 52.

ition of Alexander Delcommune (brother of Camille) started on board the *Ville de Bruxelles*. We know hardly anything of Conrad's life during the last months of 1890. Towards the end of January the following year he appeared in Brussels, then on 1 February in London.

Conrad wrote 'The Congo Diary'[4] during his trek from Matadi to Kinshasha between 13 June and 1 August, the first two months of his six-month stay in the Congo. The diary is sketchy but the parallels between the diary and the earlier phases of the novella document the factual basis that Conrad usually needed to trigger off his imagination. Conrad's 'Up-river Book', which consists almost exclusively of navigational notes from the bridge of the *Roi des Belges* from 3 to 19 August, is of much less interest to the reader.

Relations between Conrad and Camille Delcommune and other employees of the SAB were marked by mutual antipathy. His thinking was incompatible with theirs: he expected some basic decencies and found none. His attitude of moral superiority may have been irksome to the others. His aloofness, deriving from his aristocratic origins, was not conducive to popularity. But the decisive reason for Conrad's premature departure from the Congo was probably grave illness. Suffering from dysentery and fever, his plight is illustrated by an incident from his Congo experience that he later related to Edward Garnett but did not include in his fictionalized version:

> lying sick to death in a native hut tended by an old negress who brought him water from day to day, when he had been abandoned by all the Belgians. 'She saved my life,' Conrad said, 'the white men never came near me.'[5]

Conrad was a physical wreck and convalescence seems to have been a slow process, especially under the conditions of his existence in the Congo. The hiatus in evidence for Conrad's last months in Africa seems to me no 'mystery',[6] but merely the physical consequences of an illness from which he never recovered, which curtailed his career as a seaman and, in part, confirmed him in his already emerging vocation as a writer (he took the opening chapters of *Almayer's Folly* with him to the Congo). Like Pip in Dickens' *Great Expectations*, this period of illness was for Conrad, as for Marlow in *Heart of Darkness*, also a period of mental awakening and not totally negative. Edward Garnett reports of Conrad:

> in his early years at sea he had 'not a thought in his head.' 'I was a perfect animal,' he reiterated, meaning of course that he had reasoned and reflected hardly at all over the varieties of life he had encountered.[7]

Judging by the promise of *Almayer's Folly* and *An Outcast of the Islands* and the complexities of *The Nigger of the 'Narcissus'* and *Lord Jim* (*Heart of Darkness*

4   Conrad, in *Tales of Hearsay and Last Essays*, London: Dent, 1955 edn; *G:HD*, pp. 160-5.
5   Garnett, 'Introduction', *Letters from Conrad 1895–1924*, London: Nonesuch Press, p. xiii; *G:HD*, p. 167.
6   Zdzislaw Najder, *Joseph Conrad: A Chronicle*, Cambridge: Cambridge UP, 1983, p. 139.
7   Garnett, 'Introduction', *Letters from Conrad 1895–1924*, p. xii; *G:HD*, p. 168.

was composed while Conrad was engaged in writing *Lord Jim*), Conrad's Malayan and sea experiences stimulated him and contributed to his maturation. He was hardly 'a perfect animal' before the Congo; the Congo nevertheless shook him to the core and induced a kind of enlightenment, even if a dark enlightenment.

Norman Sherry asserts that the passage up the Congo was 'a routine, highly organized venture along a fairly frequented river-way linking quite numerous settlements of trading posts and factories.'[8] Zdzislaw Najder provides (more convincing) evidence to the contrary:

> About two hundred miles above Kinshasa the Congo becomes a huge elongated lake, interspersed with islands and shoals, with the other bank often invisible . . . In parts the Congo measures a few miles in width; in others it spreads over ten, ... several missions hundreds of miles apart . . . no more than six villages over a distance of more than five hundred miles.[9]

Regarding Conrad's projection of the Congo, the issue is not whether *Heart of Darkness* is realistic (in the sense of 'true to life') or not. It would be legitimate for Conrad to highlight isolation (of the single steamer and Marlow as Captain) to heighten the narrative's impressiveness and focus. Stanley Falls (Kisangani, Kurtz's Inner Station) was a small permanent settlement, but, in Conrad's novella, it had to be projected as the type of lonely outpost which was a hacked-out clearing. Finally, the reader may have to accept Conrad's own statement in his 'Author's Note' (1917): '*Heart of Darkness* is . . . experience pushed a little (only a very little) beyond the actual fact of the case.'[10] The experience in the narrative is after all convincing on a realistic plane. When Albert J. Guerard introduced it to one of Roger Casement's consular successors in the Congo in 1957, he 'remarked at once that Conrad certainly had "a feel for the country".'[11] Conrad wisely does not pinpoint the time of the action precisely and thus presents the jungle as symbolic of dark urges; his inexactitude enables him to incorporate Marlow's sensation that 'instead of going to the centre of a continent, I was about to set off for the centre of the earth' (Ch. I, p. 79) and that 'going up that river was like travelling back to the earliest beginnings of the world' (Ch. II, p. 105).

In late 1898 when Conrad was struggling with depression and weary of his residence in Essex, northeast of London, and despite disruptive experiences such as quarrelling with his old friend Adolph P. Krieger and plagued by financial problems, he found emotional security in friendship with Ford Madox Ford. Ford helped him to find a more congenial residence, Pent Farm in South Kent, within easy visiting distance of Stephen Crane, Henry James and H.G. Wells, where Conrad wrote most of his best works. He soon received the powerful patronage of William Blackwood, of the famous publishing company and literary journal

8 Sherry, *Conrad's Western World*, Cambridge: Cambridge UP, 1971, p. 61.
9 Najder, *Joseph Conrad*, p. 134.
10 Conrad, 'Author's Note', p. xi, in *Youth: A Narrative and Two Other Stories*, London: Dent, 1923; G:HD, p. 64.
11 Guerard, *Conrad the Novelist*, Massachusetts: Harvard UP & London: Oxford UP, 1958, p. 45.

Blackwood's Edinburgh Magazine ('*Maga*'); and, in 1900, began his twenty-year association with his literary agent J.B. Pinker – which helped to make the period 1898–1902 a flowering of Conrad's talent. Conrad called this his 'Blackwood's' period, which in turn led to the fruiting period when he wrote works of remarkable control and compass (*Nostromo, The Secret Agent, Under Western Eyes*) yet without manifesting the same degree of intensity as *Heart of Darkness* and *Lord Jim*.

The period of 'flowering' saw Conrad's discovery of his famous narrator/character, Marlow, the classic instance of a writer so thrilled with the possibilities of a single character that he re-uses this creation and in multiple ways. Marlow offered Conrad firstly a narrative strategy of objectifying experience and presenting multiple points of view. These became increasingly sophisticated as both Conrad and Marlow matured. In *Youth* (1898), Marlow the character (20 years old) is indeed 'a perfect animal' projected by an older (42 years), wiser Marlow, the narrator. In *Heart of Darkness* (1898), Marlow becomes more open to experience, more perceptive and critical both as character and narrator. *Lord Jim* (1900) presents most far-seeing Marlow as narrator, though he is more peripheral as a character. He appears one more time, much later in *Chance* (1913), in which his portrayal is somewhat inconsistent with his earlier characterisation.

During his early years as a writer, Conrad was fortunate both in having the support of literary friends and contacts such as Edward Garnett, John Galsworthy, Henry James, Stephen Crane, R.B. Cunninghame Graham, H.G. Wells and Arnold Bennett, and in receiving generally favourable reviews. But his works did not achieve commercial success until the publication of *Chance*, with the result that he was plagued by financial problems for the greater part of his literary career. These contributed to depression, a nervous breakdown in 1910 and premature death.

When Conrad settled in England, the influence and pressure of his immediate environment would have made him choose English as his medium of artistic expression rather than his first language, Polish, and his second, French, though he learnt English only as an adult and, in the beginning, from such seemingly unpromising sources as navigation manuals and seamen's talk. But Conrad would not have dreamt of writing in English if he had not known the English reading public through his reading of English writers, first in translation, and later in the original. He knew what was marketable and characteristically struck a compromise between the 'popular' and the 'artistic' without sacrificing his artistic integrity. He wrote for journals such as *Blackwood's* to build up his readership, reputation and finances; the first part of *Heart of Darkness* was published in *Blackwood's* 1000th anniversary number. Conrad's position today as a 'popular classic', whose books are issued in paperback form, is the perfect realization of his aims as a writer.

Literary contexts

Conrad was writing for a reading public habituated to the masculine and habitually pro-imperial tradition of late nineteenth-century romance and adventure exemplified in the works of Frederick Marryat, G.A. Henty and R.M. Ballantyne

– as well as H. Rider Haggard, R.L. Stevenson and Rudyard Kipling who might be considered more sophisticated and 'adult'. Because he focused on Africa, I will take Haggard as my example of a writer in this tradition, and *King Solomon's Mines* (1885) as a landmark text. Haggard's experience of life and landscape in (South) Africa was wide (he was a civil servant there, 1875–79, and an ostrich-farmer, 1880–81), while Conrad's was very narrow but more intense. Conrad's very newness to Africa affected his responses, so that the differences of sensibility between himself and Haggard are marked. In *King Solomon's Mines*, Haggard is able to traverse large tracts of Africa and penetrate African culture. The opening chapters introduce the hero, Sir Henry Curtis, his friend Captain John Good, the narrator, Allan Quatermain, and Sir Henry's quest for his lost brother, George, who had gone in search of King Solomon's treasure. These phases are presented in a realistic mode. The next stages – the quest itself, struggle, success and homecoming – are projected romantically. Haggard deliberately aims to create a pleasant experience to make his novel a best-seller and so provides a palatable and appealing picture. His characters see a 'glorious panorama ... The landscape lay before us like a map, in which rivers flashed like silver snakes, and Alp-like peaks crowned with wildly twisted snow-wreaths rose in solemn grandeur ...'[12] (Haggard's comparison of rivers to 'silver snakes' is a contrast to Marlow's identification of the river Congo as a menacing snake mesmerizing a bird. Ch. I, p. 73, 76.) The Africans from Kukuanaland who first confront the whites are 'very tall and copper-coloured and some of them wore great plumes of black feathers and short cloaks of leopard skins.'[13] Such touches of realism regarding African dress, food, customs, warfare and topography induce in the reader a suspension of total disbelief.

The native characters in adventure stories are usually of two types: the loyal and brave servants or helpers, and enemies, courageous or cowardly. In *King Solomon's Mines*, Umbopa the porter (actually, Ignosi, the legitimate king of Kukuanaland, incognito) and Khiva the Zulu boy, who shows courage in trying to save Good from a charging elephant and dies in the attempt (he recalls Kipling's Gunga Din in the poem of that name) fit the former stereotype. Twala, the usurper, is an example of the enemy, courageous and wicked, his single eye emblematic of his villainy. African ferocity is brought out in the battle between Ignosi's and Twala's warriors, while African cruelty and blood-thirstiness are evident in the tribal ceremonies. The whites are shown as intellectually more advanced than the blacks: when Good removes and replaces his false teeth, the Africans regard this as magic; when the whites use the eclipse of the sun, of which they had prior knowledge, as a sign of their supernatural powers, the Africans are awed. The whites are shown as superior to the Africans in contests of strength too: Sir Henry kills Twala, the strongest warrior in Kukuanaland, in single combat. In race relations on a personal level, too, colonial attitudes and views prevail. As the whites prepare to enter King Solomon's mines, Foulata, the Kukuana beauty who is devoted to Good, pauses:

---

12 H. Rider Haggard, *King Solomon's Mines*, London: Minster Classics, 1968 edn, pp. 97–8.
13 Haggard, *King Solomon's Mines*, p. 104.

'I fear, my lord,' the girl answered timidly.
'Then give me the basket.' [Good]
'Nay, my lord, whither thou goest, there will I go also.' [14]

Foulata's racist humility is a contrast to the pride of Kurtz's African woman. In King Solomon's treasure chamber, Foulata, on the verge of death after being stabbed by Gagool the witch who betrays them by closing the door, tells Quatermain:

> 'Say to my lord . . . that – I love him, and that I am glad to die because I know that he cannot cumber his life with such as me, for the sun cannot mate with darkness, nor the white with the black.' [15]

Kukuanaland is a remote, mysterious place, far removed from imperialism. How does Foulata know of the imperial race barrier? But the question does not arise if we are caught in the grip of Haggard's narrative. Ivory is one of the items in Solomon's treasure chamber, and it is regarded as a positive and accepted source of wealth. The whites escape and Quatermain gets away with a quantity of diamonds, small but sufficient insurance for his son and himself. The quest is an unmitigated success, for on the way back Sir Henry stumbles on his brother. Haggard provides a happy ending.

Quatermain the narrator is far more racist than his creator. Haggard's attitudes and views on imperial matters are mixed, some imperialistic and others not. As early as 1885, Haggard through Quatermain objects to the term 'nigger' and pleads for racial equality: 'What is a gentleman? . . . I've known natives who *are*, . . . and mean whites . . . who *ain't*.' [16] [Quatermain's emphasis] The whites assist in restoring Ignosi as king and he agrees to follow the white man's rule of law, but his farewell to them is significant:

> 'I do perceive that thy words are as ever, wise and full of reason, Macumazahn [the African name for Quatermain]; that which flies in the air loves not to run along the ground; the white man loves not to live on the level of the black. Well, ye must go, and leave my heart sore . . . But listen, and let all the white men know my words. No other white man shall cross the mountains . . . I will see no traders with their guns and rum. My people shall fight with the spear and drink water . . . I will have no praying-men to put fear of death into men's heart, to stir them up against the king, and make a path for the white men who follow to run on. If a white man comes, I will send him back; if a hundred come, I will push them back . . .' [17]

Ignosi, physically splendid, fearless, is a model man though black. Having lived in colonized areas and joined as porter, he is aware of the colour bar; and is against

14 Haggard, *King Solomon's Mines*, p. 236.
15 Haggard, *King Solomon's Mines*, p. 254.
16 Haggard, *King Solomon's Mines*, p. 13.
17 Haggard, *King Solomon's Mines*, p. 275.

the forces of imperial penetration and corruption – trade, Christianity, military might and alcohol – and thereby Haggard reveals his own anti-imperialistic side. Haggard suggests racial equality by drawing parallels between African and European life. He says of the Kukuana women: 'They were as well-bred in their way as the habitués of a fashionable drawing-room.'[18] Linda Dryden observes how Haggard makes the point in *Allan Quatermain* (1887) that the social behaviour of the European woman was not very different from the African 'savage' (see Critical readings, p. 87).

Magazines in which much of Conrad's fiction first appeared – *The Illustrated London News, Cosmopolis* and, especially, *Blackwood's* – regularly included items about life in colonial outposts for exiles and stay-at-homes as well. In fact, *'Blackwood' Tales from the Outposts* were published as collected volumes. Blackwood's middle- and low-brow readers (it had its own highbrows) would be seduced by the adventure element in *Heart of Darkness*. Martin Green rightly argues that 'the adventure tales that formed the light reading of Englishmen for two hundred years and more after *Robinson Crusoe* were the energizing myth of English imperialism.'[19]

The pre-eminent voice of Empire during its heyday (1880–1920) was Kipling. 'The Ballad of East and West' (1889) opens with his now notorious line:

Oh, East is East, and West is West, and never the twain shall meet –

and this is followed by:

But there is neither East nor West, Border, nor Breed, nor Birth,
When two strong men stand face to face, though they come from the
     ends of the earth.

Kipling's masculine, militaristic approach permits white/black equality only at the point of courage. 'The White Man's Burden' (1899) was written in the same year as Conrad's *Heart of Darkness*. Kipling's famous poem illustrates the contemporary urge to colonize and current views regarding cross-racial differences. Its purpose was to encourage the Americans to invade the Philippines. Kipling exhorts the USA to partner Britain in the colonial enterprise as well as share the ideals of responsibility and service that Marlow and Kurtz at the beginning of his career seem to have espoused:

Take up the White Man's burden –
    Sent forth the best ye breed –
Go bind your sons to exile
    To serve your captives' need;
To wait in heavy harness
    On fluttered folk and wild –
Your new-caught, sullen peoples,
    Half devil and half child.

18 Haggard, *King Solomon's Mines*, p. 120.
19 Green, *Dreams of Adventure, Deeds of Empire*, New York: Basic, 1979, p. 3.

The native people are regarded as 'half devil and half child', in need of the better-ment that comes only from contact with white civilization.

Heart of Darkness takes off from the tradition of late nineteenth-century romance and adventure, and would be read on this level by the majority of readers of Conrad's time. Their cultural/moral position would be formed by the fiction and poetry in this tradition. The novella, however, also relates to the high brow fiction and poetry of its period. Conrad learnt from the French masters (see Texts and contexts, **p. 3**) directly and also indirectly through Henry James, whom he regarded as 'notre bon maître'. This is linked with Conrad's semi-independent interest in literary form. Critics have speculated as to how Conrad came to adopt the convention of the first-person narrator. Several have ascribed this to the influence of James' use of the central observer.[20] This is, probably, partly true, but Conrad was subject to other influences too in this regard (see Text and contexts, **p. 31**) and he also departs from James. What distinguishes the central consciousness characteristic of James' fiction is its fineness, whereas what distinguishes Marlow in *Heart of Darkness* is his openness to impressions. The novella is connected to somewhat later classics of modern nihilism. Both the African wilderness and the Marabar Caves in Forster's *A Passage to India* (1924) engender 'ou-boum' – the ultimate nullity. 'Mistah Kurtz – he dead' was used by Eliot as an epigraph for 'The Hollow Men' (1925). Kurtz's cry, 'The horror! The horror!', could well have been an appropriate epigraph to *The Waste Land* (1922), given Eliot's view of the depravity of man and the deadness of Western civilization as well as the darkness beyond good and evil, though he was dissuaded from using it by the less perceptive Ezra Pound.[21]

Heart of Darkness abounds in allusions and associations. Reminiscences of Dante[22] are present in Marlow's rendering of the 'grove of death'. The last thing Dante sees in the Inferno is the devil, a parallel to the last thing Marlow sees in the Congo – Kurtz, who is, from one perspective, a devil. Conrad projects different kinds of (imperial) devils (see Text and contexts, **p. 39**), a parallel to Dante's different circles of hell. *Heart of Darkness*, ironically, alludes to fairy tales such as the Sleeping Beauty and tales of a princess in an isolated castle awaiting deliver-ance – in Marlow's bid to rescue Kurtz. From one perspective, Kurtz is a descend-ant from a tradition that features the hero-villains of Gothic tradition such as Ann Radcliffe's Montoni in *The Mysteries of Udolpho* (1794) and Emily Bronte's Heathcliff in *Wuthering Heights* (1847) and goes back to Milton's Satan and Faust. Kurtz is guilty of pride, pride of self, in keeping with the Christian legend of Lucifer which has something in common with the Classical concept of *hubris*, the arrogance resulting from excessive pride that brings on destruction. Lucifer means 'light-bearer', and Kurtz is one such, so that the inspiring woman in his painting carries a torch and is a light-bearer. Like Kurtz, Lucifer is the brightest of the angels who fell. Marlow's quest for Kurtz also alludes to Aeneas' descent into the underworld in Virgil's *Aeneid*, Book VI.

20 For example, Ian Watt, *Conrad in the Nineteenth Century*, London: Chatto, 1980, p. 204.
21 Valerie Eliot (ed.), *T.S. Eliot, The Waste Land: A Facsimile and Transcript of the Original Drafts*, London: Faber, 1971, p. 125.
22 Dante (1265–1321) the Florentine whose *Divine Comedy* reveals a scathing awareness of politics as well as his vision of the working of the universe and of man's place within the eternal order.

Cultural context

The white supremacist attitudes and views expressed by writers such as Haggard and Kipling were held in their time by the majority of Europeans. Joseph Chamberlain, Secretary of State for the Colonies, stated: 'In the first place, I believe in the British Empire and, in the second place, I believe in the British race. I believe that the British race is the greatest of the governing races the world has ever seen.'[23] Cecil Rhodes, the explorer of Africa, introduces the note of *hubris* when he claims that 'the world is not quite big enough for British trade and the British flag.'[24]

These attitudes and views received ideological support from Social Darwinism, encapsulated in Herbert Spencer's phrase 'survival of the fittest'. Although Charles Darwin's interest in *Origin of the Species* (1859) was in biological evolution and not the evolution of societies, he claimed in Chapter 6 that 'At some future period not very distant . . . the civilized races of men will almost certainly exterminate and replace throughout the world the savage races.' In *The Descent of Man* (1871), he concluded: 'There can hardly be a doubt that we are descended from the barbarians.'[25] In *Social Evolution* (1894), Benjamin Kidd the sociologist argued: 'The weaker races disappear before the stronger through the effects of mere contact.'[26]

Conrad was one of a minority of critics of imperialism. In regard to South Africa, Haggard displayed an anti-imperial attitude, while Wilfred Blunt, assigned to evaluate public opinion in Egypt when the Arab nationalists rebelled in 1881, favoured Egyptian independence. In respect of Leopold's Congo, the first public clamour was raised by the Afro-American historian George Washington Williams. The most active opponent was E.D. Morel who praised Conrad's 'picture of Congo life' in his denunciation of *King Leopold's Rule in Africa* (1904), in which he enlists Conrad's name. On a visit to America, Morel stirred Mark Twain who then wrote *King Leopold's Soliloquy* (1905), a scathing satire on Leopold's misdeeds. Both Morel and Twain drew heavily on the findings of Sir Roger Casement's report to parliament in 1904 on conditions in the Congo. This was the best factual account in its day.[27] When Casement was finishing his report, Conrad sent him an endorsement, underlining the 'ruthless, systematic cruelty towards the blacks', and concluding: 'my best wishes go with you on your crusade. You may make any use you like of what I write to you.'[28] *Heart of Darkness* stimulated the reformers who terminated Leopold's rule. Morel, head of the Congo Reform Association (it had an American chapter), wrote to Arthur Conan

23 Chamberlain, 'A Young Nation', in *Foreign and Colonial Speeches*, London: George Routledge, 1897, p. 89; *G:HD*, p. 210.
24 'Vindex' ed., *Cecil Rhodes: His Political Life and Speeches*, London: Chapman & Hall, 1900, p. 643; *G:HD*, p. 209.
25 Darwin, *The Descent of Man, and Selection in Relation to Sex*, 2 vols., Princeton: Princeton UP, 1981, 2, p. 404.
26 Kidd, *Social Evolution*, New York: Macmillan, 1894, p. 46.
27 Morel, *King Leopold's Rule in Africa*, London, 1904; Morel, *Great Britain and the Congo*, London, 1909; Twain, *King Leopold's Soliloquy: A Defense of his Congo Rule*, Boston, 1905; see *G:HD*, pp. 220–1, 221–5, 214–19.
28 Conrad, letter to Casement, 21 December 1903, in *The Collected Letters of Joseph Conrad: Vol. III 1903–1907*, ed. Karl & Davies, Cambridge UP, 1988, p. 97.

Doyle, a member and author of *The Crime of the Congo* (1909), that the novella was 'the most powerful thing ever written on the subject.'[29]

To turn to a different area, it is likely that the ideas of Friedrich Nietzsche (1844–1900) had something to do with the creation of Kurtz (see Text and contexts, pp. 34f.). Nietzsche attacked Christianity, liberalism, democracy and socialism alike as embodying a 'slave morality'. Christianity's antithesis was 'beyond good and evil' – a morality appropriate to superior individuals who were capable of rising to greater heights. These 'overmen' or 'supermen' – Nietzsche's ideal world was if anything more sexist than mainstream nineteenth-century European society – would embody the 'will to power', the height of self-assertion and self-mastery. We know Conrad read Edward Garnett's essay on Nietzsche in the *Outlook* of 8 July 1899, and criticized Nietzsche's 'mad individualism' in a letter to Helen Sanderson of 22 July 1899.[30] A much later antipathetic reference occurs in 'The Crime of Partition' (1919) when Conrad wrote, referring to Germany's role in beginning World War I, 'The Germanic Tribes had told the whole world in all possible tones carrying conviction ... Nietzschean, war-like, pious, cynical, inspired, what they were going to do to the inferior races of the earth.'[31] We have no proof that Conrad actually read Nietzsche; yet a profound writer's concepts, when these are a part of the climate of thought and animate discussion, debate and intellectual comment, seep into the awareness of the intelligentsia.

Conrad anticipated certain ideas of Sigmund Freud (1856–1939). In 1921, three years before Conrad's death, H.R. Lenormand, a young French playwright and admirer of Dostoevsky and of psychoanalysis, met Conrad at Ajaccio and was shocked by his refusal to read Freud, whose books he had lent him, or to discuss the subconscious motives influencing the behaviour of his characters.[32] Man's unconscious plays an important role in the thematics of *Heart of Darkness*. From a Freudian perspective, Kurtz in the African wilderness discards the superego, in the form of the sense of right and wrong, and instead expresses to the maximum the ego, the sense of himself, his identity or individuality, and consequently gives free rein to the id, the part of the unconscious mind where basic urges exist.

Historical context

The Congo refers both to Africa's second-largest river and its watershed and the third-largest country on the continent (an area of 2,344,858 square kilometers). The earliest inhabitants were Pygmies who were largely displaced between 500 and 1000 AD by Bantu invaders. The Bantu peoples were mining copper in the south (now Katanga province) as early as 700 AD and formed a variety of independent kingdoms, many of these of considerable complexity. The Congo

29 Morel, *History of the Congo Reform Movement*, ed. William Roger Louis & Jean Stengers, London: Oxford UP, 1968, p. 205, n.
30 Conrad, in *Collected Letters II*, p. 188.
31 Conrad, 'The Crime of Partition', in *Notes on Life and Letters*, London: Dent, 1949 edn, pp. 124–5.
32 Najder, *Joseph Conrad: A Chronicle*, p. 460.

River was named during the colonial period for the Kongo people, who inhabit the area along the river's mouth on the Atlantic Ocean. The first contact with Europeans came in 1482 with the visit of Diogo Cam of Portugal. The slave trade began to affect the coastal regions thereafter, and while it was eliminated in most areas of Africa by the late 1860s, some slave trading (primarily by Arabs) continued in the Congo, Nigeria and Nyasaland (now Malawi) until about 1903; slavery enters Conrad's 'An Outpost of Progress' (1898).

Leopold II of Belgium entered Europe's late-nineteenth century 'scramble for Africa' obliquely. In 1876 he convened a grand conference of African explorers, geographers, missionaries, anti-slavers and businessmen in Brussels. He did not chair the conference but made certain it would set up an International African Association (of which he was elected chairperson).

Shortly afterwards, Henry Stanley, more celebrated than ever after crossing the African continent via the Congo River, but having failed to interest the British in the commercial potential of the Congo, was in Leopold's employ – or, more precisely, in the employ of yet another body with another splendid name, the Committee for Studies of the Upper Congo. That Committee was succeeded by the International Association of the Congo which, according to an article anonymously contributed by Leopold to the London Times, was a sort of 'Society of the Red Cross; it has been formed with the noble aim of rendering lasting and disinterested services to the cause of progress.' His instructions to Stanley were in a different vein. Stanley was to return to the Congo and make 'treaties as brief as possible', giving 'everything', with all the native chiefs he came across.[33]

Leopold stated that he was establishing 'a confederation of negro republics' in the Congo. These independent 'republics' were then combined into a single 'state', which in early 1885 declared itself to be the Free State of the Congo. Leopold, who had funded the entire project, and had been the only subscriber to the International Association in its last form, became head of state and owner in his private capacity of the whole property, larger than England, France, Germany, Spain and Italy combined, styling himself 'King-Sovereign'. The Berlin Conference of 1884–5 was the central event in the later colonization of Africa, at which the colonial powers carved up the continent among themselves and sanctioned the Congo as Leopold's, even though other colonies were set up as subject to European nation-states.

Leopold had neither the capital nor the desire to develop his colony except in relation to extorting ivory, copal and wild rubber from the indigenes. These activities were conducted on a commission basis by administrators of the state or by companies in which the state usually held a substantial share. Turning officials into profiteers was an incentive to cruelty and recklessness. The Africans were paid only in kind – cloth, beads, rations – or in lengths of brass wire which were declared to be a form of currency appropriate for them. The Africans thus had every reason to withhold their labour, and Leopold's agents to obtain it by the cheapest means: through raids, press-gangs, floggings, the taking of hostages (especially women and children), the destruction of villages and cultivated fields,

---

33 Quoted from Adam Hochschild, *King Leopld's Ghost*, London: Pan, 2002 edn, pp. 66, 71.

the murder and mutilation of those who attempted to rebel or escape. The result was a shattering drop in the population – estimates range from 20 per cent of its original population to 10 million (or half).

Leopold professed a paternal concern for his people, whether in Belgium or the Congo, while his real focus was on power and the spoils of power. Stanley made altruistic professions in Europe and America,[34] but, in Africa, he was guilty of flogging, murder, looting, collusion with the slave trade and other crimes. In 1908, Leopold was compelled to sell the Congo – he had never set foot there – to the Belgian government because of the exposures of the campaigners against his rule and because the 'independent' report ordered by him was negative.

It is important to remember both that *Heart of Darkness* was in no way intended to provide an accurate description of Africa and that the Africa that does appear in the novella is a version of the continent as seen through late nineteenth-century European eyes. However, the Congo has probably altered less in the past 100 years than have most areas of the world. As late as the 1970s V.S. Naipaul observed: 'The airplane that goes from Kinshasa to Kisangani flies over eight hundred miles of what still looks like virgin forest.'[35] The country did not emerge from the colonial rule of Belgium until 1960, after which five years of unrest culminated in a military coup facilitated by Belgian forces and the American Central Intelligence Agency, which brought General Mobutu Sese Seko to power. Mobutu ran one of the world's most corrupt governments and he became one of the world's richest men, but his people remained among the poorest in the world. In 1971, he changed the country's name to Zaire, an attempt to return to the source of the nation's identity and authenticity ('Zaire' is a variation of traditional African names for great rivers and specifically the Congo). Mobutu was deposed in 1997 by Laurent Kabila, who restored the country's name to the Congo. He was assassinated by rebels in January 2001 and was succeeded by his son, Joseph.

To turn to generalities, since 'imperialism' and 'race' are integral to discussions about *Heart of Darkness*, it would be useful to define these terms. There has been a controversy as to whether it was the idealogues (see Text and contexts, **p. 11**, Cultural context, **p. 13**) who played the decisive role in unleashing imperial expansion or material factors (economic and political). Probably, self-interested economic motives form the primary factor in imperialism, while self-interested political considerations are the secondary factor. Altruism was often proclaimed most loudly and simple-mindedly as a motive of imperialism, but it is clearly subsidiary in imperial practice yet has a place. Much of the altruism is inseparably mixed with economic and political aims. For instance, the European powers did develop roads, railways and harbours in their colonies, but such developments were motivated mainly by the need to expand the spheres of economic and political influence. Yet whether in Asia, Africa or the Pacific, imperialism destroyed the old social system as well as providing the beginning of a new modern order. It

34 Henry M. Stanley, *Through the Dark Continent*, London: George Newnes, 1899, pp. xii–xv; speech in *The Times*, 4 October 1892; 'Through the Dark Continent' in *The World's Great Speeches*, ed. Lewis Copeland, New York: Dover, 1958, pp. 667–8; see *G:HD*, pp. 204–9.
35 Naipaul, 'A New King for the Congo: Mobutu and the Nihilism of Africa' (1975), in *The Return of Eva Peron with the Killings in Trinidad*, New York: Knopf, 1980, p. 179.

caused this social revolution and brought these regions into the stream of modern international life.

'Race is a classification based on traits which are hereditary. Therefore, when we talk about race we are talking about heredity and traits transmitted by heredity which characterize all the members of a related group.'[36] The key traits are skin colour, quality and colour of hair, eye form, shape of nose and blood groups. Using these as criteria, one can distinguish between a Chinese with his yellowish skin and marked epicanthic fold and a Negro with his dark skin and wide, flat nose. Races can be distinguished, but one race is not congenitally superior or inferior to another. Racism or racialism is the delusion that one ethnic group is innately superior or inferior to another. Racism and imperialism usually go together; racist propositions such as the innate superiority of the white over all other races were often put forward to justify imperialism (see Text and contexts, p. 13).

The text

Heart of Darkness, imperialism and race

Conrad's (and Marlow's) Congo journey took place at the high tide of imperialism and racism in European history (1880–1920). Imperialist and racist sentiments are typically founded on simplistic dichotomies. As Abdul R. JanMohamed points out:

> the colonial mentality is dominated by a Manichean allegory of white and black, good and evil, salvation and damnation, civilization and savagery, superiority and inferiority, intelligence and emotion, self and the other, subject and object.[37]

Conrad subverts this Manichean allegory in his novella, by blurring or inverting from the beginning the conventional duality. He does so in Marlow's comparison of the Roman Empire and contemporary empires. Both Conrad and Marlow are fascinated by Africa before they go there – for both a childhood response to a map is the relatively innocent motive for their joining the imperial presence in Africa. Yet Conrad goes on to suggest in the novella that the white men have turned the map of Africa, 'a white patch', into 'a place of darkness',[38] or a 'Dark Continent' (Stanley's phrase that passed into general parlance), and thus inverts the conventional view of Europeans as harbingers of light. (Later in the tale, Kurtz's painting may be taken to intimate the same inversion of roles.) But if these

---

36 Ruth Benedict, *Race and Racism*, London: Routledge, 1959 edn, p. 6.
37 JanMohamed, *Manichean Aesthetics: The Politics of Literature in Colonial Africa*, Amherst: Massachusetts UP, 1983, p. 4.
38 D.C.R.A. Goonetilleke (ed.), *Joseph Conrad, Heart of Darkness*, Peterborough, Ontario, Canada & New York: Broadview Press, 2003 edn, I, p. 73. All references to *Heart of Darkness* in this part are taken from this edition. Subsequent references will appear in the body text, taking the form of a section number and page number in parentheses.

elements imply a negative critique of imperialism, is the text still imperialist at all? To what extent (if at all) is it racist?

It has become a commonplace of Commonwealth literary criticism to condemn works such as *Heart of Darkness* and Joyce Cary's *Mister Johnson* because they are alleged to distort cultural or political reality and hence are wanting in 'truth' which is considered a necessary quality of good literature. Such criticism is based on a perceived discrepancy between the real world and the world created by the writer in his work. Chinua Achebe is impassioned on this point:

> Conrad was a bloody racist ... And the question is whether a novel which celebrates this dehumanization, which depersonalizes a portion of the human race, can be called a great work of art. My answer is: No, it cannot.[39]

Achebe has maintained his position (see Critical history, **p. 61**). And Edward Said, for his part, even argues that: 'Achebe's well-known criticism of Conrad ... does not go far enough.'[40]

Those critics who disagree with Achebe and Said (and it may be noted that among their number are many African writers[41]) recognize the value that Achebe's perspective brings to analysis of the text; the book *is* in important ways about imperialism and racism, and these issues can no longer be brushed aside. Today even those critics who feel that the most important meanings of the text concern the souls of individuals, or the heart of humanity as a whole rather than being narrowly connected with Africa or race, must nevertheless recognize that the text emerges out of the very centre of racism and imperialism, and that no matter how much it may say on one level about humanity as a whole, at another level it has a lot to say about the treatment of black Africans by white Europeans. As much as it may say something about individuals it also says something about groups; as much as it says something symbolic it also says something about the palpably real, hovering as it does between realist representation and allegory.

It is significant that the darkness we are first introduced to is not in Africa but in England. The narrative gathers momentum as the centre shifts from London to Brussels, headquarters of the Belgian empire. Neither London nor Brussels are named, but are recognizable through many references and allusions. Neither does Conrad identify the continent, Africa, nor the country and the river, Congo: but these can be inferred from the description of the journey and topography. The absence of names as well as dates or hints of dates simply imposes no limits of place or time on the tale's significance.

The scene in Brussels in which Marlow bids farewell to his aunt, who had exercised her influence to obtain for him an appointment as the captain of a

---

39 Achebe, 'An Image of Africa', in *The Massachusetts Review*, 18, 1977, 788.
40 Said, *Culture and Imperialism*, London: Chatto & Windus, 1993, p. 200.
41 'In conversations with me Lewis Nkosi ... and Matthew Buyu, the Kenyan poet and scholar, have both defended *Heart of Darkness*, emphasizing that by the standards of its times it offers a valuably sceptical account of imperialism.' Cedric Watts, 'Introduction' to *Heart of Darkness*, Oxford: OUP, 1990. Nkosi also makes his case in *Tasks and Masks*, Harlow: Longman, 1981, p. 80. Watts also offers further instances of Third World scholars who have defended *Heart of Darkness*; see also *Conradiana*, 14, 1982, 163–87.

river-steamboat, is by no means irrelevant. Conrad introduces conventional Western notions of imperialism (naturally more prominent in the metropolitan countries than in the colonies) through the aunt, and exposes their falsity through Marlow. Marlow sees the difference between her conception of his role as 'an emissary of light' and the real pettiness of his job. He is aware that the underpinnings of imperialism were economic and not altruistic. Conrad dramatizes the actual working of the head office of an imperial company. There are the memorable figures of the two unconcerned women at the door knitting black wool, who go with such an office. They recall the classical Fates (the Moerae), who were also spinners. Clotho, the youngest of the spinners, presided over men's births: 'People were arriving, and the younger one was walking back and forth introducing them' (Ch. I, p. 76). Lachesis, the second sister, was chance: 'The swift and indifferent placidity of that look troubled me. Two youths with foolish and cheery countenances were being piloted over, and she threw at them the same quick glance of unconcerned wisdom' (Ch. I, pp. 76–7). Death in the Congo is chance, a possibility, not inevitability, and, therefore, the third sister, Atropos, who cut the thread, has no equivalent in the novella. Moreover, the slim knitter is 'herself a fate – a dehumanized death in life to herself and to others, and thus a prefiguring symbol of what the trading company does to its creatures'.[42] There is Conrad's presentation of the medical examination with its suggestions of callousness and of the likelihood of derangement and death for employees in the colony, the doctor's interest in craniometry, popular at that time, adding to the black humour of the scene. The whole city, in fact, seems to Marlow 'a whited sepulchre' (Ch. I, p. 75). Its deathlike attributes, along with the implications of hypocrisy, link up with the inhumanity of the empire, and Conrad suggests how the 'achievement' of the metropolitan country is founded on imperialism.

Despite Marlow's common sense view of extravagant rhetoric and these disquieting experiences at the beginning, his enthusiasm for Empire and the Congo journey remain. The realities *en route* are as much an integral part of Conrad's portrayal of imperialism as are the realities in Belgium and in the Congo itself. The scales fall from Marlow's eyes as he approaches Africa. The French man-of-war 'incomprehensible, firing into a continent ... a touch of insanity in the proceeding' (Ch. I, p. 81) produces the first significant jolt. More important is Marlow's first contact with black Africans, in a scene crucial for establishing the novella's underlying attitude. These 'black fellows' in boats give Marlow 'a momentary contact with reality':

> The voice of the surf heard now and then was a positive pleasure, like the speech of a brother. It was something natural, that had its reason, that had a meaning. Now and then a boat from the shore gave one a momentary contact with reality. It was paddled by black fellows. You could see from afar the white of their eyeballs glistening. They shouted, sang; their bodies streamed with perspiration; they had faces like grotesque masks – these chaps; but they had bone, muscle, a wild vitality, an intense energy of movement, that was as natural and true as the surf

---

42 Ian Watt, *Conrad in the Nineteenth Century*, p. 192.

> along their coast. They wanted no excuse for being there. They were a
> great comfort to look at.
>
> (Ch. I, p. 80)

Though these descriptions are a variation of the 'Noble Savage' myth (as is the later description of Kurtz's native woman), the attitudes expressed are hardly racist. Even the phrase 'like grotesque masks' merely serves to intensify the sense of their alienness, their otherness, to Marlow. It thus gives additional grip and emphasis to the response drawn from him, the instinctive approving recognition: 'natural and true as the surf along *their* coast. *They wanted no excuse for being there*' [my emphasis]. The natives are like the surf, and the voice of the surf is to Marlow 'like the speech of a brother'. If these natives are alien to him, he is clearly entirely at peace with them – and perhaps closer to them than he is to 'all these [white] men with whom he had no point of contact' or to those on the French man-of-war.

This passage sets the tone for the attitude taken throughout towards native Africans. Conrad breaks with nineteenth-century stereotypes of unrestrained savagery. The Africans at first are seen only as strange, and then as akin. Conrad not only deploys and deconstructs the binary opposition between the self and the Other but also brings them together.

The contrast between this image of natives still free from oppression and the next image of black men could hardly be more marked: this is the chain gang, enslaved labourers who are there for the purpose of building a railway. Here for the first time Marlow's tale brings the reality of imperialism in the colony itself home to the reader. In this context of radical oppression Western terms and concepts such as 'criminals', 'rebels', 'labourers' do not fit and law itself is outraged by the oppression of the colonizers:

> Another report from the cliff made me think suddenly of that ship of
> war I had seen firing into a continent. It was the same kind of ominous
> voice; but these men could by no stretch of the imagination be called
> enemies. They were called criminals, and the outraged law, like the
> bursting shells, had come to them, an insoluble mystery from the sea.
>
> (Ch. I, p. 83)

Marlow confides to his audience that 'you know I am not particularly tender', but clearly even he is shocked by the brutality of the 'devils that drive the men who are responsible' (Ch. I, p. 83).

Marlow continues to record the series of 'definite images'[43] of his river journey, what Conrad called his starting-point for writing. These are images projected apparently haphazardly, elliptically, presented just as they strike Marlow. Their total effect, however, once they fall into an integrating perspective, is a powerful picture of what Conrad would later call 'the vilest scramble for loot that ever disfigured the history of human conscience and geographical exploration.'[44] In the

---

43 Conrad, letter to R.B. Cunninghame Graham, 8 February 1899, in *Collected Letters II*, p. 158.
44 Conrad, 'Geography and Some Explorers', in *Tales of Hearsay and Last Essays*, p. 17; *G:HD*, p. 160.

grove of death, the Africans are described in terms such as 'black shapes', 'black shadows', 'bundles of acute angles', so as to suggest that they have been so victimized by Belgian imperialism that they have been reduced to a level scarcely human. The stark restraint intensifies the horror. Marlow observes a dying boyish-looking labourer and 'found nothing else to do but offer him' a ship's biscuit (Ch. I, p. 85) – a gesture of sympathy and fellow-feeling even while Marlow is aware of its futility. Conrad too is aware that any gesture of this sort is ineffectual and meaningless in the face of the vastness of the situation. The litany of appalling human acts continues. In vivid detail Conrad brings out the suffering caused by imperialism to Africans. They are tortured, killed, exploited and dehumanized. A middle-aged man with a bullet hole in his forehead has been abandoned in the road. A man blamed for starting a fire is beaten horribly, and his cries provide a recurring reminder of the savagery of the 'pilgrims'. Conrad conveys Marlow's appalled consciousness of the callousness of the 'pilgrims' and his recognition that the only quality that gave them life was greed, which is ironically underlined by contrast with the religious associations of their descriptive epithet. Again and again the whites are shown to be crude, sordid and violent. Perhaps the most extreme example of their casual brutality is presented with a devastating understatement that only adds to its power:

> I pulled the string of the whistle, and I did this because I saw the pilgrims on deck getting out their rifles with an air of anticipating a jolly lark. At the sudden screech there was a movement of abject terror through that wedged mass of bodies. 'Don't! don't you frighten them away,' cried someone on deck disconsolately. I pulled the string time after time. They broke and ran, they leaped, they crouched, they swerved, they dodged the flying terror of the sound. The three red chaps had fallen flat, face down on the shore, as though they had been shot dead. Only the barbarous and superb woman did not so much as flinch, and stretched tragically her bare arms after us over the sombre and glittering river.
>
> And then that imbecile crowd down on the deck started their little fun, and I could see nothing more for the smoke.
>
> (Ch. III, p. 146)

It would be hard to imagine a more damning indictment of imperialism than the novella's litany of horrors perpetrated by the Europeans. The effect is to undermine for the reader the self-justifying catch phrases of imperial subjugation – 'civilizing influence', 'blood-thirsty natives', 'light-bringers' and so on. Marlow records incomprehensibility, meaninglessness, the absence of communication and clarity between natives and whites – all presented as a phantasmagoria.

The figure of Kurtz is the most extreme example of the savagery of the white man. It is Kurtz who hides beneath his veneer of 'enlightened imperialism' the sentiment 'Exterminates all the brutes!' – a horrifying revelation of the naked racist brutality at the heart of Kurtz and the heart of imperialism, and perhaps the ultimate expression of the essentialist extremes of imperialist discourse: 'they' are 'brutes', different from 'the civilized' in every essential quality, irredeemable and expendable. It is Kurtz who has been the most ruthless of ivory-traders, Kurtz who arranges for the heads of the dead to be displayed on poles, Kurtz who had ordered the attack against the steamer. Here again we may see how the text subverts traditional stereotypes. The attack by spear-throwing natives is almost a cliché, a page from what Said has termed the 'library of Africanisms'.[45] But as we learn after the fact, the chief responsibility for the savagery does not lie with the 'savages':

> He informed me, lowering his voice, that it was Kurtz who had ordered the attack to be made on the steamer. 'He hated sometimes the idea of being taken away – and then again ... But I don't understand these matters. I am a simple man. He thought it would scare you away – that you would give it up, thinking him dead.
>
> (Ch. III, p. 140)

By comparison with the brutality of the imperialists, the savagery of the blacks is a paltry thing indeed. They never initiate violence, and even the discussion of cannibalism inverts conventional notions of savagery. Eating other human beings is to the Western imagination perhaps the ultimate in savagery, but Conrad does not make an undue moralistic fuss over cannibalism. Indeed, Marlow's nonchalant tone almost seems to assume that it is simply a part of the African way of life and as such more or less 'acceptable'. In contrast to the pointless cruelty of the Europeans, the savagery of the natives is regarded as both understandable and excusable:

> I would no doubt have been properly horrified, had it not occurred to me that he and his chaps must be very hungry: that they must have been growing increasingly hungry for at least this month past.
>
> (Ch. II, p. 113)

Marlow's 'Aha!' to the headman of his African crew is 'just for good fellowship's sake' (Ch. II, p. 113) – not a command or request. Marlow is aware of him as a person, not just a tool of convenience. Nor is the African subservient: he is curt, dignified – and businesslike. Marlow is so far from attributing any positive qualities to the whites that he coolly considers the possibility that it is disgust which keeps the cannibals from eating their employers and rejects it only because he realizes that disgust is not a sufficient barrier for starving men. In this text, then, the blacks do not fit the racist stereotypes of the time any more than the Europeans fall into the mould of Empire builders.

It is hard to find support for Said's assertion regarding Conrad's standpoint, that 'the lesser or subject peoples were to be ruled'.[46] Conrad not only shows compassion for the Africans as victims, he also admires certain positive qualities in them: the sinewy vitality of the men in the coastal boat, the dignity of the cannibal headman, the sense of honour and restraint of the cannibals, and the majesty of Kurtz's woman. He respects African culture, and, indeed, places it on a par with the European. Marlow takes the same reverential attitude to the rhythm

---

45 Said, *Culture and Imperialism*, p. 79.
46 Said, *Culture and Imperialism*, p. 26.

of African drums as to the sound of bells in a Christian country (Ch. I, p. 88). That is, he is able to imagine the tables turned, the roles of the blacks and whites reversed:

> The population had cleared out a long time ago. Well, if a lot of mysterious niggers armed with all kinds of fearful weapons suddenly took to travelling on the road between Deal and Gravesend, catching the yokels right and left to carry heavy loads for them, I fancy every farm and cottage thereabouts would get empty very soon. Only here the dwellings were gone, too.
>
> (Ch. I, pp. 87–8)

It is almost impossible for the modern reader not to be brought up short by the word 'nigger' in this passage. We almost have to force ourselves to go beyond the understanding we now have of the racist connotations of the word to understand what the sentence as a whole is saying: 'no wonder these people are making themselves scarce; we would too if they had invaded our country in the way we have invaded theirs and were treating us in the fashion we are treating them.' The anti-essentialist attitude is plain: the difference between 'them' and 'us' is purely one of circumstance.

Conrad/Marlow does not say that what the Africans do is wrong, but that it would be wrong for people to whom such practices are taboo, like Kurtz, to join in and do, sacrificing their ingrained principles. Conrad does not connect the powers of darkness with the Africans, only with Kurtz who knows and accepts the powers of light as the Africans never have. The Africans do not infect Kurtz. Whatever they do is a part of their way of life. When Marlow sees the Africans healthy and practising their customs, he recognizes them not as the Other, but as having a 'remote kinship' (Ch. II, p. 107) with 'us'; the attraction, the urge for 'a howl and a dance' (Ch. II, p. 108), is seemingly an irrational impulse from the unconscious but, at bottom, an acknowledgement of a shared human impulse, just as the profound dying glance of Marlow's African helmsman affirms 'a claim of distant kinship' (Ch. II, p. 126). The parallel between the Roman colonization of Britain and the European colonization of Africa is partly recognition of shared historical experience.

Conrad's portrayal of the African under Western influence is more complex. For example, this is how Marlow characterizes the fireman:

> He was an improved specimen; he could fire up a vertical boiler . . . to look at him was as edifying as seeing a dog in a parody of breeches . . . A few months of training had done for that really fine chap . . . He was useful because he had been instructed; and what he knew was this – that should the water in that transparent thing disappear, the evil spirit inside the boiler would get angry through the greatness of his thirst, and take a terrible vengeance.
>
> (Ch. II, pp. 108–9)

Marlow shares the tendency common even among the most 'enlightened' Europeans to assume that the operation of the mind of the semi-educated African was always influenced by superstition, but his respect for the fireman as a human being, a 'really fine chap', is not something common. But Conrad goes beyond that common tendency. He shows that, unlike the cannibal crew, the fireman, 'a dog in a parody of breeches', is warped by an alien, unfamiliar technology, that his view of the boiler is a response of a man to whom this technology is a not a part of his history. He has submitted to white influence as a passive recipient, and, unlike Makola in Conrad's earlier short story 'An Outpost of Progress' (1897), has not really appropriated the white man's culture and skills. Makola not only sees himself as an equal of the white men but holds them in contempt, though he hails from a tribal, and feudal, culture. He represents the hybrid as a menace to the white man. Except for the germ of Makola in the manager's insolent African boy who announces Kurtz's death, there is hardly any African presence to disturb Conrad's white readership in respect of his pro-African stance.

Recent postcolonial theorists have formulated a concept of the Other as the embodiment of the unsatisfactory qualities within the colonizer which he projects on to the native inhabitant. In the novella, Conrad not only anticipates this concept but subverts it by indicating that there is a bond between the self and the Other, and breaks it down completely by suggesting that the Other represents a stage through which the colonizer himself has passed before arriving at his present stage of development. At a time when the view of history was melioristic,[47] inevitably he saw Africa as the childhood of human history – childhood being given to whirling, howling, strong grief and rages, but neither condemned nor condoned. Conrad does not accept a hierarchy of races or cultures, but does believe in evolutionary stages in cultural development.

A key phrase employed to describe imperialism in the tale is 'fantastic invasion', which carries connotations of forcible, wrongful intrusion, and displacement. While the text portrays the Africans as primitive, it also suggests that they are best left to themselves – the white man should not be in Africa. The Africans in the coastal boat, the deserted villages, the dignified cannibals, all seem as if they functioned perfectly well without 'civilizing'. The glow cast over the images of Africans free of European control and influence, the cannibal headman and Kurtz's woman could suggest that Conrad harbours nostalgia for the earlier stage of culture. Conrad was uncomfortable with contact between diverse cultures, as this portended the worst fate for the Africans: in this tale, partaking only a little of the 'white man's learning' is to be on the periphery of hybridity, and like Marlow's fireman, to be labelled ironically as 'an improved specimen'. (In 'An Outpost of Progress' an even worse fate overtakes the African who becomes hybrid. Makola is cunning, manipulative, and even evil.) Like Rider Haggard, though more subtly, Conrad objected to imperialism on the grounds that it disrupted, violated and harmed indigenous culture (see Text and contexts, **p. 10**). It should not be forgotten that Marlow assigns even to the disparaged helmsman a higher moral value than he does to Kurtz: 'I can't forget him [Kurtz], though I am not prepared to affirm the fellow was exactly worth the life we lost [the helmsman's] in getting to him' (Ch. II, p. 125). Moreover, the European 'pilgrim' who replaced the African proved 'a hopeless duffer at the business' (Ch. II, p. 120).

---

47 Meliorism is the doctrine that the world is capable of improvement.

Eloise Knapp Hay thinks that the chief among the drawbacks of *Heart of Darkness* as a teaching text is 'Conrad's deliberate obscurantism, hiding the part that England played in opening the Congo for free trade in the 1880s'.[48] But Conrad does take this into account imaginatively: the young African in the grove of death has 'a bit of white worsted[49] round his neck' (Ch. I, p. 85);[50] Kurtz's disciple is equipped with a Martini-Henry and Towson's *An Inquiry into some Points of Seamanship*; one of his pockets is bright red, and the other dark blue and white, a veritable Union Jack!

It should be admitted that Conrad downplays the active opposition of blacks to the imperialists in the Congo. In Conrad's presentation of the death of Fresleven, the reader sees the white Fresleven, 'the gentlest, quietest creature' (Ch. I, p. 74), beating a passive chief, whereas in the original, actual incident a ruffled, offended chief repudiated a gift of two brass rods to his child and threatened to attack a steamer captain called Freiesleben; the dispute was not about a trivial matter of hens as in the novella but one of pride, followed by the threat of a native rising.[51] Conrad transforms a dignified episode into a farcical, domestic fracas; white dignity goes to pot as Fresleven haggles over hens and hammers a feeble old negro, revealing the petty undignified stances into which whites are thrown by arrogance and a sense of what is due to them, the absolute frustration of the white who wants to behave as god and is thwarted by the native. Fresleven is killed because the chief's son is virtually pushed into it to save his father and, then, *both* sides panic. This is hardly native resistance; the heroics are nil. The Fresleven incident is crucial because it enabled Marlow to come to Africa. Moreover, Fresleven is one of the three characters (the others being Marlow and Kurtz) who are named. [The characters are usually given generic names as it is their representative status and how they contribute to the general thematics that matter.] Yet he is more important as a symptom than a person, and illustrates the changes in attitude and behaviour of the whites brought about by the colonial situation. The episode prefigures the beating of the African who was alleged to have burnt a shed full of calico and other items (Ch. I, p. 92). Similarly, although Arthur Eugene Constant Hodister[52] was one of the models for Kurtz, the novella includes nothing suggestive of the fate of the 1892 Hodister expedition as it was reported in *The Times*: 'The reception at Riba Riba was distinctly unpleasant. Arabs and natives refused absolutely to recognize the Government of the Congo State and insisted that the flag should be hauled down.'[53]

Readers today, however, should be careful to see such narrative details in the context of the time. Whereas it might seem to us inappropriate to downplay the

---

48 Hay, Abstract for 'Rattling Talkers and Silence Soothsayers: The Race for *Heart of Darkness*', in *Joseph Conrad Today*, 16, 1&2, 1991, 3.
49 'Worsted' named from 'Worsted', now 'Worstead', in Norfolk, England, where it was first manufactured.
50 The Congolese were, understandably, reluctant to work for Leopold's companies and these had to import labour mainly from British colonies.
51 Sherry, *Conrad's Western World*, pp. 17–20.
52 Hodister was a highly successful commercial agent and collector of ivory, an explorer, a man of wide abilities, a man of principles, and also charismatic (he inspired the trust and friendship of Africans and had a harem of African women) – around the time of Conrad's Congo journey. See Sherry, *Conrad's Western World*, pp. 95–118.
53 Sherry, *Conrad's Western World*, p. 110.

importance of resistance to oppression on the part of Africans, at the time Conrad was writing any suggestions of 'aggression' by blacks could be – and were – taken as justification for further oppression. Conrad wishes to avoid giving the conventional impression of Africans as 'blood-thirsty'. He takes their side and usually presents them as victims.

But it should also be admitted that there is no sustained attempt in the text to represent African culture. Given the role of Marlow, this project may not have been possible. Marlow sees no more than a man on a river trip can see and understand of 'native' life. Marlow's ignorance may be explicable and defensible, especially as he does not condemn what he does not understand. He commits himself only addressing the culture he knows, which is European culture. Abdul JanMohamed states that: 'Africans are an incidental part, not the main objects of representation.'[54] But rather than playing only 'an incidental part', I would say the Africans are integral to the narrative, even though their presence is sufficient for the position they occupy in the thematics. They are present less for their own sake than for the reader to perceive the reactions of the Europeans to them.

We have seen that in almost everything said about the Europeans the text subverts the melioristic view of history with a damning critique of 'progress' and civilization. Marlow's contemptuous dismissal of imperialism is conveyed early, during the Freseleven episode, when he says 'I should think the cause of progress got the hens, anyhow' (Ch. I, p. 75). The steamer is a symbol not only of the incursion of the Europeans but also of what was considered progress and civilization, a symbol V.S. Naipaul develops as an intertextual motif in *A Bend in the River* (1979). The steamer was tearing the face of the waters, while the wilderness was waiting to sweep back. The images of modernity/development in the novella are uniformly damning: the steamer is dilapidated, the railway-building inefficient, the management of labour and the commercial transactions (such as worthless European goods in exchange for ivory) are all discrediting. The steamer travels through a white fog, which has been interpreted symbolically. Equally, this episode shows a strong adventure story element typical of its period and the adventure novel – of threatened attack, fear and suspense. Imperialism harms the colonized (physically and spiritually) as well as the colonizer (corruption, disease, madness and death all take their toll); of the colonizers, it is the most idealistic of them (Kurtz) who is most deeply affected, though it is the colonized 'natives' who suffer most. Man was savage in Roman times, he is savage in the present: there is no such thing as progress, in the moral sense. Conrad almost seems to be exposing the nullity of all civilizations from the Roman onwards, a pessimistic assessment. He sees the ironies of technological change and development without moral advancement.

Conrad and the text

So far we have spoken of the attitude of the text to these political questions. But it is difficult to make claims for an attitude the text in its totality expresses from the

---

54 JanMohamed, 'The economy of Manichaen Allegory: The Function of Racial Difference in Colonialist Literature', in *Race, Writing and Difference*, ed. Henry Louis Gates, Jr., Chicago: Chicago UP, 1986, p. 90.

attitudes of the narrator, the expected attitudes of the reader, and the intentions of the author, and to separate these consistently from one another. It may be impossible to settle such questions conclusively, but posing these is fruitful. How do the attitudes of Marlow differ from those of Conrad? Is the reader led towards any stable position? On this point Edward Said argues:

> Conrad's readers of the time were not expected to ask about or concern themselves with what became of the natives. What mattered to them was how Marlow makes sense of everything, for without his deliberately fashioned narrative there is no history worth telling, no fiction worth entertaining, no authority worth consulting. This is a short step away from King Leopold's account of his International Congo Association, 'rendering lasting and disinterested services to the cause of progress,' activities described by one admirer in 1885 as the 'noblest and most self-sacrificing scheme for African development that has ever been or ever will be attempted.'[55]

But can we find any basis for these assertions in the text? Said in fact here takes Marlow as totally other than he is as a character. Far from being represented as infallible or as a moral guru, he is often a voice of shifting uncertainties. He sits Buddha-wise, but the 'enlightenment' he has received is the awareness of an ineluctable darkness; the only positives he clings to – work, duty and restraint – are constructs, deliberately set up and used to save a mind from disintegration.

From the beginning we are told that Marlow is distinguished from other seamen by stories that lack the neat and satisfying conclusions of the sort that listeners normally expect. And while Marlow's comments make it clear that his audience does indeed hold attitudes that place little value on 'what became of the natives', Marlow repeatedly asks them to rethink their position:

> I missed my late helmsman awfully – I missed him even while his body was still lying in the pilot-house. Perhaps you will think it passing strange this regret for a savage who was no more account than a grain of sand in a black Sahara. Well, don't you see, he had done something.
>
> (Ch. II, p. 125)

It is Marlow's audience, and by extension Conrad's original readers, who could be expected to think of a native as of 'no more account than a grain of sand'; the text, through Marlow, consistently works against that view.

Marlow's tale must act to some extent to subvert the imperialistic reality it describes. But the evidence Marlow presents sometimes acts to subvert his own assessment of it. We see some of his attitudes towards the natives – enlightened though they may have been at the time – as patronizing or condescending. We see that, to some extent, Marlow has been conditioned by the then current notions of Africa and responds to Africans in unflattering terms. He refers to them as

---

55 Said, *Culture and Imperialism*, p. 200.

'savages', 'niggers'; uses adjectives such as 'horrid', 'ugly', 'fiend-like', 'satanic' to describe their appearance or behaviour; compares them to insects/animals such as 'ants', 'hyenas'; finds their speech 'a babble of uncouth sounds', 'resembled no sounds of human language'. [Interestingly, Marlow extends his use of animal imagery to Europeans, to convey his assessment of the Eldorado Exploring Expedition, a naked attempt at plunder. He rates its members 'less valuable' than their donkeys, while its leader has a 'short flipper of an arm' (Ch. II, p. 104).] Even more centrally, 'the idea' of a higher purpose behind the exploitation of the natives, which Marlow at least intermittently seems to want to believe in, is for the modern reader entirely discredited.

But is this the way Conrad intended the text to work? Did he in fact share Marlow's views pretty much in their entirety? What do we know of the author's own beliefs and intentions? We have observed his pro-British sentiments but also noted that he is more critical of the British than Marlow who is, after all, British. Haggard's Ignosi damns all imperialists, including the British (see Text and contexts, **p. 10**). Conrad's criticism of British imperialism is implicit, oblique, qualified, yet, ultimately, more comprehensive than Haggard's. He is opposed to all imperialisms, in the past, the present, and of whatever stripe. Yet, it should be admitted that Conrad's other writings are not entirely free of the sort of racism that was conventional in his age. In his earlier tale *The Nigger of the 'Narcissus'* (1897), for example, he describes James Wait as having 'a face pathetic and brutal: the tragic, the mysterious, the repulsive mask of a nigger's soul'.[56]

But if he was occasionally prey to the prejudices of his time, in his best writings at any rate Conrad seems to have had the integrity and courage to follow through to the full the implications of his vision even when they may have challenged aspects of his own prejudices. (It may well have been the case that in *Heart of Darkness* he was even able to transcend, in a sense, his own persona.) There is also ample evidence that his lapses into prejudice were precisely that – lapses – and that Conrad for the most part genuinely believed that imperialistic oppression was a moral outrage.

Said argues that Conrad 'does not give us a fully realized alternative to imperialism'.[57] True; Conrad would have found it hard to envisage decolonization. But was this possible in 1900, especially in regard to the Congo? Kipling, in 'Recessional' (1897), foresaw the inevitable dissolution of the British Empire, but not necessarily the resurgence of subject countries or a viable alternative to imperialism. *The Daily Telegraph*, the London newspaper, published a pamphlet which protested against African independence – in 1969! To me, it seems that Conrad was intensely aware of differences between whites and Africans, but not systematically to the disparagement of the latter. He sees the Africans as having a past and, unlike V.S. Naipaul, sees them as possibly having a future. He sees the 'fantastic invasion' as 'passing' (Ch. I, p. 92). Moreover, Marlow's relaxed relationship with his 'cannibal' crew on his steamer allows for the possibility of relationship between black and white.

56 Conrad, *The Nigger of the 'Narcissus', Typhoon and Other Stories*, London: Penguin, 1963 edn, p. 27.
57 Said, *Culture and Imperialism*, p. 28.

Narrative strategies

The form of *Heart of Darkness* and its thematics are so closely intertwined as to be virtually inseparable. Ambiguities, uncertainties and ironies are echoed in the layered narrative structure of the novella, through which it is often impossible to be sure of one's bearings – and indeed, often difficult to be sure on first reading of what is happening or who is speaking. In its density the style has tellingly been likened to a tropical forest. This is most obviously the case with Conrad's strategy of including narratives within Marlow's narrative, and enclosing Marlow's narrative itself within that of another narrator.

Marlow is in a group of five on board a yawl, *Nellie*, on the Thames. The frame narrator's location is not mentioned (perhaps a club); he is not identified by name but his occupation is or has been, presumably, that of a merchant seaman because between the five 'there was the bond of the sea' (Ch. I, p. 67). He seems to be addressing a larger audience and mediating between Marlow and the reader. He begins by introducing Marlow's narrative. The *Nellie* was making a river journey from the open sea into the interior, a parallel to Marlow's Congo journey, and waiting for the turn of the tide, in mid journey – a non-conclusive moment that gestures towards the future. The Thames is like 'an interminable waterway' (Ch. I, p. 67), that thus places no limits of place or time on the tale's significance. The focus extends to the city, London 'the biggest, and the greatest, town on earth' (Ch. I, p. 67) (literally true or believed so in Conrad's time), the acme of civilization and the metropolis of the largest and most important of the empires in world history; civilization and imperialism are central questions of the novella. The later description of London as 'monstrous' (Ch. I, p. 69) strikes an ominous note.

The first person to be introduced is the Director of Companies, who represents Commerce, and thus embodies the stability and organization as well as the loot/ profit motive of civilization. Appropriately he is 'our captain' (leader) and host (provider), and is followed by the Lawyer and the Accountant, who connects with the accountant in the Congo to underline the profit motive in Empire. The Accountant's dominoes are made of ivory, and so form a link with the Intended's piano keys, also made of ivory, to underscore that ivory is not exotic but an article of daily use. This is its first and unobtrusive appearance as a commodity that is to become a prominent focus of the narrative, and, symbolically, links European high culture with imperial exploitation in Africa. From the beginning of the novella Conrad's language is rich, full of echoes and patterned with recurrent phases. The hour of day is dusk, with a 'brooding gloom' (a phrase repeated four times on the first three pages). The constantly stressed references to 'dark' and 'light', in physical, metaphorical and symbolic senses, appear to arise naturally from the atmosphere and setting, and continue, often paradoxically, till the end as the dominant leitmotif. The novella, like Kurtz's painting, is done in chiaroscuro, to achieve a third dimension that can house the reality of history. Conrad's presentation of the imperial theme begins not in the Congo or even Brussels but in London.

Marlow's audience on the *Nellie* consists of successful, intelligent men of affairs, all connected to the enterprise of Empire. Their standing suggests that Conrad intended his tale to be taken as a serious social analysis. Marlow is addressing his peers and kindred spirits, but he is also an adventurer who has gone into the darkness. His tale, necessarily and inevitably, bypasses his audience (as Conrad and Marlow are aware) because of this experiential gap. The audience cannot perceive or respond to Marlow's narrative because the experience is alien to them. Marlow protests:

> 'Absurd!' he cried. 'This is the worst of trying to tell . . . Here you all are, each moored with two good addresses, like a hulk with two anchors, a butcher round one corner, a policeman round another, excellent appetites, and temperature normal . . . And you say, Absurd!'
>
> (Ch. I, p. 122)

Nothing comes home to those who only hear. Marlow's ultimate view is:

> '. . . it is impossible to convey the life-sensation of any given epoch of one's existence – that which makes its truth, its meaning – its subtle and penetrating essence. We live, as we dream – alone.'
>
> (Ch. I, p. 97)

The *Nellie* group felt 'meditative' (Ch. I, p. 68), falling into a mood appropriate for the introduction of the Buddha tableaux, which encloses the tale. Through the comparison to the Buddha, the frame narrator suggests Marlow's role is that of a seeker after enlightenment and explorer of the self; he must needs possess an openness of mind that is not conditioned by religion nor even by culture. Indeed, 'the complex and humane outlook represented by Marlow', which Cedric Watts regards as a 'valuable feature of European civilization', seems to me an individual rather than a cultural trait.[58] The tale is really open-ended and 'inconclusive' (Ch. I, p. 72), and thereby involves the reader in active exploration and assessment, thus ensuring that 'continued vibration' which as Conrad hoped in his 'Author's Note', 'hangs in the air and dwells on the ear after the last note had been struck' (p. 65).

In his opening long speech, the frame narrator from one perspective reveals his jingoism (the strong belief that his own country is best), from another his idealism. He is a British character and projects a quintessentially British view, evoking 'the great spirit of the past upon the Thames' (Ch. I, p. 68). His meditation casts an aura of fame, romance and splendour around the history of those who had ventured to explore the unexplored. But Conrad introduces a disturbing critical undercurrent beyond the narrator's consciousness. There are suggestions that these were really financial undertakings (the Americas were milked at secondhand by marauding Spanish galleons), and that the British expansion overseas was actually a colonial enterprise. [The age of Elizabeth I saw the beginnings of British imperialism.] The contrast between Francis Drake's '*Golden Hind* returning with her round flanks full of treasure' and Sir John Franklin's *Erebus* and *Terror* 'that never returned' (Ch. I, pp. 68–9) symbolizes wealth, prosperity and

---

58 Watts, ' "A Bloody Racist": About Achebe's View of Conrad', in *Yearbook of English Studies*, 13, 1983, p. 414.

triumph on the one hand, and destruction, death and even cannibalism (Franklin's reversion out of necessity), on the other. 'Hunters for gold or pursuers of fame [They prefigure Kurtz who wanted both.] . . . bearing the sword, and often the torch . . .' (I, p. 69). In a patriarchal society, military glory was accepted as worthwhile, but Conrad adds a critical note by placing 'the torch' (a symbol of 'light', knowledge, civilization) second, and by evoking the negative suggestions implicit in 'the torch' too (torches can be destructive as well).

Marlow's sudden statement, 'And this also has been one of the dark places of the earth' (Ch. I, p. 69), cuts across and contradicts the aura of the frame narrator's words. Britain, once a colony, is now a colonizer; at a general level, the argument can imply that not only in Britain's past and present but in all imperial ventures there is an exploration of darkness. This provides the motivation for Marlow to narrate his story to an audience implicated in imperialism. 'Dark places' was a charged, rich phrase in its time. Originally found in the Bible (Psalm 74: 20–1), it was used in missionary and colonial discourse to signify unchristian, uncivilized and uncharted, and in particular Africa. Redolent of all these significations when Marlow uses it, it jolts the reader.

The anonymous frame narrator is a beneficiary of imperialism, and, like Marlow before his river journey, is ignorant of imperial realities. As he listens to Marlow's tale, he undergoes a process of education yet at the very beginning he possesses the intelligence to characterize it accurately:

> The yarns of seamen have a direct simplicity, the whole meaning of which lies within the shell of a cracked nut. But Marlow was not typical (if his propensity to spin yarns be excepted), and to him the meaning of an episode was not inside like a kernel but outside, enveloping the tale which brought it out only as a glow brings out a haze, in the likeness of one of these misty halos that sometimes are made visible by the spectral illumination of moonshine.
>
> (Ch. I, p. 70)

The narrator establishes himself as a reliable agent to relay Marlow's narrative. From one perspective, the narrative structure subverts the seaman's yarn; from another, Conrad employs the narrative mode of the sahib recounting his colonial experiences, a mode established in *Blackwood's Edinburgh Magazine* – to which Conrad contributed *Karain, Youth, Lord Jim* and *Heart of* Darkness – to subvert the sahib view of imperialism. By lingering over Marlow's technique of storytelling, Conrad warns the reader that s/he must be prepared to hunt for meaning even as he undertakes the task of introducing something new, profound and wonderful, which he felt he had performed in *Heart of Darkness*. After reading Edward Garnett's review of the *Youth* volume, Conrad wrote:

> your brave attempt to grapple with the fogginess of *H of D*, to explain what I myself have tried to shape blindfold, as it were, has touched me profoundly . . . it's a high water mark.[59]

---

59 Conrad, letter to Garnett, 22 December 1902, in *Collected Letters II*, pp. 467–8; *G:HD*, p. 171.

Aware of the difficulty of his technique, through the frame narrator's explanation Conrad teaches how *Heart of Darkness* needs to be read. Conscious of the difficulty of being understood, Marlow repeats himself on this score and does not minimize the difficulty. The use of two narrators that play off two different points of view helps Conrad to gain in precision. The frame narrator sometimes performs the role as of a commentator like a Greek chorus. At other times, he reports Marlow's story not as indirect, but as direct, speech. Marlow's story is heard at two removes, through two parallel sets of narrators and audiences, but both narrators speak in the first person which ensures a total immediacy of impact. Among other things, *Heart of Darkness* is the story of a story.

Marlow's opening remark is elaborated when he proceeds to compare the Roman Empire and the British, underlining the suggestion that the relevance of the tale is not time-bound.

> But darkness was here yesterday. . . . think of a decent young citizen in a toga ... Land in a swamp, march through the woods, and in some inland post feel the savagery, the utter savagery had closed round him ... Mind, none of us would feel exactly like this. What saves us is efficiency – the devotion to efficiency. But these chaps were not much account, really. They were no colonists; their administration was merely a squeeze, and nothing more, I suspect. They were conquerors, and for that you want only brute force – nothing to boast of, when you have it, since your strength is just an accident arising from the weakness of others ... The conquest of the earth, which mostly means the taking it away from those who have a different complexion or slightly flatter noses than ourselves, is not a pretty thing when you look into it too much. What redeems it is the idea only. An idea at the back of it; not a sentimental pretence but an idea; and an unselfish belief in the idea – something you can set up, bow down before, and offer a sacrifice to . . .
>
> (Ch. I, pp. 70–2)

As early as 1884 it was a fashion to compare England to the later Roman Empire.[60] But Conrad is taking an unusual approach in imagining Britain as savage colony rather than imperial power. In the genre of travel narrative, travellers to foreign lands cater to the home audience's sense of cultural superiority. Yet Marlow does not do so. In fact, Conrad subverts the normal travel narrative from the beginning by emphasizing the fact that imperialism began in Europe with the British as 'natives'. Moreover, he brings together the self and the Other on the basis of a shared experience in historical terms. It was a long-standing British imperial tradition to admire the Roman Empire and emulate it: Cecil Rhodes 'liked to picture himself as [Roman] emperor'![61] Conrad also departs from tradition by condemning the Romans. He distinguishes between conquest and

60 Stephen Donovan, ' "Figures, facts, theories": Conrad and Chartered Company Imperialism', in *The Conradian*, 24, 2, 1999, p. 43.
61 René Maunier, 'The Sociology of Colonies' in *British Imperialism*, ed.Robin W. Winks, New York: Holt, Rinehart & Winston, 1966 edn, p. 69.

colonialism. Marlow is aware that British colonialism, too, is unsatisfactory but thinks that it is redeemed by 'efficiency', and 'the idea'. These explicit criteria sound vague, wishy-washy and feeble today but would not have been so in Conrad's day when the Social Darwinist (see Text and context, p. 13), pro-imperial values these refer to, were fervently and widely held and also readily identifiable. Yet through the hints of 'primitive' rituals in Marlow's concluding words, Conrad makes a critical suggestion beyond Marlow's consciousness that to justify imperialism is to justify savagery. The narrative that follows implicates the British Empire in its exposure of the evils of imperialism and brings out the sheer hollowness of these ideals. After all, England (like 'all of Europe') contributed to the making of Kurtz.

In presenting the British as the colonized, Marlow also elicits sympathy for them. His justification of imperialism, especially British, is confirmed when he speaks of himself in the waiting-room of the Belgian imperial company, observing a map of the world with all the colonies marked: 'There was a vast amount of red – good to see at any time, because one knows some real work is done in there' (Ch. I, p. 76). Red represents British colonies, and Marlow sees some hopeful possibilities in Empire, especially of the British kind. This view provides him with the necessary motivation to accept colonial employment.

Marlow's view and the frame narrator's jingoism/idealism are designed to appeal to British readers. Fearing rejection as an alien (see Text and contexts, p. 4), Conrad had to identify with the society around him to gain a hearing. He could not afford to be too open in his critique of imperialism. He also needed to gain popularity as a writer; money was important to him, and his income was grossly insufficient at this time. But the pro-British passages in the novella are not solely or wholly gestures to Conrad's audience. After all, he *chose* to live and work in Britain, and was a genuine Anglophile. During the Boer War, and two days after he began writing the novella, he wrote to a cousin, Aniela Zagorska, who was living in Brussels where Belgian and British sentiments were in conflict, 'that they [the Boers] are struggling in good faith for their independence cannot be doubted; but it is also a fact that they have no idea of liberty, which can be only found under the English flag all over the world'.[62] That said, both the frame narrator and Marlow are more pro-British than their creator.

The frame narrator's long introduction of Marlow and his peculiarities establishes Marlow as an inquirer and gives him authority. His acceptability as a narrator is crucial to the success of the novella. At one point, however, as he ruminates on his experiences at the Central Station in the Congo, he confesses that his temperament is such that he hates lies. Yet Marlow lies four times. He intimidates the brick-maker by allowing him to imagine that he has the power to harm his career through influence in Europe and obtains the rivets he needs to repair his steamboat and get to Kurtz. Later Marlow appeases Kurtz's disciple even though he disagrees with his views in regard to Kurtz; the disciple thus re-enters the wilderness with his sunny temperament intact. Marlow also lies to Kurtz, who is on the verge of death, saying that his 'success in Europe is assured' in order to persuade him to return to the steamer. Most noteworthy, on Marlow's

---

62 Conrad, letter to Zagorska, 25 December 1899, in *Collected Letters II*, p. 230.

return to Europe, he lies to Kurtz's Intended. In these instances, Marlow is impelled by the pervasive power of the current system to yield to the dishonesties imperialism imposes, though minimally. Kurtz, visualized as an idealist, exacts support against sordid opponents. The desire to save Kurtz, protective pity for the Russian and the Intended overcome his revulsion. But while his dissimulations are not of the sort to impair integrity and he is candid about them, his kind of honesty is one reason why the reader accepts his tale. Moreover, Marlow remains a man with values and ideals, and he sticks to these.

That Marlow is a certain type of Englishman is also important, just as it is true that Conrad and Marlow overlap. Like Conrad, Marlow is an introspective and private man, analytic, and extraordinary in his openness to impressions and capturing these. But Marlow is essentially a projection of an English character. His class affiliations do not matter in Africa. He recalls to his audience how he had returned from 'a regular dose of the East . . . invading your homes as if I had got a heavenly mission to civilize you' (Ch. I, p. 72). He has the bantering air of one behaving in London as an imperialist would do in a colony, and so takes a swipe at the civilizing mission of Empire. Marlow is not totally unaware of imperialism pre-Congo, but is nevertheless enthusiastic about the British Empire. Through Marlow Conrad can examine British attitudes to imperialism; Marlow in turn remains the most appropriate narrative vehicle for this story because his nationality does not inhibit his clear-sightedness and frankness in confronting the colonialism represented by a foreign nation, Belgium. It is true that he is an employee of a Belgian company, but only marginally, newly and briefly contractually bound, and though he is aware that he is implicated in their deeds, he does not adopt the perspective of the exploiters.

Marlow's narrative is presented precisely from his perspective and it includes a degree of unreliability because of Marlow's own limitations. The major one is that he spends only a short time in Africa. He is, besides, shown to be chauvinistic in a national sense. His understanding of women is conventional. Because Marlow is Kurtz's secret sharer, his account of Kurtz is not fully objective. Conrad exposes these limitations and thereby underscores the distinction between the authorial voice and that of the character.

Kurtz, Conrad and Nietzsche

Marlow's encounter with Kurtz is the climax of Conrad's story. Kurtz is the chief character of the tale, not Marlow as the generality of critics have argued. Here the imperial theme expands to include an account of moral isolation – Kurtz's story in the heart of Africa – from one perspective. The direct presentation of Kurtz occupies only a few pages, his eloquence is described, not recorded, but he is extensively discussed both before and afterwards. He is presented mainly through the eyes of others, both as a great man and as the most absolute of sinners. His 'greatness' is, ironically, linked to completely ordinary facts. He is socially disadvantaged, being poor; his main purpose in finding colonial employment is to 'make his pile', the common motivation of colonial employees, and shine in Europe. Yet he is also a painter, a poet, a musician, a journalist, an orator – a man of varied talents. And he comes to the Congo 'equipped with moral ideas'. It is this, not his outstanding success in gathering ivory (which is what matters to the other colonial employees), that impels Marlow's interest. One of Kurtz's stated ideals is: 'Each station should be like a beacon on the road towards better things, a centre for . . . humanizing, improving, instructing' (Ch. II, pp. 103–4). Stephen Ross thinks that 'Kurtz approaches his endeavour with full-blown naiveté'.[63] It seems to me that Kurtz was by no means ignorant. He has an intellectual grasp and knowledge: he was in journalism and politics; he thinks each station should be a centre for trade as a matter of course. He voices ideals, yet he was driven, primarily, by material motives. Therefore, in his idealism lurks an element of hypocrisy. There were Europeans in the metropolitan countries who were idealistic without hypocrisy, such as Marlow's aunt, while in the colonies, missionaries who risked disease and death acted independently of the basic acquisitive motivations of imperialism. But Kurtz was no innocent who simply became a victim of Africa.

Given the exploitative adventurism of the period, critics have argued for a number of models for Kurtz – Klein[64] (see The author, **p. 5**), Hodister[65] (see Text and contexts, **p. 25**), King Leopold II and Stanley[66] (see Historical context, **pp. 15–16**), Captain Léon Rom.[67] In addition, many actual white men in the Congo and elsewhere (including the famous instance of Gauguin, 1848–1903, who abandoned Paris for Tahiti) 'went native' (in the Victorian phrase) or underwent moral disintegration. Yet Conrad's debt is to several people rather than to an individual, and, above all, to his own shaping imagination. The dynamics of Conrad's tale demand a figure such as Kurtz.

The key to the transformation of Kurtz is found in Marlow's realization that 'he had kicked the very earth to pieces' (Ch. III, p. 144). Kurtz is perhaps a specimen of the 'free spirit' who has gone 'Beyond Good and Evil' and answered in the affirmative the question of Zarathustra, 'the destroyer of morality': 'can'st thou give thyself thine own evil and thy good, hanging thy will above thee as a law?'[68] (see Text and context, **p. 14**). The strong drives in human nature are allowed to emerge. Lust results in 'gratified and monstrous passions' (Ch. III, p. 144). Marianna Torgovnick thinks: 'Kurtz has apparently mated with the magnificent black woman and thus violated the British code against miscegenation.'[69] The 'code' is not only British but Western. 'Apparently' is unnecessarily tentative, given that Kurtz is likely to have 'mated' with more. The lure of the alien is permitted to affect Kurtz. He is both drawn and repelled by a culture he despises; it is he who orders the Africans to attack Marlow's steamer which was intended to rescue him. Their arrows 'might have been poisoned but they looked as though they wouldn't kill a cat' (Ch. II, p. 119) – it does not avoid the realistic possibilities of the arrows being lethal, yet leaves a flavour of harmlessness, very much in tune with the fact that it is an attempt to repel, not kill, the whites. Kurtz's

---

63 Ross, *Conrad and Empire*, Columbia and London: Missouri UP, 2004, p. 52.
64 Jocelyn Baines, *Joseph Conrad*, London: Weidenfeld, 1993 edn, p. 117.
65 Sherry, *Conrad's Western World*, p. 95.
66 Ian Watt, *Conrad in the Nineteenth Century*, pp. 142–6.
67 Rom, an officer in Congo's Force Publique, was 'known for displaying a row of severed African heads around his garden, wrote a book on African customs, painted portraits and landscapes, and collected butterflies.' – Hochschild, *King Leopold*, p. 117.
68 Nietzsche, *Ecce Homo: How One Becomes What One Is*, pp. 40–1.
69 Torgovnick, *Gone Primitive: Savage Intellects, Modern Lives*, Chicago & London: Chicago UP, 1990, p. 146.

avarice and lust for power, whose seeds precede his life in Africa, and of which the human skulls around his dwelling are a symbol, are unrestrained. He betrays the natives, corrupting and ruthlessly exploiting them. He employs African villagers to fight their fellow men exclusively for his benefit, so that he can amass the maximum possible quantity of ivory. He perverts 'pure, uncomplicated savagery' into 'some lightless region of subtle horrors' (Ch. III, p. 134), including 'unspeakable rites offered up to him' (Ch. II, p. 124).

Robert Baker raises the question whether 'unspeakable rites' refers to homosexuality.[70] Kurtz has possibilities of expressing homosexuality with the Harlequin and the Africans. In Victorian times, homosexuality was considered as 'the love that dare not speak its name', in the words of the poem 'Two Loves' by Lord Alfred Douglas (1870–1945), intimate of Oscar Wilde. But it could not be considered so serious a transgression as to be viewed as one of Kurtz's 'unspeakable rites'. After all, the European cultural tradition has been quite ambivalent on the question. As Jonathan told David: 'Very pleasant hast thou been to me; thy love to me was wonderful, passing the love of women.'[71] Stephen A. Reid, using Sir James George Frazer's The Golden Bough, A Study in Magic and Religion (1890), has suggested that 'Kurtz's unspeakable rites and secrets concern (with whatever attendant bestiality) human sacrifice and Kurtz's consuming a portion of the sacrificial victim.'[72] Marianna Torgovnick thinks: 'In collecting heads he acted out a Western fantasy of savagery.'[73] But the practice may have been simply for punishment, or even intimidation; further, collecting heads as such is not specified in the text. Indeed, to specify Kurtz's 'unspeakable rites', which Conrad deliberately does not (he would have known of factual works to substantiate these, if he wished to do so),[74] would be to trivialize these and trivialize Kurtz. The un-named, therefore unlimited, is always more awful.

Nietzsche (see Text and contexts, p. 14) wrote:

> For these same men, who, amongst themselves, are so strictly constrained by custom, worship, ritual, gratitude, and by mutual surveillance and jealousy, who are so resourceful in consideration, tenderness, loyalty, pride and friendship, when once they step outside their circle become a little better than uncaged beasts of prey. Once abroad in the wilderness, they revel in the freedom from social constraint and compensate for their long confinement in the quietude of their own community. They revert to the innocence of wild animals … Deep within all these noble races there lurks the beast of prey, bent on spoil and conquest. The hidden urge has to be satisfied from time to time, the beast let loose in the wilderness.[75]

70 Baker, 'The Nature of Morality and Desires of Male Homosexuals in Conrad', in Joseph Conrad Today, 27, 2, 2002, p. 2.
71 'Judges', in The Old Testament, 1.26.
72 Reid, 'The "Unspeakable Rites" in Heart of Darkness', in Conrad: A Collection of Critical Essays, ed. Marvin Mudrick, Upper Saddle River, NJ: Prentice-Hall, 1966, p. 45.
73 Torgovnick, Gone Primitive, p. 141.
74 These were available by 1899 – e.g., Sir Edward Burnett Tylor's Primitive Culture, 1871, Frazer.
75 Nietzsche, trans. Francis Golffing, 'The Genealogy of Morals', in The Birth of Tragedy and The Genealogy of Morals, New York: Doubleday, 1956, p. 174.

Kurtz, as an imperialist, would have seen himself as of 'these noble races', Nietzsche's point of view fits him. It is useful to compare it with Marlow's analysis, addressed to his *Nellie* audience:

> How can you imagine what particular region of the first ages a man's untrammeled feet may take him into by the way of solitude – utter solitude without a policeman – by the way of silence – utter silence, where no warning voice of a kind neighbour can be heard whispering of public opinion?
>
> (Ch. II, p. 123)

Marlow thinks that Kurtz's problems are 'solitude' and 'silence'. In fact, Kurtz's solitude is not absolute, like Decoud's in the Gulf in *Nostromo*. It is tempered by the presence of the Harlequin, his African woman and other Africans. 'Solitude' and 'silence', what Nietzsche calls 'the freedom from social constraint', point to what Conrad's tale suggests is Kurtz's chief problem: freedom. Deprived of the protective power of his society, as well as its civilized restraints, Kurtz is faced with the terrible challenge of his own self, the knowledge that he is free, with all the dangers that attend this awareness. The discovery of the self is the discovery of one's freedom. It is then that the strong drives in human nature emerge in Kurtz in all their force. There are visible signs of the atavistic transformation in the wilderness of this missionary of civilization ['the wilderness ... had taken on him a terrible vengeance for the fantastic invasion' (Ch. III, p. 134)]. Conrad knows but, like Marlow, refuses to accept the Nietzschean 'option' – or even to treat Nietzsche with respect. In fact, Kurtz can be seen as both a demonstration and a repudiation of the Nietzschean vision of a 'free spirit.' Kurtz's kind of progress is a circular regression: to rely totally on intellect and will, to reject all religious and social taboos, is to be beyond man – but also to be less than man. He regresses to the level of a brute, at the end literally 'crawling on all fours' (Ch. III, p. 142). He is wasted, bald, undignified, a verbal gas-bag. The 'insolent' African boy who announces Kurtz's death is not a primitive unsophisticated type. In Marlow's words, he adopts 'a tone of scathing contempt', and has sized up Kurtz, just as Makola does Kayerts and Carlier in 'An Outpost of Progress'. To him, Kurtz is just another exploiter. The boy is so dismissive that Kurtz's dream of being a god collapses, suggesting the utter futility of all aspiration and achievement. In the end, Kurtz is nothing, a nonentity. We might even recall how Marlow at the beginning of the narrative, first referred to Kurtz as 'the poor chap' (Ch. I, p. 72). This view of Kurtz has come full circle. Ironically, the civilization which gave Kurtz his (fragile) idealism is a sterile death-in-life (Brussels is a 'sepulchral city', Ch. III, p. 150). Yet Kurtz's daring, his daemonic vitality and strength of spirit/personality are never denied but are powerfully presented. The spell he has cast over the Russian, his African woman, other Africans and even Marlow remains. His role in the novella suggests meanings on political, moral, psychological, philosophical and also archetypal levels.

Kurtz is remarkable in that he can win loyalties and appeal to fellow human beings even during moments of darkest savagery. Achebe is critical: 'The aggravated witch-dance for a mad white man by hordes of African natives may accord with the needs and desires of the fabulists of the Africa that never was.'[76] But the Africans are not shown as worshipping any and every white man (for instance, the Russian), but they worshipped Kurtz – just as the Russian and the Intended did – because he was exceptional, a magnetic personality. How did Kurtz control the blacks? By remaining remote and dignified or by relating to them? There was no question of 'relating' to them via sex (a form of domination) or violence, since this was the common behaviour of whites. But, instead of changing African culture as he originally set out to do, he exploits his own culture, his 'superior position'; without impairing his imperial image, he identifies with them via religion – not as a fellow worshipper, of course, which would be beneath the dignity of a white man, but as a deity himself; not the God of the missionaries but a God neverthe-less. Kurtz thereby embodies blasphemy, but Marlow does not employ Christian terms in presenting this (indeed, he does not think in a religious framework at all).

The Intended holds on to the conventional façade of her man and venerates Kurtz as a hero. She is inviolable in her ability to ignore realities. The Russian on the other hand is light – like a harlequin. His buoyancy and optimism are fantastic in the context of his situation, with hostile Belgian officials and unpredictable natives. He has decency: he repays with ivory the old Dutchman, Van Shuyten, who equipped him. It would be a recommendation especially to British readers that he knows English, has served on English ships and has a taste for English tobacco. He values Towson's *An Inquiry into some Points of Seamanship*, which, to Marlow, is something familiar, reliable, true – reassuring in a situation that makes him question all that he has hitherto taken for granted. The Russian refers to Marlow as a 'brother seaman' (Ch. III, p. 139) and as being 'of the same profession' (Ch. III, p. 140). Conrad thus promotes the notion of the faith, the freemasonry of mariners worldwide, not only British. The Russian is appealing, warm and a loyal follower of Kurtz; in providing wood for the steamer he follows a Towson-like work ethic. He has been threatened by Kurtz and Kurtz is thereby shown as demanding and without limits. His admiration for Kurtz is leavened with realism. Partly, this reflects Kurtz's impressiveness, yet this is discounted by his volatility.

It is Marlow's reactions to Kurtz that carry most weight in terms of appraising his character. Kurtz's character has developed from its early idealism as suggested in flashbacks in the course of the narrative, but, when Marlow encounters him, his character is fully formed, a *fait accompli*. Marlow is a character in the process of being formed by his experiences. He is open to African experiences as shown by his wanting to go to Africa and meet Kurtz. Marlow is attracted to Kurtz in an ambivalent way and is impressed (not necessarily favourably) by the force of his personality (cavernous mouth etc.). He follows Kurtz into the empty heart of darkness, but denies it. Death would prove it. Kurtz goes further into emptiness, via death, than Marlow does. Marlow throws the bulwark of Victorian values such as restraint, responsibility, integrity, and the work ethic – work gives man and time value; Marlow's professional integrity requires him to pay attention to his steamer and navigation – against the disruptive knowledge he has acquired

---

76 Achebe, 'Africa's Tarnished Name', in *Another Africa*, photographs by Robert Lyms, Essays and Poems by Chinua Achebe, London: Lund Humphries, 1998, p. 114.

through Kurtz's consciousness rather than his own. He desperately clings to old ideals despite his shared glimpse of the abyss which shows their inadequacy. The novella thus enacts the transition from the Victorian to the modern age in the intellectual climate, just as it does in the area of literary form. At the beginning of his journey into the interior, Marlow makes an important distinction between the 'strong, lusty, red-eyed devils, that swayed and drove men', on the one hand, and 'a flabby, pretending, weak-eyed devil of a rapacious and pitiless folly', on the other (Ch. I, p. 83). He prefers the former category, which Kurtz falls into, while the 'pilgrims', the Manager and the brick-maker all belong to the despicable second category. In Marlow's view, Kurtz is a genuine devil who can inspire horror, whereas we are told the Manager 'was obeyed, yet he inspired neither love nor fear, nor even respect. He inspired uneasiness' (Ch. I, p. 90). He keeps up appearances and pretences continuously, whereas Kurtz commits himself totally to the free expression of the self and a belief in action. The *postscriptum* to his report for the International Society for the Suppression of Savage Customs 'Exterminate all the brutes!' has to be taken seriously because it figures as a principle of action. While the Manager plots against Kurtz and plans to prevent help from reaching the sick man till he perishes, he is very cautious; even his evil is negative, weak and mean. Marlow calls the 'first-class agent', also known as 'the brick-maker', a 'papier-mâché Mephistopheles' (Ch. I, p. 96). The ordinary unidentified pilgrims are the worst. They are all essentially alike in that they suffer from moral impotence and vacancy. They cannot do evil for they are never involved in making a moral choice for good or evil, and, certainly, cannot go beyond morality as Marlow suggests Kurtz does. In Marlow's view, Kurtz is man enough to make a decision and peculiarly honest in acting by it. It is to this honesty in Kurtz that Marlow turns 'for relief'. He thus proceeds to choose the 'nightmare' of Kurtz before that of the other colonial employees, even though it is far more unsettling, because Marlow, like Kurtz, wants *to see*. Conrad's view here is an extension of T.S. Eliot's:

> So far as we are human, what we do must be either evil or good; so far as we do evil or good, we are human; and it is better, in a paradoxical way, to do evil than to do nothing: at least, we exist. It is true to say that the glory of man is his capacity for salvation; it is also true to say that his glory is his capacity for damnation.[77]

From this vantage point, Kurtz is man enough (or *human* enough) to be damned. The other colonial employees are not; they can neither be saved nor damned. It is Kurtz's soul that goes mad (Nietzsche literally lost his sanity), whereas the other employees do not possess souls and so cannot go mad. In Marlow's words,

> You may be too much of a fool to go wrong – too dull even to know you are being assaulted by the powers of darkness. I take it, no fool ever made a bargain for his soul with the devil.
>
> (Ch. II, p. 123)

77 Eliot, 'Baudelaire', in *Selected Essays*, London: Faber, 1951, p. 429.

Alternatively, instead of 'soul', the vital faculty that marks Kurtz out from the other colonial employees could be termed 'imagination'. It is part of Conrad's detached scepticism to see the intellectually superior persons as more vulnerable – Marlow, Kurtz, like Decoud in *Nostromo*.

Conrad's strategy in presenting Kurtz involves a gradual building up of Kurtz's character, whereby mystery accumulates and a delayed appearance follows. The deferred climax leaves Kurtz as the focal point of the narrative and the apex of Conrad's tale. The episode of Marlow's encounter with Kurtz reaches its culmination with Kurtz's death. His final cry, 'The horror! The horror!', is rich in meaning. It is interpreted by Marlow as 'complete knowledge' (Ch. III, p. 148) and 'a moral victory' (Ch. III, p. 150). The reader glimpses the 'fascination of the abomination' (Ch. I, p. 71) with Kurtz, who denied progress and civilization, and went back to savagery, uttering a cry of recognition, repudiation, even repentance. He remains silent, not calling out to the drummers and participants at primitive rites, but returning to civilization (the steamer) with Marlow, seemingly damning his past atavism, 'a moral victory' (a phrase repeated and stressed). The cry may also refer to 'the approach of death'.[78] But the 'privileged' reader, Marlow's and Conrad's secret sharer, will catch more disturbing intimations in this bleak vision. The 'horror' represents the gap between the ideals of civilization – the ideals that Kurtz had mouthed – and the reality (domination, torture, exploitation) as well as recognition of their common source. The cry, at its deepest, is an assessment of the sum total of life as recognition of the emptiness of a world without moral criteria, the vacuity of all ideals and all endeavour, a nihilistic vision of life and death, or what Nietzsche called 'the ghastly absurdity of existence'.[79] Even the Nietzschean superman is pathetically helpless to come to terms with it, while the ordinary reader of *Heart of Darkness*, otherwise blind to the realities of imperialism (greed and brutality), at the very least receives a shock by Conrad's revelation of the true face of Empire.

For the most part, Kurtz is projected as a voice, and only given life through Marlow's narrative. There are repeated references to his 'eloquence'. The implied promise is that Kurtz, with his gift of expression, will articulate the secret of, and solution to, the problems that the journey has posed. Indeed, Marlow's quest for Kurtz, his stated desire to hear him ('I had never imagined him as doing . . . but as discoursing' Ch. II, p. 121), reminds me of people who go far to hear oracles, even as far as Delphi. What the oracle says, is of immense importance. Finally, Marlow hears Kurtz, and all that Kurtz expresses is the novella's radical scepticism about the possibility of explanations and values.

Kurtz is paradoxically seen as a representative or symbol of the acme of European civilization and of imperialism ('His mother was half-English, his father was half-French. All Europe contributed to the making of Kurtz.' Ch. II, p. 124). But he also acquires a wider significance as a human being. The title of the novella is inclusive. The heart of darkness is the centre of Africa but more important is the suggestion that it is all that is unknown: the corruptibility of and the evil in man;

---

78 Lionel Trilling, *Beyond Culture: Essays on Literature and Learning*, London: Secker & Warburg, 1966, p. 24.
79 Nietzsche, *The Birth of Tragedy*, p. 51.

the hidden self; the non-validity of moral standards and ideals; and the negation at the back of things.

Style, image and symbol

Two statements by Conrad help explain the style that he employs:

> . . . explicitness . . . is fatal to the glamour of all artistic work, robbing it of all suggestiveness, destroying all illusion.[80]
>
> I wish at first to put before you a general proposition: that a work of art is very seldom limited to one exclusive meaning and not necessarily tending to a definite conclusion. And this for the reason that the nearer it approaches art, the more it acquires a symbolic character.[81]

These principles are at work behind his methods of description and suggestion as much as they are behind his narrative structures. Ian Watt, Cedric Watts and other critics have remarked on Conrad's technique of delayed decoding, by which events are described in such a way that what is happening only gradually becomes clear to the protagonist/narrator and/or the reader.[82]

More obvious, perhaps, is Conrad's penchant for adjectives that attempt to describe the indescribable: 'ineffable', 'incomprehensible' and so on. This tendency has often been criticized, beginning with F.R. Leavis' strictures on the 'overworked vocabulary', 'the adjectival insistence upon inexpressible and incomprehensible mystery' as applied to the Congo and to 'the evocation of human profundities and spiritual horrors'.[83] Later critics (for instance, C.B. Cox and James Guetti[84]) argue that Conrad's kind of language represents not a failed attempt to capture experience but rather an effort to suggest an experience for which normal language is inadequate. Moreover, Marlow's insistence on the incommunicability of the story is, from one perspective, due to the inadequacy of language to express the experience. (It is also meant to signal to the receptive reader the need for active imagination to enter into the experience narrated.) Conrad, like Eliot, was occupied with frontiers of consciousness beyond which words fail, though meaning itself still exists. There is a fascinating balance of two basic styles – long undulating sentences, used in the brooding descriptions of the river and the wilderness, elaborate and intense with farcical humour (for instance, when the sick agent is tipped out and abandoned by his bearers, during the Fresleven incident and in focusing on Kurtz's baldness); and crisp dry sentences, that often undercut the apparent seriousness of a situation with a kind of grim

---

80 Conrad, letter to Richard Curle, 24 April 1922, in *Conrad to a Friend*, ed. Richard Curle, New York: Doubleday, 1928, p. 113.
81 Conrad, letter to Barrett H. Clark, 14 May 1918, in G. Jean-Aubry, *Life and Letters*, London: Heinemann, 1927, pp. 204–5.
82 See Watt, *Conrad in the Nineteenth Century*; Watts, *The Deceptive Text*, Sussex: Harvester, 1984; and Bruce Johnston, ' "Conrad's Impressionism" and Watt, "Delayed Decoding" ', in *Conrad Revisited*, ed. Ross C. Murfin, Tuscaloosa: Alabama UP, 1985.
83 Leavis, *The Great Tradition*, London: Penguin, 1962 edn, pp. 196–7.
84 Cox, 'Introduction', in *Conrad: Heart of Darkness, Nostromo and Under Western Eyes: A Casebook*, London: Macmillan, 1981, pp. 16–17.

levity/black humour (for instance, in the presentation of the 'pilgrims', the Eldorado Expedition and the Harlequin).

Heart of Darkness quickly came to be regarded as an important text in the development of modern symbolism. Marvin Mudrick has gone so far as to suggest that 'after *Heart of Darkness*, the recorded moment – the word – was irrecoverably symbol'.[85] The ways in which light and darkness are employed, for example, contain an extraordinary symbolic complexity (see Text and contexts, **p. 29**), while ivory forms an important real and symbolic leitmotif in the tale. Ivory is to the Congo what silver is to Costaguana in *Nostromo*. It is both the actual raw wealth that private individuals, colonial companies and imperial powers covet and a symbolic centre for their self-aggrandizing motives. Amidst pretences, the white man's desire for ivory is unmistakably real and prominent. The search for it is the expression of Kurtz's baser impulses, his brutality towards the natives as well as his greed.

Ivory has a wider symbolic application too. It is white and shiny on the outside but it is really dead matter, and thereby points to a paradox at the heart of Western civilization, impressive in appearance but sterile. (It is significant that the Accountant keeps up appearances, but his accounts are false and he is insensitive, callous and dried-up within.) Conrad chooses to focus on ivory rather than rubber, because in the Congo in 1890 it was more important than rubber (rubber became more important after the ivory dried up) and because ivory provides richer thematic and metaphorical possibilities.

In discussing the structure of the tale, many commentators have remarked that Marlow's journey into the interior becomes, at the same time, an interior journey; at a symbolic level the journey into the Congo becomes also a journey into the depths of man's unconscious, revealed in all its darkness.

It is quite clear that Conrad intended the reader to draw such symbolic inferences – though almost certainly he would not have been comfortable with a thoroughly Freudian or Jungian approach of the sort that some critics have attempted,[86] analyzing the perceived connections between the tale and Conrad's own psyche. The connections between the Congo journey and Conrad's boyhood dreams (reported in 'Geography and Some Explorers'[87]) have been made much of by some, for example, and others have suggested that Conrad may have been in part motivated by a desire to expiate guilt at the part he had himself played in the imperialistic adventure.

Heart of Darkness functions, on one level, as popular adventure fiction: exotic setting, a quest, suspense, unexpected attack by savages, escape, mystery (regarding Kurtz), sex, romance, and a happy ending (Marlow prevents Kurtz from returning to his abominations and redeems the lost Kurtz; a white man goes native, recants and dies in the odour, if not sanctity, of white opinion) (see Text and contexts, **pp. 9–10**). Conrad uses the adventure tradition to win a ready

---

85 Mudrick, 'The Originality of Conrad', in *Conrad: A Collection of Critical Essays*, ed. M. Mudrick, Upper Saddle River, NJ: Prentice-Hall, 1966, p. 44.
86 See, e.g., Guerard in *Conrad the Novelist*; Frederick R. Karl, 'Introduction to the *Danse Macabre*: Conrad's *Heart of Darkness*', in *Heart of Darkness: A Case Study in Contemporary Criticism*, ed. Ross C. Murfin, New York: St. Martin's, 1989.
87 *Last Essays*, in *Tales of Hearsay and Last Essays*, London: Dent, 1955 edn, pp. 16–7; *G:HD*, pp. 159–60.

response from the (contemporary) reader, while at the same time complicating
and subverting this tradition which espoused imperial values and assumptions.
For instance, Blackwood's (see Text and contexts, **p. 11**) middle- and low-brows
(it had its own high-brows) would expect the mysterious depravity of Kurtz going
native to be unveiled at last, but what is presented is a darker, starker revelation
than mere paganism. Blackwood's was gendered, in that its tales were meant
mainly for a male readership. Marlow, as a male chauvinist (see below, **p. 43**),
would appeal to this audience. Moreover, Marlow belongs to the British
Merchant Service and, as such, is a positive figure, an embodiment of the positive
qualities of this masculine Service. He also waves the flag.

Heart of Darkness and gender

An aspect of *Heart of Darkness* that many modern readers find problematic is the
attitudes towards women that are displayed in it – from the frank lusts of Kurtz to
the patronizing tone that Marlow adopts:

> Then – would you believe it? – I tried the women. I, Charlie Marlow, set
> the women to work – to get a job.
>
> (Ch. I, p. 74)

> I ventured to hint that the Company was run for profit.
>
> 'You forget, dear Charlie, that the labourer is worthy of his hire,' she
> said, brightly. It's queer how out of touch with truth women are. They
> live in a world of their own, and there has never been anything like it,
> and never can be. It is too beautiful altogether, and if they were to set it
> up it would go to pieces before the first sunset. Some confounded fact we
> men have been living contentedly with ever since the day of creation
> would start up and knock the whole thing over.
>
> (Ch. I, p. 79)

As at so many other places, though, at this point the text as a whole acts to
subvert the sentiments being expressed. Marlow good-humoredly belittles the
idealistic sentiment of the woman who suggests that the value of the labourer
should be placed above the profit motive. Yet the text as a whole shows with
appalling clarity the effects of the profit motive being let loose without restraint –
and the effect in particular of unrestrained *male* capitalism. In the sphere of
gender too, it is important to distinguish between Marlow and Conrad, and recognize the gap between them. In this respect, Marlow is obviously presented as a
typical Victorian male chauvinist. Conrad shows how Marlow's aunt exercises
more social power than he does, and Marlow, in describing her as out of touch
with the world, appears a little comic. Conrad is conscious of the real power
women wield in the world of action (in *Nostromo*, Antonia is presented as a
strong character who is involved in politics). Marlow will not tell the truth to a
woman such as Kurtz's Intended – too pure and noble to have dreams tarnished –
and, in any case, no decision-maker, totally apart from the actions of imperialism.
But he does tell it to men – to men involved in it – revealing realities that may be
hidden from them, the policy-makers. Conrad, of course, is addressing the totality

of his meaning to men as well as women. Carola M. Kaplan complains that the women are given 'no names, play minor parts'.[88] Yet the men, too, apart from Marlow, Kurtz and Fresleven, are given no names (the stress, then, falls on the representative/professional function of the characters) and the fact is that imperialism was a male enterprise.

The contrast between Kurtz's black woman – whose portrayal may remind us of the 'Noble Savage' motif but is yet more than that – and his Intended has often been commented on as a fairly conventional dichotomy of Whore/Virgin. But this is misleading. The real antithesis in the text is between the Intended as virginal, cerebral, idealistic (her forehead is highlighted) and the African as passionate, yet with dignity as her distinguishing trait: she is theatrical, statuesque, sensuous, yes, but not a whore, not cheap or mercenary in sex. The African woman has often been called a 'mistress',[89] suggesting an illegal relationship. But the fact is that Kurtz was not married to his Intended and he has shelved her – at least, for the moment, because he does entertain dreams of a triumphal return to Europe. 'Mistress' has the wrong period flavour, slightly old-fashioned and middle-class, and suggests a social rather than the elemental background of the novella. Torgovnick thinks 'the woman is decked with leggings and jewelry that testify to a high position among the Africans – the position, one assumes, of Kurtz's wife'[90] – or rather, it seems to me, of the ruler of the tribe which raids ivory for him, since the tribe is deferential to her even after Kurtz's departure. She is queenly and definitely a black African; Rider Haggard (see Text and contexts, **p. 9f.**), in contrast, makes his Ayesha, 'the mighty queen of a savage people', imperious, awe-inspiring, but panders to his pro-imperial readers by also making her 'a white woman of peculiar loveliness'.[91] Kurtz's African woman 'had the value of several elephant tusks upon her', wears brass wire and glass beads (Ch. III, p. 137) and is, thereby, metaphorically and literally connected to the imperial theme via the basis of imperialism, its economy of unequal exchange. She appears both as a victim of imperialism and pre-eminent among her own people. She conducts herself as Kurtz's equal. When he leaves her, she acquires a tragic stature, like that other African queen, Dido, in Virgil's *Aeneid* seemingly contemplating suicide ('. . . dumb pain mingled with the fear of some struggling, half-shaped resolve . . .', Ch. III, p. 138) once her Aeneas deserts her – not necessarily fact, but Marlow's impression. The intertextual echo of Queen Dido elevates the African woman whereas the intertextuality regarding Aeneas works ironically at the expense of Kurtz. Aeneas succeeds in fulfilling his obligations whereas Kurtz repudiates his past and is, ultimately, a failure. Torgovnick surmises: 'The woman presumably dies'.[92] But Conrad visualized no death, only the contrast between the blacks' terrified fight and her steadfast dignity as Marlow blows the steamer's whistle and

88 Kaplan, 'Women's Caring and Men's Secret Sharing: Constructions of Gender and Sexuality in "Heart of Darkness" and "The Secret Sharer" ', in *Approaches to Teaching Conrad's 'Heart of Darkness' and 'The Secret Sharer'*, ed. Hunt Hawkins and Brian W. Shaffer, New York: Modern Language Association of America, 2002, p. 97.
89 E.g., Kaplan, 'Women's Caring', p. 99; Peter Edgerly Firchow, *Envisioning Africa: Racism and Imperialism in Conrad's 'Heart of Darkness'*, Kentucky: Kentucky UP, 2000, p. 25.
90 Torgovnick, *Gone Primitive*, p. 146.
91 H. Rider Haggard, *She*, Oxford: OUP, 1991 edn, p. 11.
92 Torgovnick, *Gone Primitive*, p. 155.

the 'pilgrims' squirt lead. The blacks' response to the whistle – like the response to Good's false teeth (see Text and contexts, p. 9) – is not infantile or childish but an understandable reaction to something outside their experience. Conrad takes so much care in building up the African woman that it would be incongruous if she were a casual casualty, especially of the mindless, undignified 'pilgrims'. Kurtz's disciple presents the woman, from *his* perspective, as a shrew, a virago, reading her as a mindless savage who 'kicked up a row about those miserable rags I picked up in the storeroom to mend my clothes with' (Ch. III, p. 132), but to the reader it appears that he misinterprets her rage (he admits he does not understand her dialect), a rage likely to have been prompted by his appropriation of Kurtz's time and attention, not something petty. The reader's view of Kurtz's woman is thus not contradicted or impaired. In the final scene, she and the Intended appear to Marlow not as antithetical types but complementary sides of a single archetypal woman.

What of the final scene? Does it imply that women as a group are naïve and must be protected from horror, sheltered from the truth? Johanna M. Smith has plausibly argued that the scene embodies 'the ideology of separate spheres' for men and women,[93] and there can be no question that gender roles have an important part to play. It would be difficult, however, to suggest that the final scene holds *only* a gender-related message. Indeed, insofar as a message concerning the necessity of protecting ourselves from 'the appalling face of glimpsed truth' is concerned, it is surely at least as plausible to see such a theme running throughout the book: to see it surface as much in the illusions that Marlow constructs for himself as in those he allows to remain undisturbed in the heart of Kurtz's Intended. It is Marlow, after all, who in the face of the purest horror strives desperately to find his 'Idea', to find somehow in this evil,

> an affirmation, a moral victory paid for by innumerable defeats, by abominable terrors, by abominable satisfactions. But it was a victory! That is why I have remained loyal to Kurtz to the last, and even beyond, when a long time after I heard once more, not his own voice, but the echo of his magnificent eloquence thrown to me from a soul as translucently pure as a cliff of crystal.
>
> (Ch. III, p. 150)

If the Intended is deemed unable to truly face the horror, may we not say the same of Marlow himself? In terms of 'protection' it could be said that the novella's final statement is not that women must be somehow protected from too much reality, but all humanity 'cannot bear very much reality', in the words of T.S. Eliot.[94]

Marlow's African journey ends at the key places from where he set out – Brussels, the headquarters of the Belgian Empire, and London, the headquarters of the British Empire. The final phase in Europe is pitched on a lower key than the events that happened in Africa. This is appropriate and necessary to convey and under-line the tale's final wisdom. Conrad directs his irony at conventional, ordinary living and the values of work, duty and restraint found in it, and suggests a preference for the kind of exploration of the self that occupied Kurtz in Africa. Through Marlow's account of his return to 'the sepulchral city' – during which he refers to physical details in the Intended's house such as the fireplace with 'a cold and monumental whiteness', a piano like a 'sarcophagus', and even the woman's perfect but pallid skin – Conrad is able to confirm that the secure opulence of Europe is only able to maintain itself by a radical ignorance of the raw savageries that ultimately pay for it.

The Intended is a rich pun. It refers to Kurtz's fiancée, to his intentions regard-ing her, to Africa and to himself, and to his will, which he wanted to use to better Africa and which he used to break free of Western morality. Marlow thought that 'the culminating point' (Ch. I, p. 72) of his experience was the Kurtz episode. This was so in regard to Africa as well as to wider life. The final scene with the Intended is a necessary extension of his experience. In his conversation with her, he suppresses the dark truth of Kurtz and concludes by uttering the biggest of his white lies, that Kurtz's last words were not 'The horror! The horror!', but her name. Marlow has become more aware of deeper and darker things, but now he sees that illusions, ethics and ideals are necessary for the survival of the individual and of civilization itself, however debatable its value.

> The lights must never go out,
> The music must always play,[95]

even if on the keys of the dead and deathly ivory that grin like a death's head in the Intended's drawing-room. A sustained illusion is necessary to all but the strongest minds – like Marlow who has found a Buddha-like 'enlightenment', the knowledge of the dark.

Mark A. Wollaeger thinks that Marlow's lie to the Intended may be viewed as an attempt to 'impose the false closure of popular romance on a radically inconclusive story'.[96] The conventional Victorian pieties of the Intended are in beautiful ironic juxtaposition with fact and Marlow's knowledge of 'the darkness outside and within',[97] suggesting a yawning gap between these. Marlow is, then, trapped into uttering the lie. For the scope of the Intended's understanding, he supplies the right answer to her yearning, a closure of the view of the stay-at-home woman who saw her man as an agent of civilization in the dark continent. But it is not a closure for the reader because s/he knows that Marlow's lie is a lie. The tale thus remains inconclusive because it is left for the reader to complete its meanings. Conrad himself was acutely aware of the essential and rich obscur-ity of his tale and, anticipating postmodernism, looked upon the reader as an

95 W.H. Auden, 'September 1, 1939', in *Poetry of the Thirties*, ed. Robin Skelton, London: Penguin, 1964, p. 282.
96 Wollaeger, *Joseph Conrad and the Fictions of Skepticism*, Stanford, CA: Stanford UP, 1990, p. 76.
97 Eliot, 'Chorus from the Rock', in *Collected Poems 1909–1935*, London: Faber, 1956 edn, p. 170.

imaginative collaborator. 'For one writes only half the book,' he insisted to Cunninghame Graham in 1897, 'the other half is with the reader.'[98]

At the very end of the novella, the Thames merges with the Congo (one is reminded of Marlow's opening words, 'This also has been one of the dark places of the earth'), linking the rivers physically and symbolically, and suggesting the shared humanity as well as condemning imperialism as a 'black' tendency of civilization. Conrad leaves the reader gazing at the heart of darkness, still in the grip of the world of the novella.

---

98 Conrad, letter to Graham, 5 August 1897, in *Collected Letters I*, p. 370.

2

Critical history

Early responses

The initial reception of *Heart of Darkness* was divergent, and some of it is now only of passing 'period' interest. Most reviewers read the novella on a topical level as a critique of Belgian imperialism, but a minority asserted that it should not 'be supposed that Mr. Conrad makes attack upon colonization, expansion, even upon Imperialism'.[1] John Masefield complained that 'the author is too much cobweb and fails to create his central character'.[2] The *TLS* reviewer referred to 'an indulgence in the picturesque horror of the villain, his work and his surroundings . . . quite extravagant according to the canons of art'.[3] Both Masefield and this reviewer judge the novella according to the then current expectations of nineteenth-century realism, rather than (say) seeing Kurtz as a vast death's head dominating a worldscape of egoism, avidity, cruelty, squalor, all equally meaningless in the face of the ultimate nullity. Masefield, who was to become England's Poet Laureate in 1930, also thought the narrative of *Heart of Darkness* 'most unconvincing', for it was not 'vigorous, direct, effective, like that of Mr Kipling', nor was it 'clear and fresh like that of Stevenson' – judging it against the standard of the adventure fiction of the time.[4]

Some contemporary critiques, however, contained the seeds of later developments. Edward Garnett considered the novella a 'psychological masterpiece' and 'the high-water mark of the author's talent',[5] echoed in Hugh Clifford's praise for Conrad's unrivalled appreciation of the 'why' of 'going Fantee' and for the novella as representing 'Conrad at his very best'.[6] Garnett's perceptions also show that Conrad's opposition to imperialism is intrinsic to the novella and not something later imposed by postcolonial critics. A.J. Dawson judged the novella as

---

1 Unsigned, 'Mr. Conrad's New Book', in *Manchester Guardian*, 10 December 1902, 3; *G:HD*, p. 177.
2 Masefield, 'Deep Sea Yarns', in *The Speaker*, 7, 31 January 1903, p. 442.
3 *Times Literary Supplement*, 48, 12 December 1902, 372; *G:HD*, p. 178.
4 Masefield, 'Deep Sea Yarns', p. 442.
5 Unsigned, 'Mr. Conrad's New Book', in *Academy and Literature*, 6 December 1902, 606; *G:HD*, p. 172.
6 Clifford, 'The Art of Mr. Joseph Conrad', in *The Spectator*, 29 November 1902, 827–8; *G:HD*, pp. 175–6.

'a big and thoughtful conception',[7] while Frederick Taber Cooper referred to 'crumpling up a world-wide theme into the limits of a few pages'. Cooper's racist reading lends support to Achebe's accusation that the novella reinforces racist attitudes:

> The Heart of Blackness [sic] . . . pictures the subtle disintegration of the white man's moral stamina, under the stress of the darkness, the isolation, the promiscuity of the African jungle, the loss of dignity and courage and self-respect through daily contact with the native man and native woman.[8]

In a famous passage from his review of Conrad's *Notes on Life and Letters* (1921), E.M. Forster wrote:

> What is so elusive about him is that he is always promising to make some general philosophic statement about the universe, and then refraining with a gruff disclaimer . . . Is there not also a central obscurity, something noble, heroic, beautiful, inspiring half-a-dozen great books, but obscure, obscure? . . . These essays do suggest that he is misty in the middle as well as at the edges, that the secret casket of his genius contains a vapour rather than a jewel; and that we needn't try to write him down philosophically, because there is, in this direction, nothing to write. No creed, in fact. Only opinions, and the right to throw them overboard when facts make them look absurd. Opinions held under the semblance of eternity, girt with the sea, crowned with stars, and therefore easily mistaken for a creed.[9]

Forster's critique is partly endorsed by F.R. Leavis in *The Great Tradition* (1948)[10] and later echoed by V.S. Naipaul:

> I felt with Conrad I wasn't getting the point. Stories, simple in themselves, always seemed at some stage to elude me. And there were the words, the words that issued out of a writer's need to be faithful to the truth of his own sensations. The words got in the way; they obscured.[11]

In a letter to Maryan Dobrowski (1914), Conrad said:

> English critics – for indeed I am an English writer – speaking about me always add that there is something incomprehensible, impalpable, ungraspable in me. You (Poles) alone can grasp this ungraspable element,

7 *Athenaeum*, 2, 20 December 1902, 824.
8 Cooper, 'The Sustained Effort and Some Recent Novels', *The Bookman*, New York, 18 November 1903, pp. 310–11.
9 Forster, 'Joseph Conrad: A Note' (1921), in *Abinger Harvest*, London: Penguin, 1957 edn, pp. 152–3.
10 Leavis, *The Great Tradition*, London: Penguin, 1962 edn, pp. 192–3.
11 Naipaul, 'Conrad's Darkness' (1974), in *The Return of Eva Peron with the Killings in Trinidad*, New York: Alfred A. Knopf, 1980, p. 211.

comprehend the incomprehensible. This is my Polishness. The Polishness which I took to my works through Mickiewicz and Slowacki.[12]

This is an explanation, but it does not take away much from the misunderstanding of Forster, Leavis and Naipaul. When Conrad over-works adjectives of excess and overt mystery (as in *Arrow of Gold*, 1919), he can be weak in a way common to many writers. Conrad, in his strength, is poetic and different, though not simple, as I have tried to bring out in discussing the language of *Heart of Darkness* above. I would also point out a special kind of mystery – that which attends 'the intolerable wrestle with words and meanings'[13] when Conrad suggests in his fiction the ultimate mystery of human existence and of human destiny, as in *Heart of Darkness*, *The Secret Sharer* or *Nostromo*.

The rise of the novella – 1930–1959

The general revival of interest in Conrad's work after his death in 1924 began with Edward Crankshaw's *Joseph Conrad: Some Aspects of the Art of the Novel* (1936), but he makes only brief references to *Heart of Darkness*. Interest in the novella, shown by M.C. Bradbrook in *Joseph Conrad: England's Polish Genius* (1941), had to await F.R. Leavis' *The Great Tradition* (1948) for major stimulus. Leavis chose Conrad, along with Jane Austen, George Eliot and Henry James, as representing 'the great tradition' of English novelists, but while he acknowledged that *Heart of Darkness* was 'by common consent, one of Conrad's best things', he judged it as flawed even if it sometimes embodied 'Conrad's art at its best'.[14] I have discussed Leavis' strictures on Conrad's language and their refutations (see Text and contexts, **p. 41**). Leavis, like Bradbrook, being free of the historical/colonial considerations affecting Conrad's contemporaries never refers to imperialism.

Albert J. Guerard in his landmark study *Conrad the Novelist* (1958), concedes that *Heart of Darkness* 'has its important public side, as an angry document on absurd and brutal exploitation',[15] but his emphasis is on the psychological. For him, 'the story is not primarily about Kurtz or about the brutality of Belgian officials but about Marlow its narrator' – and, more precisely, about Marlow's 'night journey into the unconscious, and confrontation of an entity within the self', 'the waking dream of a profoundly intuitive mind' (p. 37f.). Thomas Moser in *Joseph Conrad: Achievement and Decline* (1957) had written that 'going into the jungle seems to Marlow like travelling into one's own past, into the world of one's dreams, into the subconscious'.[16] Moser and Guerard anticipate a concern of the following decades, encouraged by the psychiatrist R.D. Laing in the 1960s – the journey into the dark and divided self. Moser also anticipates later feminist concerns: his argument is that Conrad's writing is inferior in quality when he attempts to write about love. Moser is also of interest on Conrad's technique in

12 Quoted from Eloise Knapp Hay, *The Political Novels of Joseph Conrad*, Chicago: Chicago UP, 1963, p. 30.
13 T.S. Eliot, 'Four Quartets', in *The Complete Poems and Plays of T.S. Eliot*, p. 179.
14 Leavis, *The Great Tradition*, pp. 193, 196.
15 Guerard, *Conrad the Novelist*, p. 34.
16 Moser, *Joseph Conrad: Achievement and Decline*, Cambridge, Massachusetts: Harvard UP, 1957, p. 81.

the novella: 'It is difficult to discuss Conrad's technique without referring to its effect upon the reader, for Conrad's masterly control of the reader's responses is one of the most significant results of his unorthodox methods. By holding back information and moving forward and backward in time, Conrad catches up and involves the reader in a moral situation, makes the reader's emotion follow a course analogous to that of the characters.' (p. 42) He points out that the usual pattern of imagery is reversed: 'darkness means truth, whiteness means false-hood'. (p. 47) It reflects the racial situation in the Congo, a psychological truth (the truth is within, and dark) and other matters such as the ivory trade. Guerard challenges Leavis in regard to the language of *Heart of Darkness*:

> If my summary [of the novel as a dream] has even a partial validity it should explain and to an extent justify some of the 'adjectival and worse than supererogatory insistence' to which F.R. Leavis (who sees only the travelogue and the portrait of Kurtz) objects. I am willing to grant that the unspeakable rites and unspeakable secrets become wearisome, but the fact – at once literary and psychological – is that they must remain *unspoken*.[17]

In order to render a dream powerfully, a language that is imprecise is an appropriate vehicle, in Guerard's view.

Politics, philosophy, ethics – 1960s–1970s

By the 1960s, *Heart of Darkness* had been 'given a kind of canonical place', in the words of Lionel Trilling.[18] Jocelyn Baines' respected critical biography, *Joseph Conrad* (1960), stimulated Conrad studies and, though his account of the novella is not in itself penetrating, he reaffirms its standing and asserts that its 'power and fascination . . . rest upon moral elusiveness and ambiguity'.[19] Unlike Guerard, Eloise Knapp Hay in *The Political Novels of Joseph Conrad* (1963) foregrounds the political and reads it as 'a vehement denunciation of imperialism and racism' that nevertheless did not damn 'all men who through accident of their birth in England were committed to these public policies'.[20] Hay separates Marlow from Conrad (rather rigidly), differing from the tendency to identify the two: Walter Allen takes Marlow as a kind of 'self-dramatization' on the part of the author; though more up-to-date, Wayne C. Booth and Ian Watt make essentially the same mistake in regarding Marlow as usually a 'reliable reflector of the clarities and ambiguities of the implied author', and Frederick R. Karl's view is similar to theirs.[21]

Heart of Darkness was regarded as the classic anti-imperial text, 'perhaps the

17 Guerard, *Conrad the Novelist*, p. 42.
18 Trilling, *Beyond Culture: Essays on Literature and Learning*, London: Secker & Warburg, 1965, 1967 edn, p. 32.
19 Baines, *Joseph Conrad: A Critical Biography*, London: Weidenfeld & Nicolson, 1969 edn, p. 224.
20 Hay, *The Political Novels of Joseph Conrad*, p. 112.
21 Allen, *The English Novel*, London: Penguin, 1962 edn, p. 306; Watt, *Conrad in the Nineteenth Century*, p. 103; Karl, *Joseph Conrad: The Three Lives*, London: Faber, New York: Farrar, Straus and Giroux, 1979, p. 298.

most horrifying description of imperialism ever written', in the words of Arnold Kettle[22] – until Achebe launched his native attack on 18 February 1975 at the University of Massachusetts in Amherst. That came in the wake of the wave of decolonization in the previous decade and the upsurge of demand for equal rights for blacks in USA. He sparked off debates over imperialism and racism in *Heart of Darkness* that have raged to this day. At stake in the debates is not just our appraisal of the text but also our understanding of the culture in which Conrad lived and wrote as well as our understanding of ourselves. The year 1975 thus marks a watershed moment in Conrad criticism.

Achebe's postcolonial critique implied that critics who did not note Conrad's racism themselves shared in it. Indeed, C.B. Cox in *Joseph Conrad: The Modern Imagination* (1974) can be blindly racist in his reading of Kurtz's African woman:

> there is something detestable, even loathsome about this primitive crea-
> ture ... Co-habitation with this superb but mindless creature degrades
> Kurtz; for Conrad's total response to her, as to the wilderness, mixes
> together the attractive and the repellent.[23]

Among other things Conrad does not imply mindlessness or repulsiveness in this woman. But Cox can also take stock of received criticism and be discriminating: *Heart of Darkness* exemplifies 'an art concerned to express a profound meta-physical scepticism, to be coherent about what must remain incoherent' (p. 16); 'Like Marlow, we are offered a choice of nightmares, but the strategy of the novel suggests that final commitment is possible only for the simple and the deluded' (p. 47). In fact, Marlow can neither accept Kurtz's exploration of the self nor adopt a completely contrary view.

Bruce Johnson in *Conrad's Models of the Mind* (1971) takes a philosophical and ethical rather than psychological approach. He dissents from the notion that Conrad entertained a low opinion of tribal life. He argues that in *Heart of Darkness*

> because the native is at one with nature and feels no sense of alienation,
> he does not sense the need to create his own contingent values and sanc-
> tions and so can readily accept what presents itself as divine sanction; he
> has the capacity to create gods and to worship them (as Kurtz is wor-
> shipped). The Marlovian[24] white man who has undercut easy notions
> of natural moral purpose has little or no capacity for this categorical
> belief.[25]

Referring to Jean-Paul Sartre (1905–80), the French philosopher and writer, he suggests that Conrad anticipated existential thought.[26] He also raises questions

---

22 Kettle, *An Introduction to the English Novel*, Vol. 2, London: Hutchinson, 1953, 1972 edn, p. 64.
23 Cox, *Joseph Conrad: The Modern Imagination*, London: Dent, 1974, p. 46.
24 'Marlovian' applies to Kurtz's similarity to Christopher Marlowe's over-ambitious protagonists like Faustus.
25 Johnson, *Conrad's Models of the Mind*, Minneapolis: Minnesota UP, 1971, p. 72.
26 Existentialism is the philosophy that human beings are free and responsible for their own actions in a world without meaning.

related to the problematics of language, underlining the impossibility of defining (and limiting) knowledge gained via experience, and suggests that comprehension may never come.

Beyond formalism – 1970s–1980s

The biographical and historical context of the novella was first examined by G. Jean-Aubry in *Joseph Conrad in the Congo* (1925–6), then superseded by Norman Sherry's *Conrad's Western World* (1971) and supplemented by M.M. Mahood's *The Colonial Encounter* (1977) and Hunt Hawkins' essays. Hawkins' research and conclusions are the most helpful work of this period in understanding the text from new political perspectives. In 'Conrad's Critique of Imperialism in *Heart of Darkness*' (1979),[27] for instance, the topographical and political factors (of which Marlow was ignorant) provide a solid substructure of causes for the nightmare muddle he witnesses. What seems 'objectless blasting' is necessitated because the railway line to the central station at Kinshasa had to run over Palaballa Mountain, 525 metres high, because the Congo river blocked a detour to the north while the border with Portuguese Angola, only three miles away, blocked the south. Leopold lacked the political leverage to have the unfortunate border, drawn at the Berlin Conference five years earlier, changed. Hawkins also notes 'the transfer of cargo from ocean steamers to small-draft steamers (a shift Marlow himself makes). The transshipment, necessary because Leopold could not afford to dredge the river above Boma, accounts for the poor condition of the machinery in *Heart of Darkness*.' (p. 291)[28] Hawkins possesses a fine grasp of the imperialist economy and its effect on the natives. He accounts for the presence of the Russian 'harlequin' outfitted by the Dutch trader Van Shuyten,

> a fictional counterpart of Antoine Greshoff, the chief agent as early as 1888 of the Dutch house Nieuwe Afrikaansche Handels-Vennootschap, the largest trading company after the Belgian SAB. The manager of the Central Station, who describes the Russian as 'a species of wandering trader – a pestilential fellow, snapping ivory from the natives', expresses the attitude of Leopold and the then favoured SAB when he says, 'We will not be free from unfair competition till one of these fellows is hanged for an example' (Ch. II, p. 103). Despite Leopold's promise at Berlin to preserve free trade, he saw such trade as 'unfair competition', which he intended to crush.
>
> (pp. 292–3)

In 'Joseph Conrad, Roger Casement and the Congo Reform Movement' (1981–82),[29] Hawkins shows how Conrad wished to assist, yet not participate in, the movement. Hawkins perceptively notes, for instance, that 'as in *Heart of Darkness*, Conrad's sense of the larger tragedy of the universe overshadowed his

27 Hawkins, in *PMLA*, 94, 1979, 286–99.
28 See *G:HD*, Ch. I, pp. 81–2.
29 Hawkins, in *Journal of Modern Literature*, 9, 1, 1981–82, 65–80.

outrage against specific social wrongs' (p. 76). In 'Conrad's *Heart of Darkness*: Politics and History' (1992),[30] Hawkins argues that 'Conrad manages to have it both ways: he presents an absurd universe in which the writing of history is impossible and he writes the history of the Congo with [a] political purpose' (p. 212); and that

> the most intimate relation exists between Conrad's 'further' and his 'nearer' vision, between his metaphysical skepticism and his practical involvement in life, his 'nearer' vision is an antidote to the 'further', and the struggle between the two generates all his work. Conrad may have shared Kurtz's vision of the void, but he refused to endorse or submit to it.
>
> (p. 214)

In '*Heart of Darkness* and Racism' (2005),[31] Hawkins makes a complex, qualified defence of the novella against Achebe's charges. Hawkins and Brian W. Shaffer edited *Approaches to Teaching Conrad's 'Heart of Darkness' and 'The Secret Sharer'* (2002).

By the 1970s, the assumptions about literature of the formalist school, whose focus was analyzing only 'the words on the page,' were set aside by scholars who went beyond the text into context and biography. A combination of these approaches – critical, biographical, historical, ideological – is adopted by Ian Watt in his monumental *Conrad in the Nineteenth Century* (1979). Impressive in its scholarship and insights, it is nevertheless traditional in offering 'a fairly literal account of how Conrad's narrative, thematic and symbolic structures develop' in *Heart of Darkness*[32] at a time when the 'literal meaning' of a text was being called into question by new theories of literature, and regressive in asserting that the novella is not 'essentially concerned with the colonial and racial issue in general' (p. 159); Watt added that it 'is not essentially a political work' (p. 160) at a time when these aspects seemed increasingly important. The most influential aspect of Watt's examination of *Heart of Darkness* is his analysis of 'delayed decoding' (see Text and contexts, **p. 41**) and impressionism:

> . . . the connection between delayed decoding and impressionism: it reminds us of the precarious nature of the process of interpretation in general; and since this precariousness is particularly evident when the individual's situation or his state of mind is abnormal, the device of delayed decoding simultaneously enacts the objective and the subjective aspects of moments of crisis. The method also has the more obvious advantage of convincing us of the reality of the experience which is being described; while we read we are, as in life, fully engaged in trying to decipher a meaning out of a random and pell-mell bombardment of sense impressions.
>
> (pp. 178–9)

---

30 Hawkins, in *Conradiana*, 24, 3, 1992, 207–17.
31 Hawkins, in *Joseph Conrad: Heart of Darkness*, ed. Paul Armstrong, New York: Norton, 2005 edn.
32 Watt, *Conrad in the Nineteenth Century*, 1979, p. 214.

Watt's most combative onslaught is directed against certain types of symbolic interpretations such as those of the two knitters:

> One obvious practical objection to this kind of symbolic interpretation is that it alerts our attention too exclusively to a few aspects of the narrative – to those which seem to provide clues that fit the assumed unitary and quasi-allegorical frame of symbolic reference. This leads us to interrogate the text only in those terms and to ask such questions as: Why does Conrad give us only two fates? Which one is Clotho the spinner? and which is Lachesis the weaver? Did the Greeks know about knitting anyway? Where are the shears? . . .
>
> (p. 191)

It seems to me that Conrad's text does not prompt tight, narrow allegorical reading – just suggestions and hints that expand variously in the mind. Watt follows earlier critics in arguing that 'both the form and content of *Heart of Darkness* are centred on the consciousness of Marlow' (pp. 201, 209). This, in fact, becomes a general line of thinking. Robert O. Evans had thought: 'Conrad's hero is Marlow and the story deals with change in his character.'[33] Benita Parry and H.M. Daleski regard Marlow as 'the central protagonist', 'the principal mediator', and 'a protagonist-narrator', respectively.[34]

In the same year Watt's book appeared, Frederick R. Karl published his massive biography *Joseph Conrad: The Three Lives* (1979). Influenced by Freudian and post-Freudian theories of the unconscious, Karl stresses the psychological. In his view, while writing *Heart of Darkness* 'Conrad began to split into pieces, and the result was Charley Marlow, the middle-aged seaman'. Some of the differences between Marlow and Kurtz – 'between Marlow's moderation and Kurtz's anarchy', for example – are not unlike 'divisions' that were present 'within [Conrad] himself'.[35] Karl has also been influenced by the then current interest in myth, legend and the family tree concept of literary production. He connects *Heart of Darkness* not only with Conrad's experiences but with these areas. For Karl, the Inner Station 'has a totemic value as the lair for a dragon or primitive beast, as the mythical hiding place for Loke or another satanic figure of evil' (p. 296). The scene in which Marlow observes 'a wasted landscape of industrial junk' in which 'a chain gang of indentured Africans . . . clink, deathlike, indifferent' is, he claims, 'Inferno-like, a descent, whether that of Dante, Odysseus, or Aeneas, into the underworld of human existence' (p. 270). According to his view, Kurtz is a later version of Faust and Marlow of Ulysses.

Another landmark work appeared a few years later, the English version of Zdzislaw Najder's *Joseph Conrad: A Chronicle* (1983), completed in 1977 then brought up to date and supplemented in early 1983. This is still the most authoritative biography of Conrad. Najder stresses Conrad's cultural background and

33 Evans, 'Conrad's Underworld', in *Modern Fiction Studies*, II, May, 1956, quoted from *Joseph Conrad: Heart of Darkness*, ed. Robert Kimbrough, New York: Norton, p. 190.
34 Parry, *Conrad and Imperialism*, London: Macmillan, 1983, p. 26; Daleski, *Joseph Conrad: The Way of Dispossession*, London: Faber, 1977, p. 52.
35 Karl, *Joseph Conrad: The Three Lives*, pp. 425, 488.

resources, especially the Polish political, intellectual and literary milieu from which he emerged. Najder's command of English and French in addition to Polish informs the fullness of his account. His sub-title is important: he chronicles Conrad's life, year by year, recording every important event, friendship and writing. His work supports a major notion of G. Jean-Aubry, Norman Sherry and M.M. Mahood that Conrad possessed a kind of talent that fed mainly on personal experiences and contacts, as in *Heart of Darkness*, but warns: 'the finished product should not be treated in the same way as raw material'.[36]

Though Watt, Karl and Najder discuss French influences on Conrad, the first book to take the full measure of Conrad's involvement with, and indebtedness to, the French literary tradition was Yves Hervouet's *The French Face of Joseph Conrad* (1990). Like others, Hervouet argues for Conrad's 'triple identity' (Polish, English, French), but the chief value of his (mainly literary) study is to illuminate Conrad's French literary connections, with Flaubert (1821–80), Maupassant (1859–93) and Anatole France (1844–1924). Hervouet suggests, for example, a source for Kurtz in Rimbaud's *Saison en enfer*, draws a parallel between Kurtz and Rimbaud, and argues for a contribution from Maupassant to the creation of Marlow.[37] The impact of Flaubert and Maupassant, he claims, occurred at the beginning of Conrad's career, but 'the influence of Anatole France was of a later date [after *Heart of Darkness* was written], slower in effect and more diffuse'. (p. 149).

The abundant scholarship shows the wide range of literary influences on Conrad that combine with his extraordinary life experiences to confirm a concept of the imagination as less a matter of pure inventiveness than complex synthesis. After all, Conrad himself wrote: 'The sustained invention of a really telling lie demands a talent which I do not possess.'[38] His is an art that develops from a rare integrating faculty operating as a shaping and unifying power of creativity.

Because of the impact of the biographical work of Najder,[39] Watt and Karl, critics like Daniel R. Schwarz discuss the author as well as the text. Indeed, Schwarz argues that Conrad's books are the history of his psyche and that Conrad uses his fiction to define himself. To Schwarz, 'Marlow is a surrogate through whom Conrad works out his own epistemological problems. Marlow's search for values echoes Conrad's.'[40] Writing specifically of *Heart of Darkness*, Schwarz asserts:

> The subject of 'Heart of Darkness' is primarily Marlow, but the presence of Conrad is deeply engraved in every scene. Marlow's effort to come to terms with the Congo experience, especially Kurtz, is the crucial activity

36 Najder, *Joseph Conrad: A Chronicle*, p. 493.
37 Hervouet, *The French Face of Joseph Conrad*, Cambridge: Cambridge UP, 1990, pp. 241, 247, 63.
38 Conrad, 'Author's Note' to *Tales of Unrest*, p. vii, in *Almayer's Folly and Tales of Unrest*, London: Dent, 1923.
39 Before he published his biography, Najder had edited *Conrad's Polish Background: Letters to and from Polish Friends*, Oxford: Oxford UP, 1964, and in the same year as his biography published his edition, *Conrad under Familial Eyes*, Cambridge: Cambridge UP, 1983. He later published *Conrad in Perspective: Essays on Art and Fidelity* – it included 'Conrad's Polish background, or from biography to a study of culture', 'Joseph Conrad's parents' and 'Joseph Conrad and Tadeusz Bobrowski' – completing an impressive, and indispensable, corpus of background work on Conrad.
40 Schwarz, *Conrad: Almayer's Folly to Under Western Eyes*, London: Macmillan; Ithaca, NY: Cornell UP, 1980, p. xiv.

that engaged Conrad's imagination ... Both the epistemological quest
for a context or perspective with which to interpret the experience and
the semiological quest to discover the signs and symbols which make
the experience intelligible are central to the tale ... Conrad transfers to
Marlow the agonizing self-doubt about his ability to transform personal
impressions into a significant tale.

(p. 63)

Post-colonial criticism

The impact of Achebe's attack was delayed, though it is true that Frances B. Singh
responded two or three years later in a woolly article 'The Colonialistic Bias of
Heart of Darkness' (1978).[41] Strangely, Hunt Hawkins in his essay 'Conrad's
Critique of Imperialism in "Heart of Darkness" ' and Ian Watt in *Conrad in the
Nineteenth Century*, both published in 1979, do not refer to Achebe. It was only
in and after the 1980s and 1990s that the impact of his attack was strongly felt.
Hawkins entered the fray in 1982 and 2005[42] and Watt in 1989.[43] So did Wilson
Harris (1981), Cedric Watts (1983), Patrick Brantlinger (1985, 1988), Mark
Kinkead-Weekes (1990), Robert Burden (1992) and R. Zhuwarara (1994) among
others.[44] Harris, the Guyanese novelist, feels 'sympathy' for Achebe's argument
but is

convinced that his judgment or dismissal of *Heart of Darkness* – and of
Conrad's strange genius – is a profoundly mistaken one ... I find it
possible to view *Heart of Darkness* as a frontier novel. By that I mean
it stands upon a threshold of capacity to which Conrad pointed though
he never attained that capacity himself.[45]

It seems to me that Conrad, in colonial times, pointed to, even anticipated,
post-colonialism but that it is unfair to expect Conrad, in his time, to be fully
post-colonial. In a slightly earlier interview, Harris asserted:

Conrad's *Heart of Darkness*, in my judgment, is a great novel because
it brings home the tormenting issue of form if the modern novel is
to sustain heterogeneous contents without one culture suppressing or

41 Singh in *Conradiana*, 10, 1978.
42 Hawkins, 'The Issue of Racism in "Heart of Darkness" ', in *Conradiana*, 14, 3, 1982; '*Heart of
    Darkness* and Racism', in *Joseph Conrad: Heart of Darkness*, ed. Paul Armstrong, New York:
    Norton, 2005 edn.
43 Watt, 'Conrad's "Heart of Darkness" and the Critics', in *North Dakota Quarterly*, 57, 3, 1989.
44 Harris, 'The Frontier on which *Heart of Darkness* Stands', in *Research in African Literatures*, 12,
    1, 1981; Watts, ' "A Bloody Racist": About Achebe's View of Conrad', in *Yearbook of English
    Studies*, 13, 1983; Brantlinger, ' "Heart of Darkness": Anti-Imperialism, Racism, or Impression-
    ism', in *Criticism*, 27, 4, 1985, revised version in *Rule of Darkness: British Literature and Imperial-
    ism 1830–1914*, Ithaca, NY: Cornell UP, 1988; Kinkead-Weekes, ' "Heart of Darkness" and the
    Third World Writer', in *Sewanee Review*, 98, 1, 1990; Burden, 'Conrad's "Heart of Darkness":
    the Critique of Imperialism and the Post-Colonial Reader', in *L'Epoque Conradienne*, 18, 1992;
    Zhuwarara, ' "Heart of Darkness" Revisited: The African Response', in *Kunapipi*, 16, 3, 1994.
45 Harris, 'The Frontier on which *Heart of Darkness* Stands', pp. 86, 87.

exterminating the other or hypocritically claiming to be liberal while maintaining its fixtures of bias.[46]

Cedric Watts carefully takes into account all Achebe's criticisms of *Heart of Darkness* and argues that 'really Conrad and Achebe are on the same side.'[47] Without naming Watts, Achebe rejects this argument outright:

> One [of my critics] actually took the trouble to write a letter to me and offer his good offices to reconcile me with Conrad because, as he said, Conrad was actually *on my side!* I did not, however, take up this kind mediation offer because I was not talking about *sides*. For me there is only one, *human*, side. Full stop! [Achebe's emphasis][48]

Achebe's stoking the fires of the controversy has greatly invigorated Conrad studies by foregrounding the currently important issues of imperialism and racism as we enter the twenty-first century and by opening up *Heart of Darkness* to post-colonial perspectives that would become increasingly important in the decades that followed his initial intervention.[49]

New theories and concerns – 1980s

Achebe's argument was based on the classic realist assumptions on which orthodox criticism at that time rested. He assumed that a novel could and should represent the real world and possess only one primary meaning, and that language is a transparent medium which hands over experience whole and without being problematic. Post-structuralism and deconstruction, on the other hand, argued that reality is mediated by language, which is a system of differences, with arbitrary connections between signifier, signified and referent, and by discourse and ideology. None of these categories are transparent, but all of them structure our sense of being and also meaning, which is multiple and unstable. As a transitional work between nineteenth-century classic realism and early modernism, *Heart of Darkness* lent itself as an exemplary text for the new theories. An early example of deconstructionist analysis of *Heart of Darkness* is Perry Meisel's 'Decentring "Heart of Darkness" '.[50] I have provided a prime example of such an analysis by

---

46 Michael Fabre, 'Wilson Harris: Interview', in *Kunapipi*, 2, 1, 1980, p. 104.

47 Watts, ' "A Bloody Racist": About Achebe's View of Conrad', in *Yearbook of English Studies*, 13, 1983, reprinted in *Joseph Conrad: Critical Assessments*, ed. Keith Carabine, Robertsbridge, East Sussex: Helm Information, 1992, Vol. 2, p. 413.

48 Achebe, 'Africa's Tarnished Name', in *Another Africa*, p. 106.

49 Achebe, 'An Image of Africa', in *Massachusetts Review*, 18, 4, 1977, revised version under title 'An Image of Africa: Racism in Conrad's "Heart of Darkness" ', in Achebe, *Hopes and Impediments: Selected Essays 1965–1987*, London: Heinemann, 1988, and in *Joseph Conrad: Heart of Darkness*, ed. Kimbrough, 1988; 'Viewpoint' in *Times Literary Supplement*, 4010, 1 February 1980; 'The Song of Ourselves' in *New Statesman and Society*, 3, 87, 9 February 1990, also published as 'African Literature as Restoration of Celebration' in *Kunapipi*, 12, 2, 1990; Karen J. Winkler, 'An African Writer at a Crossroads', in *The Chronicle of Higher Education*, 12 January 1994; Lyms, Achebe, *Another Africa*, 1998; Caryl Phillips, 'Out of Africa' in *The Guardian*, 22 February 2003.

50 Meisel, 'Decentring "Heart of Darkness" ', in *Modern Language Studies*, 8, 3, 1978; revised version in *The Myth of the Modern: A Study of British Literature and Criticism after 1880*, New Haven: Yale UP, 1987.

one of its leading practitioners by including J. Hillis Miller's ' "Heart of Darkness" Revisited' (1989) in this volume (see Critical readings, **pp. 101–12**).

By the 1980s, the theoretical revolution in literary studies in the UK and USA imparted a new impetus to work on *Heart of Darkness*, which had previously proved congenial to traditional approaches. New readings reflected symbolic, psychological, political, mythological, metaphysical, autobiographical, formalist developments, but were not contained by these. Benita Parry's *Conrad's Imperialism: Ideological Boundaries and Visionary Frontiers* (1983) is sensitive to the ideological and political implications of *Heart of Darkness*. In contrast to Achebe, however, Parry does not assume that a literary text has a single primary meaning and reveals the influence of the post-structuralist and deconstructionist view that all texts are, inherently and necessarily, contradictory. Her conclusion is that 'to proffer an interpretation of *Heart of Darkness* as a militant denunciation and a reluctant affirmation of imperialist civilization, as a fiction that exposes and colludes in imperialism's mystifications, is to recognize its immanent contradictions.'[51] I do not agree with the second half of Parry's equation. She adopts a more temperate and up-to-date literary-critical language but largely concurs with Achebe. She thinks that 'the landscape is mythic, the scenery surreal, the circumstances grotesque' (p. 24), and that the novella incorporates 'adumbrations of racist views' (p. 36). Parry also states:

> what [Marlow] sees, and this remains uncontroverted by the text, belongs not to history but to fantasy, to the sensational world of promiscuity, idolatry, satanic rites and human sacrifices unveiled in nineteenth-century travellers' tales as the essence of Africa without law or social restraint . . . (p. 29).

But Achebe's *Things Fall Apart* (1958) confirms practices of polygamy and human sacrifice within tribal law. Parry's book nevertheless remains a strong interpretation and includes many insights such as:

> It is . . . Marlow's own narration that negates his thesis on the redemptive dimensions to imperialism. His confusions about the substance of his narration, his misrecognitions, the discrepancies between what he shows and what he sees, his positing of certainties which prove to be dubious, these are the fiction's means of exhibiting that his endeavour to devise an ethical basis for imperialism is destined to fail . . . In the fiction's universe, Europe does not manifest itself as the vital force of progress proposed by imperialist propaganda, but as the parent of degenerate progeny, of sordid ambitions pursued by corrupt human agents. Yet, having detached readers from spontaneous trust in imperialism's rationale, the fiction introduces themes valorizing the doctrine of cultural allegiance as a moral imperative which is independent of the community's collective moral conduct.

> (pp. 28–39)

---

51 Parry, *Conrad's Imperialism: Ideological Boundaries and Visionary Frontiers*, p. 39.

In the 1980s, interpretations of *Heart of Darkness* were not wholly concerned with issues of imperialism, colonialism, racism and the representation or discursive construction of Africa.[52] Peter Brooks' original approach to *Heart of Darkness* in *Reading for the Plot* (1984) (see Critical Readings, **pp. 113–27**) refers to the imperialist aspect but does not make it central. He is influenced by structuralism (which sees literature as part of a range of signifying practices) as well as by psychoanalysis and narratology (the study of the way stories are related) to analyze the narrative of *Heart of Darkness*. After all, it seems to me, the ultimate reason for the continuing popularity of the novella is, probably, that it is engrossing as a story.

In the 1980s, *Heart of Darkness* was examined not only for possible racism but also for possible sexism, another controversial area that was being scrutinized for the social construction of gender and the power relations governing sexuality. Imperialism came to be seen as a hyper-masculine construct that subjugates and marginalizes not only persons of colour but also women of whatever colour. In her essay ' "Too Beautiful Altogether": Patriarchal Ideology in *Heart of Darkness*' (1989),[53] Johanna M. Smith interrogates the 'complex interrelation of patriarchal and imperialist ideologies' (p. 180). Smith argues that these shape the creation of the novella's (minor) female characters, causing them to remain silent or causing them to speak words that affirm masculinity. She argues that when Marlow depicts Kurtz's African woman as an embodiment of the jungle, he unites patriarchal and imperialist ideologies:

> As the patriarchal ideology intends with its power of image-making to distance and hence conquer the woman's body, so the imperialist ideology intends with its power for good to distance and conquer the mysterious life of the jungle. And both the savage woman and the jungle are momentarily silenced by Marlow's images of them. As these images interrupt the movement of his narrative, however, they create gaps by which the reader can see the impossibility of such containment.
>
> (p. 186)

In her essay from this perspective (which also draws on psychoanalysis and reader-response theory), 'The Exclusion of the Intended from Secret Sharing in Conrad's "Heart of Darkness" ' (1987),[54] Nina Pelikan Straus argues that Marlow's tale is directed at a male 'reader-participator': 'these words are understood differently by feminist readers and by mainstream male commentators'.[55] She thinks that 'the artistic conventions of *Heart of Darkness* are brutally sexist' (p. 200), catering to the needs and desires of male readers and extending into the sexism continued by the masculine tradition of Conrad critics. Straus also asserts: 'Marlow presents a world distinctly split into male and female realms – the first

52 See also Christopher L. Miller, *Blank Darkness: Africanist Discourse in French*, Chicago, 1985.
53 Smith, in *Joseph Conrad: Heart of Darkness*, ed. Murfin, 1989.
54 N. Pelikan Straus, 'The Exclusion of the Intended from Secret Sharing in Conrad's "Heart of Darkeness" ', *Novel*, 20, 1987.
55 Pelikan Straus, as reprinted in *Joseph Conrad's Heart of Darkness* ed. Gene M. Moore, New York: Oxford UP, 2004, p. 206.

harbouring the possibility of "truth" and the second dedicated to the mainten-
ance of delusion' (p. 199). She proceeds: ' "we exist only in so far as we hang
together" . . . there is no indication that [Marlow's] existence depends upon his
"hanging together" with a "humanity" that includes the second sex' (p. 199).
Straus overlooks the fact that the sea, like 'business', was a masculine world in
Edwardian times. She feels that 'male criticism is self-serving' (p. 201), unaware
that feminist criticism too can be regarded as 'self-serving'. It is justifiable for her
to characterize the Intended as a 'fleshless soul' [never fulfilled], but 'soulless flesh'
(p. 203) is a ridiculous epithet for the stately African woman who cries out to a
frail wreck of a man, Kurtz, as the waters carry him away from her, like Aeneas
leaving Dido. However, Straus' landmark essay is coherent. To her, Marlow's lie,
a 'chivalric, albeit ironic, sacrifice' which excludes the Intended from the truth,
'brings truth to men' and simultaneously excludes female readers unless they 'are
willing to suspend their womanliness far enough to forever disassociate themselves from the women characters in *Heart of Darkness*' (p. 207). Yet Straus does
discover a role for the woman reader: arguing that Marlow's protectiveness of
Kurtz's secret stems from unexpressible homocentric, but not necessarily homosexual, love (itself offering a paradigm of the male critic's relationship with Conrad), she claims that the 'guarding of secret knowledge is thus the undisclosed
theme of *Heart of Darkness*' (pp. 213–14). Straus represents a radical feminist
challenge to Conrad and his male critics.

Recent directions – after 1990

As we move from the 1980s to the 1990s and the immediate present, the debates
aroused by the attacks of Achebe and the feminists have continued but have also
become more complex. Approaches to *Heart of Darkness* productively employ
both traditional and more recent methodologies. In a phase when canonical texts
are more open to question than in the past and artistic quality does not enjoy the
same degree of allegiance, *Heart of Darkness* seems, in fact, to have consolidated
its position.

Marianna Torgovnick in *Gone Primitive* (1990) departs from both the traditional formalist/humanist approaches and existing critiques of Conrad as imperialist, and develops an analysis based on specifically African considerations. She
deconstructs the image of the primitive which functions in Western culture to
designate 'them' in order to define by contrast 'us'.[56] She argues that in Conrad's
novella Africa and the Africans are constructed as the primitive and set up in
antithesis to Europe and Europeans: them/us, savage/civilized, black/white. She
talks about 'what the novella refuses to discuss except in the vaguest terms – "the
horror, the horror" – what Kurtz was about in Africa' (p. 146). [In my view, 'the
horror' is not only connected to Africa.] She focuses on the heads that adorn
Kurtz's palisade and asserts that 'Kurtz chose to collect real heads' and also
engaged in 'rituals of human sacrifice and cannibalism', and concludes [dubi-
ously]: 'Africa and the Africans became Kurtz's grand fantasy-theatre for playing
out his culture's notions of masculinity and power through the controlled,

---

56 Torgovnick, *Gone Primitive*, pp. 3–4.

borrowed rituals attributed to certain groups within Africa, perverted to Western ends' (p. 151). [More acceptably] Torgovnick argues:

> In Conrad, as in Bataille, Lawrence, Eliot, and others of the genera-tion, the creation of specific versions of the primitive ... is condi-tioned by a sense of disgust or frustration with Western values. The primitive becomes a convenient locale for the exploration of Western dullness or degeneracy ... Present as sign and symbol, the primitive lacks authenticity in and of itself. It becomes grist for the Western fantasy-mill.

She adds: 'Conrad's version of the primitive is a cheat. It promises much and seems to offer tolerance and sympathy, balance and wisdom, an unlimited and unconditional exploration of experience extreme in its difference from Western norms' (p. 153). [I think Conrad makes it clear that Marlow's river-trip offers a limited view.] Torgovnick, then, states a [debatable] conclusion: 'the words con-vey only stale, familiar ideas about Africa and the West's relation to it' (p. 154), and a [startling] view, 'The African woman is the crux of *Heart of Darkness*' (p. 154). [Acceptably] Torgovnick holds: 'She is the symbol of Africa' (p. 155). [I would prefer 'a' rather than 'the' symbol though.] She surmises: 'The woman presumably dies' (p. 155). Torgovnick proceeds to argue in the vein of the newer body-based feminism: 'Her death fulfils her role as emblem of the African land-scape ... For the African landscape is death in the novella. ... Europeans enter it but leave it either dead or ill or changed and marked forever. Women are uniformly associated with the landscape and with death' (pp. 155–7).

Robert Hampson's lucid *Joseph Conrad: Betrayal and Identity* (1992) acknow-ledges his debt to Paul Kirschner[57] who 'in particular suggested a way of looking at Conrad that drew on psychological ideas without subjecting Conrad's work to the reductionism of earlier psychological approaches',[58] to Eloise Knapp Hay[59] for her perception of 'the significance of the merchant navy for Conrad' (p. 7), and to a reliance on Laingian existential psychology which 'provides a language for the precise analysis of relations within the self and relations between the self and others' (p. 10). Focused on 'Conrad's exploration of the nature of identity through his novels', it examines 'incidents of betrayal (both of one's self and of others)' (p. 8).

Conrad has played an important role in Edward Said's development. Said's doctoral study of Conrad's letters in relation to his fiction at Harvard became his first published book, *Joseph Conrad and the Fiction of Autobiography* (1966).[60] The emphasis in his interpretation of *Heart of Darkness* here is mainly metaphysical – as one of the works in which Conrad examines 'the encounter between truth and image, abstraction and concreteness, darkness and illumin-ation' (p. 147). He refers to imperialism briefly: 'Kurtz's spirit of adventure

57 *Conrad: The Psychologist as Artist*, Edinburgh: Oliver & Boyd, 1968.
58 Hampson, *Joseph Conrad: Betrayal and* Identity, London: Macmillan, 1992, p. 6.
59 Hay, *The Political Novels of Joseph Conrad*, 1963.
60 Said, *Joseph Conrad and the Fiction of Autobiography*, Cambridge, Massachussetts: Harvard UP, 1966.

and colonialism has taken him to the centre of things, and this is where Marlow hopes to find him' (pp. 147–8). Said discusses Conrad in *Beginnings* (1975), but his focus is mainly on *Nostromo*. In his essay 'Intellectuals in the Post-Colonial World'[61] he takes the 'narrative form' of *Heart of Darkness* as the 'paradigm' (p. 48) of the type of post-colonial discourse that tries to erase 'the ravages to the colonial people' (p. 47). He develops this view in his major study, *Culture and Imperialism* (1993). This is part of his examination of the cultural forms that reveal the continuing interdependent discourse between subject peoples and the dominant discourse of empire in the nineteenth and twentieth centuries.

Geoffrey Galt Harpham's original approach in *One of Us: The Mastery of Joseph Conrad* (1996) has had an impact on Conrad studies, though it seems to me, ultimately, an unstable account. Harpham announces: 'This book represents an attempt at a theory of production, a psychology of composition . . .'.[62] His overarching interest in the thematic of 'mastery' does not prevent the book from being centrifugal. He can be ingeniously silly, as when he sees Kurtz as a pun on 'Christ' and 'cursed' (p. 170). Harpham, however, repays reading. Kurtz signally lacks 'self-mastery'. He appears to be affected by the fin de siècle cultural 'degeneration' just as it affected Dorian Gray and his creator too. Harpham refers to this concern with 'degeneration' (p. 163).

Critics have continued to relate Conrad's fiction to fields of study connected with it. John W. Griffith in *Joseph Conrad and the Anthropological Dilemma* (1995) defines 'the dilemma' as the dangers caused by the inability of one culture to comprehend/ interpret due to conditioning and how 'such cross-cultural contacts would prove dangerous to the members of each society'.[63] [It does prove 'dangerous' to the African, the 'dog in breeches', as well as to the European Kurtz.] Griffith also reveals 'some fissures in what has been viewed as a confident melioristic age' (p. 2) – as does Linda Dryden in her essay (see Critical readings, **pp. 83–91**). Martin Bock in *Conrad and Psychological Medicine* (2002) reads Conrad's medical history in the context of contemporary psychological and medical discourse, and demonstrates its connection with the fiction. Peter Edgerly Firchow devotes a full-length book to *Heart of Darkness – Envisioning Africa: Racism and Imperialism in Conrad's Heart of Darkness* (2000). He provides a painstaking, copious collection of background information. Andrea White in *Joseph Conrad and the Adventure Tradition* (1993) examines the significance for Conrad's earlier work of two related genres – imperial travel writing (from Captain Cook to David Livingstone) and adventure fiction (from Captain Marryat to Haggard). She demonstrates how Conrad subverted the conventions of Victorian adventure fiction from within, continuing a process (begun by Haggard) through which the founding pro-imperial assumptions of the genre were demythologized and disrupted, and which culminated in *Heart of Darkness*. She argues that the very complexity of Conrad's work provided an alternative, and more critical, means of assessing the experience of empire. For instance, she comments:

---

61 Said, 'Intellectuals in the Post-Colonial World', in *Salmagundi*, 70–1, 1986.
62 Harpham, *One of Us: The Mastery of Joseph Conrad*, Chicago: Chicago UP, 1996, p. xi.
63 Griffith, *Joseph Conrad and the Anthropological Dilemma*, Oxford: Clarendon, 1995, 1999 edn, p. 30.

'Marlow is not so much Conrad's spokesman as a strategic innovation that served his purposes in disrupting the generic adventure story and its essentially danger-ous monolithic illusions. His use increases the dialogic possibilities and allows the story to be the site of struggle between disparate languages and outlooks.'[64] White marshals her evidence with clarity and captures our interest.

'Trauma narrative' is a theme that has been discussed a great deal in recent theory and criticism. While Lea Wernick Fridman's subject in *Words and Wit-ness* (2000) is *Narrative and Aesthetic Strategies in the Representation of the Holocaust*, her exemplary text of trauma narrative is *Heart of Darkness*. Her attempt to link her approach to the novella seems to me not particularly fertile, though her concern is with 'historical horror', and Conrad's Congo is, certainly, an instance. I would also add that Conrad suffered trauma in the Congo. But Fridman argues:

> The central quest of the novella is really about the problem of fact and how we can know fact, especially where the fact involved is cata-strophic. And it is this problematic of catastrophic fact – of fact that is, finally, unknowable – that shapes *Heart of Darkness* as a journey, not toward the object itself since, in any case, that object cannot be known, but toward Kurtz, the European agent who has participated in the hor-ror and gives testimony to that horror in his famous dying words. *Heart of Darkness* is not the story of the white man's shocking behaviour in Africa, but the story of Marlow's journey to receive Kurtz's testimony about that shocking behaviour . . . The narrative of *Heart of Darkness* is doubled. It includes an untold story – the utter horror of catastrophic experience that cannot be put into words – as well as the story of a journey to hear the story of a witness to that horror.[65]

It seems to me that Conrad understands 'the historical horror' and puts it across, ironically, through Marlow who can, and does, present it himself. It is not 'unknowable' and 'unrepresentable'. The reader does not need Kurtz's testimony. His dying words include other, wider implications.

Andrew Michael Roberts in *Conrad and Masculinity* (2000) offers the most coherent account to date of Conrad seen in terms of gender and cultural material-ism. He makes extensive use of post-Lacanian,[66] feminist, psychoanalytic, colonial discourse and narrative theories, and argues that 'any model must be liable to modification in the light of the specific instance, since neither imperial practice nor imperial discourse was unified and homogeneous'.[67] He defines masculinity, apart from gender, as 'a psychic structure, as a fantasy, as a code of behaviour, or as a set of social practices and constraints' (p. 5). Masculinity presents a

---

64 White, *Joseph Conrad and the Adventure Tradition*, Cambridge: Cambridge UP, 1993, p. 177.
65 Fridman, *Words and Witness*, New York: State University of New York Press, 2000, pp. 18–19.
66 The ideas of Jacques Lacan (1901–81), the French psychoanalyst, such as 'the mirror stage', the human tendency to be mesmerized by visual images, to live in the world of 'the imaginary', and 'the symbolic order', that it was not the stream of pictures passing across the mind's eye that determined human behaviour but the unconscious web of words and phrases that lay beneath the images, have been used by literary critics to produce novel ways of interpreting texts.
67 Roberts, *Conrad and Masculinity*, Basingstoke, UK, & New York: Palgrave, 2000, p. 22.

rewarding field for Conrad studies partly because Conrad's narrative point of view exclusively involves male narrators (most famously, Marlow) and a male audience – both fictional and 'real' or implied. In regard to *Heart of Darkness*, Roberts notes how the ways information is exchanged – via telling stories, confessing, overhearing, lying etc. – is gendered, and how women are excluded from the crucial exchange of knowledge. He writes of Kurtz's African woman: 'her lack of comprehensible voice within his [Marlow's] narrative . . . combined with the elaborate description of her visual appearance, renders her the passive object of a masterful gaze, . . .' (p. 167). He reads the novella in terms of homosexual desire as part of 'the rhetorical and symbolic structures [that] constantly evoke discourses of sexual knowledge and ignorance.' Roberts sometimes theorizes at the expense of analysis, yet his book underlines the need for coverage of *Heart of Darkness* to be alert to the ways it represents men and women.

Stephen Ross' *Conrad and Empire* (2004) announces a departure from an earlier approach and the adoption of a new one:

> Conrad's engagement (or lack thereof) with imperialism as imperialism . . . should no longer be taken as sufficient grounds for critique. Rather it must be read as a symptom of his engagement with emerging post-imperialist modernity that Michael Hardt and Antonio Negri have christened Empire.[68]

Ross explores the psychology of Empire, highlighting how Conrad projects and criticizes global modernity both as an ideological system and subjective condition.

> Taken together, these two elements – the social and psychic – of Conrad's work articulate a uniquely prescient conception of modernity not merely in terms of existing structures and dynamics of nineteenth-century nation-state imperialist politics, but as a much more sweeping shift in orientation toward an era of extra-national global capitalism
>
> (p. 8)

Ross de-historicizes and de-contextualizes Conrad's works such as *Heart of Darkness*, but his approach is not wholly new. As he himself acknowledges, his book is an extension of a trend that includes Chris Bongie's *Exotic Memories: Literature, Colonialism and Fin de Siècle* (1991) and Christopher GoGwilt's *The Invention of the West: Joseph Conrad and the Double-Mapping of Europe and Empire* (1995). GoGwilt argues that Conrad's work progresses from dealing with nation-state imperialism in the Malay fictions to dealing with European modernity on its own ground in the later works of his major phase, particularly *The Secret Agent* and *Under Western Eyes*. Building on the work of Edward Said, he offers an account of Conrad's role in shaping and reacting to notions of 'the West'. But his discussion of *Heart of Darkness* is brief.

Douglas Hewitt, a pioneer in the revival of interest in Conrad in the 1950s, was one of the first to argue that *Heart of Darkness* 'is primarily concerned with the

---

68 Ross, *Conrad and Empire*, Columbia & London: Missouri UP, 2004, p. 6.

effect of the country [Africa] and of Kurtz on Marlow'.[69] He later claimed (accurately) that Conrad's novella has 'probably had more critical attention per word than any other modern prose work'.[70] *Heart of Darkness* remains, somewhat like its author, fascinating and fertile in ideas – but ultimately elusive.

69 Hewitt, *Conrad: A Reassessment*, Cambridge: Bowes, 1952, p. 18.
70 Hewitt, *English Fiction of the Early Modern Period 1890–1940*, London: Longman, 1988, p. 31.

3

Critical readings

Ian Watt, 'Heart of Darkness and Nineteenth-Century Thought' (1978)

Watt's essay traces the many factors which led to a gradually deepening sense of pessimism in the late Victorian era that together with Conrad's own temperament, both pessimistic and ironic, and his curiously variegated experiences must have contributed to the nature of *Heart of Darkness*. The reference to Albert Camus (1913–60), the French author and philosopher, at the end is appropriate: it points to Conrad's modernity and being ahead of his time; Kurtz is obviously an existentialist (see Critical history, **p. 55**), and so is Camus and also Conrad from one perspective. The essay illuminates strands of the intellectual context in which *Heart of Darkness* has to be placed. [Incidentally, Watt (see Critical history, **pp. 57–8**) does not supply references.]

From *Partisan Review*, 45, No. 1, 1978

Conrad isn't a philosophical novelist in the way that George Eliot, Thomas Hardy or George Meredith are; we don't feel in the presence of logical arguments or moral lessons. But if Conrad doesn't present himself as a thinker, he strikes us as very thoughtful; the intimations of his fictional world steadily invite ethical and even metaphysical response.

The basic conflict in this fictional world arises from a double vision; Conrad wants both to endorse the standard Victorian moral positives, and to express his forebodings that the dominant intellectual directions of the nineteenth century were preparing disaster for the twentieth. This conflict between the endorsements and the forebodings is most comprehensively expressed in the tension between Marlow and Kurtz in Conrad's ideological *summa*, *Heart of Darkness*. It has gradually established itself for the twentieth century as the supremely modern work in the Conrad canon; and it appeared, very appropriately, in the last year of the nineteenth century, and in the thousandth number of that very representative organ of high Victorian culture, *Blackwood's Magazine*.

Scientifically, Conrad was fairly well informed and, unlike most of the other great modern writers, he neither doubted nor discounted the findings of natural science. His position about the ultimate human implications of these findings, however, was deeply sceptical, and in several ways. Like Matthew Arnold in his essay 'Literature and Science', Conrad diagnosed a deep intellectual muddle behind contemporary attempts to force a marriage between science and culture; for his own part he contemptuously rejected 'the tyranny of science and the cant of science', and concluded that 'life and the arts follow dark courses and will not turn aside to the brilliant arc-lights of science'.

Some negative inferences, however, had to be drawn from science as regards human life, and they led to radical conclusions that brought Conrad fairly close to an existentialist position: the individual consciousness was destined to be in total contradiction to its physical and moral environment. 'What makes men tragic,' Conrad wrote to Cunninghame Graham,

> is not that they are victims of nature, it is that they are conscious of it . . . There is no morality, no knowledge, and no hope; there is only the consciousness of ourselves which drives us about a world that whether seen in a convex or a concave mirror is always but a vain and fleeting appearance.

It was primarily the two forms of natural science which most affected the general Victorian outlook – physics and biology – that had been decisive in making man see himself as the victim of nature. The traditional belief that the creation of the world, and of man, was a unique manifestation of God's providence had been fatally undermined long before by astronomy. Then in the nineteenth century geology had suggested, not only that the earth itself was a transitory phenomenon, but that, as Tennyson put it in *In Memoriam*, even man himself might one day, like the fossils in the books, become extinct and 'Be blown about the desert dust, or sealed within the iron hills'. Finally Victorian physics had confirmed this vista of coming extinction. For, it now appeared, our terrestrial planet had originated not out of the hand of God but accidentally out of the cooling gases of the sun; and the formulation of the second law of thermodynamics by Lord Kelvin in 1851 seemed to mean that the destiny of the earth was to end in cold and drought through the diffusion of heat-energy.

This astrophysical pessimism, widely popularized by Balfour Stewart's *The Conservation of Energy* in 1873, soon became a standard feature of late Victorian thought. As Edward Carpenter wrote about the universe of his youth: 'one of its properties was that it could run down like a clock, and would eventuate in time in a cold sun and a dead earth – and there was an end of it.' The eighteenth century had inferred a divine watch-maker from the operations of the celestial machine; it was now discovered that there was no watch- maker and that the watch's spring was running down.

This dispiriting historical perspective pervades *Heart of Darkness*. Marlow's first remark, as the sun sets over London, is 'And this also . . . has been one of the dark places of the earth.' Dismissing from our minds both the present lights on the shore and the glories of the national past enacted along the estuary of the Thames, Marlow harks back to the darkness which had here confronted the first Roman settlers in Britain; and we are made to see civilization, not as a stable human achievement, but as a brief interruption of the normal rule of darkness; the extent and duration of civilized order are as limited and brief as 'a flash of lightning in the clouds', and, Marlow reflects, 'We live in the flicker.'

Like atomic physics in our day, however, it was biology which had the most important moral and political implications for the later nineteenth century. That some of these implications found their way into *Heart of Darkness* is not surprising, for Conrad grew up in the heyday of evolutionary theory, and Alfred Wallace was one of his favourite authors.

The main plot of *Heart of Darkness* is provided, in effect, by that aspect of the evolutionary process to which Marlow is exposed in his voyage further up-river. Marlow stumbles onto a grim historical variant of the law that ontogeny recapitulates phylogeny; the case of Kurtz demonstrates the process in reverse. His atavistic regression is brought on by the wilderness which, Marlow says, 'whispered to him things about himself which he did not know, things of which he had no conception till he took counsel with this great solitude'. At home everything conspired to keep Kurtz in ignorance of his true self; the police stopped him from devouring others or being devoured; but in the solitude his 'forgotten and brutal instincts' revealed themselves as potent forces in his biological inheritance, and therefore as powerful arguments against the widespread distortion of evolutionary theory to support the Victorian faith in economic, social, political and national progress, the faith which originally animated Kurtz.

The strongest single support for the Victorian faith in progress was economic expansion, to which both Bentham and natural science had lent a theoretical rationale and an immense public prestige. Conrad, however, rejected the material and quantitative values of a commercial and industrial society: he saw only danger in 'the blind trust in mere material and appliances'; he warned against 'carrying humility towards that universal provider, Science, too far', and he viewed the Victorian hope that progress would automatically result from 'the peaceful nature of industrial and commercial competition' as an 'incredible infatuation'.

Kurtz, of course, stands not only for the civilizing beneficence of economic progress, but for the other more spiritual components of the Victorian religion of progress. Evolution had replaced the traditional view of man's supremacy in the Divine plan with the idea that an equivalently splendid status could be attained through the working out of humanity's secular destiny. In Arthur Lovejoy's phrase, the 'temporalisation of the Chain of Being' had substituted the law of historical progress for the lost belief in the perfection of God's providential design.

During the eighties and nineties the main ideologies that supported this kind of belief were social Darwinism and imperialism, whose doctrines were closely related. Social Darwinism, of which the most famous exponent was Herbert Spencer, supported the competitive economic order at home, and utilitarian theory in general, on the grounds that – to use his phrase in *First Principles* (1862) – the 'survival of the fittest' was a law of nature, and led to human progress.

The same kind of thinking provided an ideology for colonial expansion. Merely by occupying or controlling most of the globe, it was assumed, the European nations had demonstrated that they were the fittest to survive; and the accelerating exportation of their various economic, political and religious institutions was therefore a necessary evolutionary step towards a higher form of human organization in the rest of the world. It was also widely thought – by Spencer, for example – that the dominance of the white races was itself the result of biological superiority, and this racial doctrine became particularly useful in enlisting popular political support for the imperialist adventures of the end of the nineteenth century. As Victor Kiernan has written, the 'mystique of race was Democracy's vulgarization of an older mystique of class.'

Conrad's own attitude to colonialism was complicated; but he had been lucky, from a literary point of view, in finding an ideologically perfect and patriotically unembarrassing example of the discrepancies between colonial pretence and reality. It was a pure case: first, because the Congo Free State was in theory international, and thus did not raise the question of national loyalty; second, because unlike most other colonies the Congo Free State was a conscious political creation; and third, because the whole world had listened to public professions of exalted educational, moral and religious purposes from its founders, and then been forced to discover that these verbal pretences masked what Conrad later described as 'the vilest scramble for loot that ever disfigured the history of human conscience and geographical exploration'.

During the two decades between Conrad's arrival in England in 1878 and the writing of *Heart of Darkness*, many leaders of thought were becoming convinced that the Victorian world order was collapsing. *Heart of Darkness* is an expression of that conviction; and its widely-shared rejection of earlier optimistic assumptions about progress is clearly echoed both in the literature and the evolutionary theory of the period.

A great many novels of the nineties have a note of apocalyptic gloom. Grant Allen's 1895 novel, *The British Barbarians*, for instance, pictured the twenty-fifth century as a relapse into anthropoid animality; and there is a sense of the impending collapse of western civilization both in Nietzsche's *Twilight of the Idols* (1889) and in Max Nordau's *Degeneration*, which was immensely successful in its 1895 English translation. The idea gained even wider currency from Oscar Wilde's *The Picture of Dorian Gray* (1891), where Lord Henry murmurs '*Fin de Siècle*' and his hostess knowingly answers '*Fin du globe*'.

The most immediate basis for this loss of confidence in the future was probably political, but the implications of natural science were also important.

Darwin himself had been in the main dubious about whether any political or psychological deductions about man and his future could be drawn from evolutionary theory; a good many of Darwin's followers, however, had drawn such deductions, and, in the case of the most eminent of them, Thomas Huxley, they had become increasingly pessimistic. In his influential and widely reported 1893 Romanes lecture on 'Evolution and Ethics', a lecture which had the optimism of Spencer as its main target, Huxley asserted an intractable dualism between nature and human values which is in many ways parallel to that which Conrad presented in *Heart of Darkness*.

Spencer had been sure that what he regarded as the necessary law of progress meant that 'evil and immorality' would disappear, and 'man become perfect'. Huxley had no such illusions. He conceded that

> after the manner of successful persons, civilized man would gladly kick down the ladder by which he has climbed. He would be only too pleased to see 'the ape and tiger die'. But they decline to suit his convenience,

and the unwelcome intrusion of these boon companions of his hot youth into the ranged existence of civil life adds pains and griefs, innumerable and immeasurably great, to those which the cosmic process brings on the mere animal.

The prospect of happiness or perfection, then, is 'as misleading an illusion as ever was dangled before the eyes of poor humanity'; man will always 'bring with him the instinct of unlimited self–assertion', so that his future will be 'a constant struggle . . . in opposition to the State of Nature'; and this unhappy conflict will continue until 'the evolution of our globe shall have entered so far upon its downward course that the cosmic process resumes its sway; and, once more, the State of Nature prevails over the surface of our planet.'

Five years later, in 1898, even the sanguine positivism of Herbert Spencer had apparently evaporated and he was inclined to agree, writing in a letter to Grant Allen: 'We are in the course of rebarbarisation.'

Heart of Darkness, then, expresses a perspective that was representative of many currents of thought in late nineteenth-century England; but it is representative in a very tangential way. Conrad's imaginative world seems wholly independent; the ideas don't stick out, or ask for support or confirmation. Thus the closeness of Conrad's moral and social assumptions to Huxley's later evolutionary thought is very striking if we compare Conrad's picture of man and society with that of Hardy, Wells, or Shaw; but we could hardly say that *Heart of Darkness* is about evolution; and even if one said it is about colonialism, or about the implications of colonialism for the colonizers and their civilization, the description would still seem both too analytic and too restrictive.

Yet in his own way Conrad was an intellectual, and his first mention of writing *Heart of Darkness* presented it in specifically intellectual terms: 'The *idea* in it,' he explained to his publisher, William Blackwood, 'is not as obvious as in "Youth" – or at least not so obviously presented', and added: 'The subject is of our time distinctly – though not topically treated.'

This description, written on December 31, 1898, when the story was barely begun, refers only to its most obvious ideological content: that is, as Conrad rather defensively put it in the same letter, 'the justifiable idea' of exposing 'the criminality of inefficiency and pure selfishness when tackling the civilizing work in Africa'. This anti-colonial tenor is very similar to that of Conrad's earlier story, 'An Outpost of Progress', which had led Cunninghame Graham, an avowed Marxist who shared platforms with such men as Engels and Kropotkin, to write a letter of enthusiastic praise. What Cunninghame Graham had correctly recognized was a general political perspective very similar to his own definition of 'the Imperial Mission' as 'the Stock Exchange Militant'; and Cunninghame Graham was equally enthusiastic about the anti-colonial first part of *Heart of Darkness*. Conrad, however, urged him to delay final judgment, writing that 'There are two more instalments in which the idea is so wrapped up in secondary notions that You – even You! – may miss it.'

Conrad nowhere specifies what these 'secondary notions' were; but he gives a clue in a later letter to Blackwood when he says that the final scene, where Marlow finds himself forced to lie about Kurtz's end to the Intended, 'locks in' the whole narrative 'into one suggestive view of a whole phase of life'.

One of the secondary themes 'locked in' to the conclusion is presumably Marlow's view of women. At the very beginning of the story Marlow was quite unable to convince his 'excellent aunt' who got him a job with the Trading Company that it was run for profit; and this led him to interject: 'It's queer how out of touch with truth women are. They live in a world of their own.' Marlow makes a similar comment when he first mentions the Intended: 'Oh, she is out of it – completely. They – the women I mean – are out of it – should be out of it. We must help them to stay in that beautiful world of their own, lest ours gets worse.' In the manuscript Conrad made this passage even more explicit, and anticipates Marlow's final lie to the Intended about Kurtz's actual end, by adding: 'That's a monster – truth with many maws to whom we've got to throw every year – or every day – no matter – no sacrifice is too great – a ransom of pretty, shining lies.'

Marlow's misogyny may seem a somewhat less disabling prejudice if it is set in the context of his general view of life. What he says clearly refers, not to the women who work in the office of the Trading Company, for instance, or to Kurtz's native mistress, but quite specifically to women of the well-to-do and leisured class to whom his aunt and the Intended, and presumably the womenfolk of his audience, belong. Marlow's perspective, in fact, assumes the Victorian relegation of leisure-class women to a pedestal of philanthropic idealism high above the economic and sexual facts of life. Since Marlow believes that it is only through work – more generally through a direct personal striving to master some external and objective force – that anyone can find 'his own reality', it follows that the practical truths of life are not transferable from one individual to another, whether verbally or otherwise; and it further follows that, merely by allotting its women a leisure role, bourgeois society has in effect excluded them from discovering reality. It is by no choice or fault of hers, therefore, that the Intended inhabits an unreal world; but because she does, Marlow at the end finds himself forced to lie to her about Kurtz. One reason is that if he told the truth she would not have the necessary grounds in her own experience to be able to understand it; another is that since for all his seeking Marlow himself has found no faith which will move mountains, his nostalgia inclines him to cherish the faith that ignores them.

Work versus words is an even commoner opposition in Conrad than in life; and in *Heart of Darkness* the cognitive role of work is often made the dialectical opposite of another secondary theme – the self-deluding tendency of verbal communication. Kurtz is the most obvious example; he is, Marlow discovers, 'very little more than a voice', a hollow sound-box of egotistic pretensions; and Marlow's 'memory of that time' lingers round him still 'like a dying vibration of one immense jabber'. For Marlow, women such as his aunt and the Intended are destined to be the mere echo chambers of this jabber. His aunt's illusions about the civilizing work in Africa came to her only because she lived 'right in the rush of all that humbug' which had been 'let loose in print and talk just about that time', while the illusions of the Intended are only 'the echo of [Kurtz's] magnificent eloquence'. Both Marlow's aunt and the Intended unconsciously function as the façade for the operations of the manager and his cronies; they are indeed, as Kurtz's oil painting suggests, the blind publicists for the venal hypocrisies of the sepulchral city; and words are its whitewash.

Marlow sees both the Intended and Kurtz as pitiful victims of the unreal aspirations of their century. The developing imperatives of Romantic individualism had set up the ideal of absolute liberation from religious, social and ethical norms; and this trend was later reinforced by many others – most obviously by the utilitarian view of society as composed of an aggregate of economic individuals, by the democratic egalitarianism of liberal political theory and by the thought of Herbert Spencer, who assumed that the progressive differentiation of individuals was the ultimate and sufficient aim of the evolutionary process. All these views at least agreed that progress required the removal of most established economic, political and social 'restraints', and the Harlequin's surrender to Kurtz thus represents his century's innocent but fateful surrender to that total Faustian unrestraint which believes that anything is justified if it 'enlarges the mind'.

Conrad's critical intelligence had arrived, independently perhaps, but supported, surely, by his quick sensitiveness to what he could use in the thought and speech of others, at an unformulated but resolute intellectual conviction which had much in common with that general tendency among so many of the thinkers of the later nineteenth century, who began from the assumption that reason was not the controlling factor in human affairs. This view, in very varied forms, controls the philosophy of von Hartmann, Vaihinger and Nietzsche, the psychology of William James, Bergson and Freud, the anthropology of Sir James Frazer and the sociology of Tonnies, Sorel, Pareto, Max Weber and Durkheim; all of these shared Conrad's total scepticism about progress.

As a naturalized Englishman and a sea captain, however, Conrad had also come to adopt other much more positive and conservative loyalties which supply some of the other secondary notions by which Marlow judges his experience in *Heart of Darkness*. Ford Madox Ford wrote that Conrad ideally 'desired to be . . . a member of the ruling classes of England' in the stable days of Lord Palmerston, and the positive standards in *Heart of Darkness* have something of this early Victorian quality. These standards – roughly, Duty, Restraint and Work – are those by which Marlow lives; and in various guises they were a firm, indeed a notorious, presence in early Victorian thought.

John Stuart Mill wrote in his 'The Utility of Religion' that it was characteristic of 'an age of weak beliefs' that 'such beliefs as men have' should be 'much more determined by their wish to believe than by any mental appreciation of evidence'. We can see this wish to believe both in Marlow and in Conrad. Thus in his first letter to Cunninghame Graham, Conrad wrote: 'It is impossible to know anything,' but added, 'tho' it is possible to believe a thing or two.' Marlow makes the distinction even more explicit in *Lord Jim* when he comments, 'Hang ideas! They are tramps, vagabonds, knocking at the back-door of your mind, each . . . carrying away some crumb of that belief in a few simple notions you must cling to if you want to live decently and would like to die easy.'

One of the few stable points of reference in *Heart of Darkness*, which Marlow much admires in others and what keeps him more or less sane himself, is efficiency at work. This emphasis on the psychologically stabilizing function of labour is close to Carlyle's remark in *Sartor Resartus* (1834) on 'the folly of that impossible precept, "Know thyself" till it be translated into this partially possible one, "Know what thou canst work at" '.

In Conrad's own day the idea of the supreme value of work had been made the basic social and political issue not only by Marx, but by Ruskin and Morris; while notions of group duty and discipline, a necessary component of the imperialist mission as well as of the nautical order, were advocated by W.E. Henley and Kipling. At the back of these insistences was the Victorian nightmare that the disappearance of God would destroy all social and moral sanctions for individual conduct, and that thereafter, in Tennyson's words, men would merely 'submit all things to desire'. The question, in its simplest terms, was whether in a secularized world there would remain anything which corresponded to the word 'conscience'. *Heart of Darkness* continues this Victorian preoccupation. For instance, when the dying Kurtz is said to have 'judged' his life, Marlow is surely implying the real existence of the conscience, of some inner moral constraint.

Marlow's overriding moral commitment to civilization, however deluded, weak and unjust it is found to be, is rather similar to that of Conrad's contemporary, Freud. Freud's observations had forced him to a position which dramatically undermined the accepted psychological foundations of the social and moral order, since man was shown to be unconsciously dominated, not by reason or benevolence or duty, but by the omnivorous and ultimately unappeasable appetites of the id; and so, in *Civilization and Its Discontents* and *The Future of an Illusion*, Freud wondered whether any secular mechanism could ever replace religion in controlling the aggressive drives which led to war and hatred of civilization. Freud had a deeper belief in systematic thought than Conrad, and Conrad was not interested in Freud; nevertheless, they shared not only the same dark view of man's innate constitution and the same conviction that culture was based on repression or restraint, but a similar sense that the destructive tendencies of man which their vision emphasized must be controlled as far as possible, partly by promoting a greater understanding of the inherent darkness of the self, and partly by supporting the modest counter truths on which civilization depends. As against the more absolute negations of Rimbaud or Nietzsche, or the equally absolute transcendental affirmations of Dostoyevski or Yeats, both Freud and Conrad defend a practical social ethic based on their fairly similar reformulations of the Victorian trinity of work, duty and restraint.

The general modern tendency has been to overlook this aspect of the thought of Conrad and Freud in favour of its more dramatic and original destructive side; in effect both of them have been either attacked or praised more for what they saw than for what they said about it. In the process their insistence on the need to control the unconscious and egotistic sides of man has been misinterpreted or overlooked: and this bias has often been reflected in the modern critical treatment of Kurtz.

Kurtz dramatizes Conrad's fear of the ultimate directions of nineteenth-century thought. These directions are beautifully expressed in Auden's poem 'In Father's Footsteps', which begins with a poignant valediction to the basic psychological strategy of the Victorian religion of progress as it assimilated the implications of biological evolution:

> Our hunting fathers told the story
>   Of the sadness of the creatures
> Pitied the limits and the lack
>   Set in their finished features;
> Saw in the lion's intolerant look
> Behind the enemy's dying glare,

Love raging for the personal glory
     That reason's gift would add,
The liberal appetite and power,
     The rightness of a God.

The 'rightness of a God' was a role almost automatically conferred on the white European when he left home and went out to govern colonies. 'All Europe', we are told, 'had contributed to the making of Kurtz', and his motives, as well as his fate, are deeply representative. He goes out, first of all, to make money; he is thus a representative of economic individualism, a protagonist of the career open to talent in the free marketplace; and because he finds a more effective way of exploiting the ivory of the Congo he is naturally expected to become a power in the great Trading Company. Paradoxically, however, the Benthamite, utilitarian and imperialist modes of thought turn out to be not the historical contraries but the complements of Romantic individualism as it had been transformed into its later Bohemian, Decadent and Symbolist embodiments. Kurtz is a poet, a painter, above all a man with the power of words; and his final quest for absolute liberation from all the constraints of civilization makes him a symbolic parallel to the career of Arthur Rimbaud, who had turned his back on European civilization in 1875 and ended up as a trader and explorer in Abyssinia.

The representative importance of Kurtz's surrender to the drives of the unconditioned ego has been analyzed by Lionel Trilling in his essay 'The Modern Element in Literature'. Conrad's 'strange and terrible message of ambivalence towards the life of civilization', Trilling writes, 'continues the tradition of Blake and Nietzsche'; and Kurtz is a portent of the future, for 'nothing is more characteristic of modern literature than its discovery and canonization of the primal, non-ethical energies.'

Kurtz, however, does not consciously seek to liberate these energies; he goes out as a member of the 'gang of virtue', the benevolent liberal reformers who are going to bring the light of modern educational, political, moral and religious progress to the dark places of the earth. Unlike Rimbaud, or Gauguin later, Kurtz is an envoy of civilization, not a voluntary exile; he is 'an emissary', as the brickmaker says, 'of pity, and science, and progress, and devil knows what else'. But in Africa Kurtz meets the ape and the tiger within himself, and eventually lets them loose. Given the opportunity, it appears, the autonomous individual will indeed 'submit all things to desire', and far deeper than his social instinct, it appears, is the desire to do everything he wants to do and claim 'the rightness of a God' for doing it.

This 'rightness' finds a powerful sanction in Western industrial progress. Kurtz achieves supernatural ascendancy primarily though his monopoly of firearms; the idea is prefigured, ironically enough, in his report to the International Society for the Suppression of Savage Customs, where Kurtz begins from the premise that 'we whites . . . must necessarily appear to them [savages] in the nature of supernatural beings – we approach them with the might as of a deity.' The Harlequin confirms this basis for Kurtz's power: 'He came to them with thunder and lightning, you know – and they had never seen anything like it.' So, Marlow tells us Kurtz later presided 'at certain midnight dances ending with unspeakable rites, which – as far as I reluctantly gathered from what I heard at various times – were offered up to him – do you understand? – to Mr. Kurtz himself.'

Marlow is horrified, and so, just before his end, is Kurtz, to understand what happens to a man who discovers his existential freedom under circumstances which enable him to put into practice the ultimate direction of nineteenth-century thought: to bestow on the individual all those powers and freedoms which had formerly been reserved for God. Man's last evolutionary leap was to be up to the throne that he had emptied; up, and yet, at the same time, it seemed, far down, and far back.

Heart of Darkness embodies that view of human destiny which Sartre summed up in his definition of man as 'the being whose plan it is to become God'. Conrad enacted the unreal exorbitances of the plan in the fate of Kurtz; for himself he tentatively preferred the humbler and irresolute moral alternatives of Marlow. Conrad's vision had no use for Christianity, mainly on practical grounds: 'Christianity', he wrote in 1916, 'is the only religion which, with its impossible standards has brought an infinity of anguish to innumerable souls – on this earth.' The cardinal lesson of experience is a full realization of our fragile, lonely and humble status in the natural order; and here any theoretical system, whether philosophical, scientific or religious, is likely to foster dangerous delusions of independence and omnipotence. Thus in 'Youth' Marlow prefers Burnaby's *Ride to Khiva* to Carlyle's *Sartor Resartus*, the soldier to the philosopher, on the grounds that: 'One was a man, and the other was either more – or less.' So, against all the unreal psychological, social and religious hyperboles of his waning century, Conrad decisively rejected both the more and the less; and in *Heart of Darkness* affirmed the necessity, as Camus put it, 'in order to be a man to refuse to be a God.'

Linda Dryden, 'The Vexed Question of Humanity in *Heart of Darkness*: A Historicist Reading' (2007)

In her new essay, Linda Dryden sees historicism as a reinterpretation of history, as an interrogation of history, as history viewed from a current standpoint, and offers a concise introduction to this complex critical approach which also concerns itself with the absence of determinism and of direct links between cause and effect. Her subsequent reading of *Heart of Darkness* throws light on the novella, underlining how it reflects the contemporary unease that whites were no better than blacks, Europeans no better than savages, based on happenings and writings sufficiently recent to have made Conrad aware of this atmosphere.

Dryden, author of *Joseph Conrad and the Imperial Romance* (2000) and *The Modern Gothic and Literary Doubles: Stevenson, Wilde and Wells* (2003), has contributed to the study of early-twentieth-century literature and culture.

The mind of man is capable of anything – because everything is in it, all the past as well as all the future.

Historicist criticism liberates literary texts from the confines of older historical approaches that had assumed historical facts could be objectively determined. Ross C. Murfin argues that historicism contests the notion that history can be fixed as fact: critics now wonder 'whether the truth about what really happened can ever be purely and objectively known'.[1] Challenges to traditional historical inquiry thus liberate texts from their critical shackles, propelling them into a world where no route of investigation can be exhausted, where no truth is absolute. Michel Foucault encouraged historicists to 'outwardly redefine the boundaries of historical inquiry', warning them to 'be aware that investigators are themselves "situated"'.[2] Our cultural perspective limits our powers of observation and

---

1 Murfin (ed.), *Joseph Conrad, Heart of Darkness: A Case Study in Contemporary Criticism*, New York: St. Martin's, 1989, p. 228.
2 Murfin, p. 230.

investigation: we read a text through the lens of the received culture and perception of our own time. Thus new generations of literary commentators bring new interpretations to the literary text. As Arnold Kettle says: 'a book is neither produced nor read in a vacuum and the very word "value" involves right away criteria which are not just "literary". Literature is a part of life and can be judged only in its relevance to life. Life is not static but moving and changing.'[3] Recent historicism, acutely aware of this, extends the disciplinary base available to the critic:

> It is a movement that would destabilize our overly settled conceptions of what literature and history are. It is one, too, that would define history broadly, not as a mere chronicle of facts and events but, rather as a 'thick description' of human reality, one that raises questions of interest to anthropologists and sociologists, as well as those posed by traditional historians.[4]

Criticism now traverses disciplinary boundaries at will in its quest to enrich our understanding. For Stephen Greenblatt the wider focus of criticism should 'prevent it from permanently sealing off one type of discourse from another or decisively separating works of art from the minds and lives of their creators and their audiences'.[5] However, as Paul Hamilton observes, historicism 'is suspicious of the stories the past tells about itself', but equally 'suspicious of its own partisanship': 'It offers up both its past and its present for ideological scrutiny.'[6]

In 1905 Conrad wrote that Henry James saw the novelist as a historian:

> I think that the claim cannot be contested, and that the position is unassailable. Fiction is history, human history, or it is nothing. But it is also more than that; it stands on firmer ground, being based on the reality of forms and the observation of social phenomena, whereas history is based on documents, and the reading of print and handwriting – on second-hand impression. Thus fiction is nearer truth. But let that pass. A historian may be an artist too, and a novelist is a historian, the preserver, the keeper, the expounder, of human experience.[7]

Obliquely, Conrad warns of the dangers of positing historical 'truth'. His friend Hugh Clifford was similarly aware of literature's historical significance, claiming for his work a significance reaching beyond literary worth: 'Today my tales are to be valued, not only as historical, but as archaeological studies.'[8] But Conrad is aware of something more: fiction inscribes a past unavailable in any other form, a history that, unlike bald documentation, is open to interpretation.

Edward Said famously critiqued Western views of Eastern cultures, and

3   Kettle, *An Introduction to the English Novel* [1951], Vol. 1, London: Hutchinson, 1983, p. 15.
4   Murfin, p. 226. The 'thick description' refers to a term from Clifford Geertz.
5   Greenblatt, *Renaissance of Self-Fashioning: From More to Shakespeare*, Chicago: Chicago UP, 1980, p. 5.
6   P. Hamilton, *Historicism*, London: Routledge, 2003, p. 3.
7   Conrad, 'Henry James: An Appreciation' [1905] in *Notes on Life and Letters*, London: Dent, 1949, pp. 16–17.
8   Clifford, *In Court and Kampung* [1897], Singapore: Graham Brash, 1989, Preface, p. 219.

implicated Conrad in the imperial project: 'His historicist vision overrides the other histories contained in the narrative sequence; its dynamic sanctions Africa, Kurtz, and Marlow – despite their radical eccentricity – as objects of a superior Western (but admittedly problematic) *constitutive* understanding.'[9] Peter Firchow, however, examines Kurtz through historical data, establishing new interpretations of Conrad's Congo. Firchow's data deepens our understanding of what Conrad may (and may not) have known when writing *Heart of Darkness*.[10] Similarly, Martin Bock widens the parameters of investigation by relating Conrad's work to psychological illness: a narrative of Conrad's medical crises shows how illness helped to shape his fictions.[11] Such critics offer new, often contradictory, perspectives on the novel; in each case the challenges to received criticism prove there is much still to be said.

Heart of Darkness begins and ends in London, focusing on the heart of the Congo *and* that of the British Empire. Acknowledging London as a legitimate site of analysis allows a probing of late nineteenth-century metropolitan anxiety, and how it is inscribed in the novel. Geographically, culturally and ideologically, we can range between the Congo and the metropolis and explore how the cultural perspective of *fin de siècle* London impacts on a novel whose narrative focus is Africa. In line with recent historicist approaches, this discussion examines some of the concerns dominating the late nineteenth-century British and European cultural landscape, and how these issues are inscribed in *Heart of Darkness*.

Humanity, hysteria and cultural prejudice

A perceived degeneration in the individual, and in the fabric of British society, added to a sense of instability and doubt that characterized the *fin de siècle*, contributing a defining theme to the emergent modernist imagination. Max Nordau's study of European thought and culture, *Degeneration* (English translation 1895), expressed the mood: 'Things as they are totter and plunge, and they are suffered to reel and fall, because man is weary, and there is no faith that is worth an effort to uphold them.'[12] Apocalyptically, Nordau speaks of the 'Dusk of Nations', mourning a passing age, lamenting the advent of one threatened by degeneracy. For Nordau, and Lombroso, to whom *Degeneration* was dedicated, degeneracy was manifest in characteristics that, in a pseudo-Darwinian sense, heralded the decline of a species: 'under any kind of noxious influences an organism becomes debilitated' and then the 'healthy, normal type of the species' passes on to new generations the 'morbid deviations from the normal form'.[13] Thus, deviancy threatens the persistence of the whole species. The mood of *Heart of Darkness*, and Marlow's pugnacious, sourly ironic narrative, registers a recognition of, and scepticism about, these extreme views. Yet, in this same narrative, we can detect concerns that caused such anxiety in the *fin de siècle*.

---

9 Said, *Culture and Imperialism*, p. 199.
10 P. E. Firchow, *Envisioning Africa Racism and Imperialism in Conrad's Heart of Darkness*, Lexington: Kentucky UP, 2000.
11 Bock, *Conrad and Psychological Medicine*, Lubbock: Texas Tech UP, 2002.
12 In *The Fin de Siècle: A Reader in Cultural History C. 1880–1900*, ed. S. Ledger and R. Luckhurst, Oxford: Oxford UP, 2000, p. 13.
13 Ledger and Luckhurst, *The Fin de Siècle*, p. 15.

Marlow calls Kurtz an 'initiated wraith':[14]

> And the lofty frontal bone of Mr Kurtz! They say the hair goes on
> growing sometimes, but this – ah – specimen, was impressively bald.
> The wilderness has patted him on the head, and, behold, it was like a
> ball – an ivory ball; it had caressed him, and – lo! – he had withered; it
> had taken him, loved him, embraced him, got into his veins, consumed
> his flesh, and sealed his soul to its own by the inconceivable ceremonies
> of some devilish initiation.
>
> (Ch. II, p. 122)

Kurtz is Nordau's 'debilitated' organism, a deviant. Marlow, however, explores
the moral dimensions of Kurtz's fall in altogether more complex forms than
Nordau's hysteria allowed, exhorting us to imagine ourselves cut off from civilization, from the constraints of a policed society: 'These little things make all
the difference. When they are gone you must fall back upon your own innate
strength, upon your own capacity for faithfulness' (Ch. II, p. 123). Kurtz presents
the possibility that even the most civilized individual may not be strong enough to
withstand the urge to barbarity without the moral crutches of civilization.

In July 1885 W. T. Stead exposed, in his 'Maiden Tribute of Modern Babylon',
the wealthy men who were visiting the slums of London's East End to procure
children for sex: mothers were selling their daughters for as little as £5.[15] Public
outrage ensued. Henley sent Stead's articles to Robert Louis Stevenson, who was in
the process of writing *Jekyll and Hyde* (1886).[16] Jekyll's immorality subsequently
echoed Stead's exposé; and Stead's articles may have influenced Stevenson's
imagination. Further, the 1889 'Cleveland Street affair', where telegraph boys
were prostituted for aristocrats at a gay London brothel, heightened public anxiety. Lord Arthur Somerset's involvement, and rumours implicating Prince Albert
Victor, fuelled a growing sense that the British male could be as degenerate as
the 'savage native'. Confidence in the 'gentleman' was severely shaken. A decade
later, Jekyll/Hyde's fictional depravity and the actual horrors perpetrated in
London, are amplified in Kurtz, an imperial adventurer-gone-wrong, who, like
the hypocrite Jekyll, proves that the most upright citizen is prone to the basest of
actions.

Marlow takes Kurtz for a journalist or painter, but 'even the cousin . . . could
not tell [Marlow] what he had been – exactly' (Ch. III, p. 151). Kurtz's elusive identity allies him with Jekyll, a creature of conflicting impulses and dual identities,
the good citizen 'gone bad'. Conrad, like Stevenson, was conscious of a multi-
faceted human identity, of the fact that in one breast could beat a heart of the
purest intentions, yet with the urge to perform the blackest of deeds. Kurtz's high
principles – ('By the simple exercise of our will we can exert a power for good
practically unbounded') – contrast awfully with his postscript: 'Exterminate all

---

14 D.C.R.A. Goonetilleke (ed.), *Heart of Darkness, Joseph Conrad*, Peterborough, Ontario, Canada &
    New York: Broadview Press, 2003 edn, p. 124. Unless otherwise stated, all subsequent quotations
    from this novel are drawn from the same edition.
15 See the *Pall Mall Gazette*, nos. 6336, 6337 and 6338 on 6, 7, and 8 July 1885.
16 See L. Dryden, *The Modern Gothic and Literary Doubles: Stevenson, Wilde and Wells*, Basingstoke:
    Palgrave Macmillan, 2003, pp. 76–109, for more discussion.

the brutes!' (Ch. II, pp. 124, 125) Jekyll's realization that 'man is not truly one, but truly two', that it 'was the curse of mankind that these incongruous faggots were thus bound together', is Kurtz's dilemma.[17] Like Stead's sexual predators, Kurtz is a civilized monster. The Congo wilderness awakened in him 'forgotten and brutal instincts', and the 'memory of gratified and monstrous passions' (Ch. III, p. 144). Kurtz reminds us of our repressed savage instincts, or as Wilde's Dorian Gray, puts it, of the fact that ' "Each of us has Heaven and Hell in him" '.[18]

Plumbing the depths of Kurtz's moral soul, Marlow bitterly acknowledges that this eloquent gentleman scholar was not 'exactly worth the life we lost in getting to him' (Ch. II, p. 125). Marlow's agonizing over Kurtz's depravity is symptomatic of a society no longer able to assume superiority over the colonized subject, as proven by recent scandals, including the Ripper murders. Kurtz's 'unspeakable rites' were, in the ideology of empire, evidence of the innate 'native savage'. Marlow's incredulity at Kurtz's barbarity expresses a European's distress at recognizing his own potential: if men like Kurtz can succumb to savagery, what does that tell us about ourselves, about humanity as a whole?

Late-nineteenth century anxiety about degeneration, the 'other', and the metropolis, are evident in Nordau's *Degeneration*, Le Bon's *The Crowd* (English translation, 1896), and Booth's *Darkest England* (1890). Kurtz, too, is a degenerate: 'That which nearly all degenerates lack is the sense of morality and of right and wrong. For them there exists no law, no decency, no modesty.'[19] Nordau harnessed arguments about degeneracy as a warning to 'civilized' humanity; but others were more circumspect. Recognizing that the European harboured the same impulses as the African, Rider Haggard's Allan Quatermain mocks his 'superior' readers:

> And yet, my dear young lady, what are those pretty things around your own neck? – they have a strong family resemblance, especially when you wear that *very* low dress, to the savage woman's beads. Your habit of turning round and round to the sound of horns and tom-toms, your fondness for pigments and powders, the way in which you love to subjugate yourself to the rich warrior who has captured you in marriage, and the quickness with which your taste in feathered headdresses varies, – all these things suggest touches of kinship; and remember that in the fundamental principles of your nature you are quite identical.[20]

Conrad is less dogmatic, yet, through Marlow, he challenges his reader's complacency about Africans: they were not 'inhuman', and what 'thrilled you was just the thought of their humanity – like yours – the thought of your remote kinship with this wild and passionate uproar' (Ch. II, p. 107). For Haggard and Conrad 'kinship' is fundamental, and the trappings of civilization are no proof against

17 R. L. Stevenson, *Strange Case of Dr Jekyll and Mr Hyde* [1886], in *The Strange Case of Dr Jekyll and Mr Hyde & The Merry Men and Other tales and Fables*, London: Wordsworth Classics, 1999, pp. 42–3.
18 O. Wilde, *The Picture of Dorian Gray* [1891], D. L. Lawler (ed.), London: W. W. Norton, 1988, p. 122.
19 Ledger and Luckhurst, *The Fin de Siècle*, p. 16.
20 H. Rider Haggard, *Allan Quatermain* [1887], London: Longmans, Green, 1904, pp. 4–5.

barbarity. Like Quatermain, Marlow confronts his listeners' assumptions: 'Principles won't do. Acquisitions, clothes, pretty rags – rags that would fly off at the first good shake. No.' Finally, Marlow acknowledges his inner savage in admitting his temptation to 'go ashore for a howl and a dance' (Ch. II, p. 108). He challenges his listeners to deny their kinship:

> Yes, it was ugly enough; but if you were man enough you would admit to yourself that there was in you just the faintest trace of a response to the terrible frankness of that noise, a dim suspicion of there being a meaning in it which you – you so remote from the night of first ages – could comprehend.
>
> (Ch. II, pp. 107–8)

In the middle of *fin de siècle* London, Marlow forces his listeners, and Conrad forces his readers, to confront the fact that Western humanity has the same impulses as the so-called 'savage'.

London is established as a place of darkness in the opening paragraphs where the 'air was dark above Gravesend', with a 'mournful gloom, brooding motionless over the biggest, and the greatest, town on earth' (Ch. I, p. 67). Cedric Watts observes that 'London itself is one ominous heart of darkness'.[21] Barbarism was evident on the doorstep of every London citizen. That mothers would sell their children suggested extreme measures in the face of poverty: worse still, such deprivation was being exploited by the wealthy. The East End was a foul smelling, overcrowded slum abounding in prostitution, garrotting, drunkenness and general moral depravity. Conditions were savage, and necessarily fostered savage instincts to survive. Thus, campaigners like William Booth, Henry Mayhew, Charles Booth and Andrew Mearns attempted to awaken the bourgeoisie to these appalling conditions. When Marlow says, 'And this also . . . has been one of the dark places of the earth' (Ch. I, p. 69), he binds London with Africa. Conrad's contemporaries were finding evidence in the East End rookeries that not much had changed since Roman times. The 'mysterious life of the wilderness that stirs in the forest, in the jungles, in the hearts of wild men' (Ch. I, p. 71) was amply evidenced in London's slums. Such behaviour could be understood when confined to the East End. Kurtz, however, is a cultured man who should be a shining exemplar, yet he shatters any illusion that education and breeding elevate the individual above the savage mob: faced with similar conditions, the over-refined sensibilities of Kurtz crumble, and he becomes a paradoxically, perplexing civilized savage.

Other Europeans in *Heart of Darkness* compound the issue. Le Bon had accused the metropolitan crowd of mindless mob behaviour; Marlow's 'pilgrims' export that mentality to the Congo. Attacked from the shore, they 'opened with their Winchesters, and were simply squirting lead into that bush' (Ch. II, p. 119). Like Le Bon's creatures, they act by instinct: 'Making part of a crowd, [the individual] is conscious of the power given him by number, and it is sufficient to suggest to him ideas of murder or pillage for him to yield immediately to

21 C. T. Watts, 'The Myth of the Monstrous Town', in *Conrad's Cities: Essays for Hans van Marle*, ed. G. M. Moore, Amsterdam: Rodopi, 1992, p. 24.

temptation.'[22] The 'bloodthirsty little gingery beggar' who felt that they had 'made a glorious slaughter of them in the bush' is motivated by the instinctual response of Le Bon's crowd (Ch. II, p. 126). Retreating from Kurtz's station, primitive instincts prevail: the 'imbecile crowd' on the deck 'started their little fun, and [Marlow] could see nothing more for smoke' (Ch. II, p. 146). This mob subsumes its humanity into a collective bloodlust.

European humanity is an unresolved issue: Africans are figured in animal imagery; but the white men are constituted of inanimate fabric. The brickmaker is a 'papier-mâché Mephistopheles', who when poked would reveal a 'little loose dirt', and whose eyes 'glittered like mica discs' (Ch. I, pp. 96, 94). The Chief Accountant is known only through his clothes, and Kurtz is a dead man walking, seemingly composed of fossil ivory. Kurtz problematizes notions of superior European ethics: he is more barbarous than the African. Marlow understands him only too well: the wilderness 'had whispered to him things about himself which he did not know, things of which he had no conception till he took counsel with this great solitude – and the whisper had proved irresistibly fascinating. It echoed loudly within him because he was hollow at the core' (Ch. III, p. 134). Even Marlow, becomes simply 'a voice', echoing Kurtz, who is 'indistinct like a vapour exhaled by the earth', and 'little more than a voice' (Ch. I, p. 97; Ch. III, p. 143; Ch. II, p. 122). Marlow's disgust for Kurtz, alloyed with grudging admiration, betrays a repressed suspicion that his temptation to join the 'wild and passionate uproar' signifies his dualistic humanity, bringing Marlow closer to Kurtz than he cares to admit (Ch. II, p. 107). In the repressed language, the unspeakable, of *Heart of Darkness* lies the terrible possibility that we are all potentially capable of Kurtz's depravity.

Kurtz's crimes, like the Ripper murders, are gruesomely signalled: the shrunken heads on poles are a terrible testimony. Yet like the Ripper, Kurtz is never fully known. The 1888 Ripper murders sent shock waves through London's consciousness, generating appeals for more street lighting; and this was allied to the threat posed to the Empire by the degenerate East End. As the *Star* put it: 'Unless these and other things come, Whitechapel will smash the Empire, and the best thing that can happen to us is for some purified Republic of the West to step in and look after the fragments.'[23] Such rhetoric links the 'health' of the Empire to the moral 'health' of Britain. Conrad exposes the rotten Belgian regime in the Congo; and Kurtz, Belgium's favoured son, and representative of European imperialism and civilization, is 'hollow at the core'. By 1898 the worst fears of the population a decade earlier are fictionally borne out in Kurtz's bloody career.

The Ripper was variously thought to be a Malay, a Jew, and a deranged doctor. Anxiety reached out in two directions: the murders were perpetrated either by an underdeveloped, barbarian, the primitive Malay, or by an appallingly over-developed, over-civilised member of polite society, the deranged doctor, reminding us that Kurtz is the educated painter/journalist and the barbarian crawling through the jungle to return to his 'satanic rites'. Stead suggested a 'Jekyll and Hyde' parallel for the Ripper, and many prominent citizens were suspected:

---

22 G. Le Bon, *The Crowd: A Study of the Popular Mind* [English translation 1896], Atlanta, Georgia: The Cherokee Publishing Company, 1982, p. 19.
23 L. P. Curtis, *Jack the Ripper and the London Press*, London: Yale UP, 2001, p. 263.

William Gladstone; Walter Sickert; Richard Mansfield, even Thomas Barnardo. Ten years before *Heart of Darkness* British citizens faced the possibility that too much repression of the 'savage' self may cause dangerous eruptions of the barbarian – a fact all too clearly signalled in Stevenson's hypocrite Jekyll. Kurtz had some very bloodcurdling antecedents.

An influx of European Jews caused many to view the East End as 'populated by people of darker skin and/or swarthier complexion, and therefore primitive qualities'.[24] Many blamed foreigners: 'Convinced that no true Englishman could commit such savage crimes . . . ethnocentric readers were quick to construct a Jewish "monster" or a culprit who belonged to some other "inferior race".'[25] These readers revealed their cultural prejudices, and a subconscious suspicion that 'civilization' was a sham. Conrad exposes these prejudices and fears through Marlow's complex response to Africans, and through Kurtz's 'satanic rites'. For George Bernard Shaw the Ripper murders 'were a function of class rather than gender, because they arose out of the brutal exploitation of workers by mercenary capitalists'.[26] The murders awakened the British consciousness to how the rich benefited from the labours of the poor. The *Star* complained:

> The West owes to the East something more than platitudinous gush and sentimental and spasmodic almsgiving . . . The brutalization of nine tenths of our population is too heavy a price to pay for the culture and refinement of the other tenth.[27]

These are arguments familiar to critics of imperialism: handing a biscuit to a dying African, Marlow enacts the same empty gestures that the *Star* derides. Metropolitan anxiety about the poor is echoed in Marlow's recognition of the inhumanity of the 'work' in Africa: 'The work was going on. The work! And this was the place where some of the helpers had withdrawn to die' (Ch. I, p. 84). No one stated the parallel more starkly than William Booth:

> As there is a darkest Africa is there not also a darkest England? Civilisation, which can breed its own barbarisms, does it not also breed its own pygmies? May we not find a parallel at our own doors, and discover within a stone's throw of our cathedrals and palaces similar horrors to those which Stanley has found existing in the great Equatorial forest?[28]

He is referring to the East End of London.

Ranging from Africa to Europe, Marlow's narrative emphasises the anxiety that Europeans may, after all, be no better than the Africans they seek to conquer. The stations that Kurtz avers should be like beacons 'on the road towards better things' are represented by the chaotic Central Station on 'a backwater

---

24 Curtis, *Jack the Ripper*, p. 41.
25 Curtis, *Jack the Ripper*, p. 41.
26 Curtis, *Jack the Ripper*, pp. 262–3.
27 Curtis, *Jack the Ripper*, pp. 263–4.
28 W. Booth, *In Darkest England and the Way Out*, London: International Headquarters of the Salvation Army, 1890, p. 11.

surrounded by scrub and forest, with a pretty border of smelly mud on one side, and on the three others enclosed by a crazy fence of rushes'. The 'flabby devil' that was 'running that show' comes from the 'sepulchral' city, Brussels (Ch. II, p. 103; Ch. I, p. 89). The chaos and inefficiency speaks of European cultural malaise springing from a neglected ghost-like metropolis. The white workers who 'with long staves in their hands appeared languidly from amongst the buildings, strolling up to take a look at [him], and then retir[ing] out of sight somewhere' (Ch. I, p. 89), are barely distinguishable from the Africans they have enslaved.

In the heart of the Congo, Belgian, and thereby, European, superiority is interrogated and found to be a sham. The events of the previous decade helped generate the atmosphere of anger, disillusionment, and despair that leaves Marlow unable, or unwilling to describe the actualities of Kurtz's savage rule. The cumulative effect of domestic anxiety about the possibility of progression beyond primitive savage instincts is inscribed in Conrad's hollow man, Kurtz. Marlow travels to the yellow heart of an Africa that is 'Dead in the centre' (Ch. I, p. 76). The pun deliberately betrays his disgust.

Conclusion

When Marlow avers that the 'mind of man is capable of anything – because everything is in it, all the past as well as all the future' (Ch. II, p. 108), he is, like T. S. Eliot, aware that our cumulative history defines us. In *Four Quartets* (1944) Eliot states: 'Time present and time past / Are both perhaps present in time future, / And time future contained in time past.'[29] Like Marlow, Eliot emphasizes the centrality of history in human understanding and experience, how the past and present shape the future, how the present is understood through the past. Stating that the mind is capable of anything, Marlow implies Kurtz's barbarism: a savage past is part of the sum of human history, and therefore always already available to subsume the civilized. The inescapability of this savage inheritance, of this barbarous collective memory, provides a clue to the perplexities concerning human nature in *Heart of Darkness*. It sends a terrible challenge to *fin de siècle* Europe to confront its confidence in its own civilized nature.

When Stephen Dedalus declares in *Ulysses* (1922), 'History . . . is a nightmare from which I am trying to awake', he defines a dilemma of memory.[30] Marlow's Congo journey haunts him too; recounting it betrays his own obsession with the memory. Despite the pain of memory for Marlow, and probably for Conrad, *Heart of Darkness* inscribes numerous human histories that require revisiting to reinterpret the text through the lens of the present time, and through the recovered history of the past. As Conrad said in his article on James, 'Fiction is history, human history, or it is nothing.' For Stephen Dedalus, history is the subconscious horror he is trying to avoid; for cultural and literary historians, history is the consciousness that we are always in the process of recovering. For Conrad, history provides the evidence of our own terrible potential.

29 T. S. Eliot, *Four Quartets* [1944], London: Faber, 1972, p. 13.
30 J. Joyce, *Ulysses* [1922], Oxford: Oxford UP, 1993, p. 34.

Ruth Nadelhaft, 'A Feminist Perspective on *Heart of Darkness*' (2007)

Ruth Nadelhaft is the author of the first book-length study of Conrad's work from a feminist perspective, *Joseph Conrad* (1991). Her new study simultaneously illuminates the aim and scope of the feminist project and the role of women in the novella.

Though feminist literary criticism has a long and complex history, the works of Joseph Conrad have not been the focus of much analysis from a feminist perspective. At least two separate but related reasons seem to account for the lack. First, from its earliest publication, Conrad's work has seemed to be the province of men, especially including male editors and critics (as well as close and encouraging male friends who themselves were also writers and critics). And secondly, feminist literary criticism has been through a series of changes, developments and methodologies, some of which have been unfriendly to male writers in general and Joseph Conrad in particular.

In her book *Around 1981: Academic Feminist Literary Theory*, Jane Gallop summarizes the development of feminist literary criticism as a criticism which emerged 'in the second half of the 1970s informed by an attempt to 'rethink the conjunction of "women" and "literature" '.[1] There have always been women, academic and otherwise, reading and attempting to think and write critically about literature. But the literary canon, in which Conrad's work has for long occupied a significant place, has until recently been overwhelmingly male. Part of the initial energy and thrust of feminist readings and criticism focused on opening up and adding to the recognized canon by identifying and valorizing the work of women writers, from Hildegarde of Bingen to Virginia Woolf and beyond. In 1983, for example, summarizing this development, the critic Lillian Robinson wrote that 'the very definition of feminist criticism has come increasingly to mean scholarship and criticism devoted to women writers'.[2] Most feminist writers and

---

1   Jane Gallop, *Around 1981: Academic Feminist Literary Theory*, London: Routledge, 1992, p. 21.
2   Gallop, *Around 1981*, p. 24.

critics, indeed most women readers, encounter literature initially through exposure to the accepted great writers of the western canon, a list which necessarily includes authors such as Chaucer, Shakespeare, Pope, Dickens and, of course, Conrad.

One major task for women readers, and more explicitly for feminist readers who are usually but not always women, is to distinguish the relation between women's experience in and with literature from that of men to literature. And, more deeply, it is part of the task of feminist readers to consider the criteria by which literature itself may be defined. Attacking and broadening the definition of canonical literature was (and remains) a great task for feminist criticism.

Another part of the work of feminist reading is to claim, in some cases to reclaim, accepted male writers for women readers and critics. The discovery and acclamation of neglected or undervalued women writers continues and has itself generated new avenues of critical analysis. But the reclaiming of canonically significant male writers by generations of feminist writers has resulted in a deeper appreciation of the achievements of writers such as James Joyce, Nathaniel Hawthorne, John Milton and, of course, Shakespeare himself.

Women scholars have considered the work of Joseph Conrad for many decades, though by far the majority of Conrad's important critics have been men. The major biographies by Baines and Guerard, and the critical biographies by Karl and Watt have been written by men. Ian Watt's study of *Conrad in the Nineteenth Century* was published in 1979 and was intended to be followed by a second, equally definitive volume which would bring together the life and the works to the end of Conrad's life. Some important studies of Conrad have been written by women, most notably M.C. Bradbrook, Eloise Knapp Hay and Claire Rosenfield.[3] While there have been women scholars devoted to considering Conrad's work, their approaches have not usually been identifiable as feminist approaches. That is, they have been primarily interested in the same aspects of Conrad's work as traditional male scholars, especially the political implications and the development of literary style. In fact, the prevailing psychological investigation, by Bernard C. Meyer, was especially discouraging to feminist reading and analysis. Meyer, a psychoanalyst, made use of biographical information which was incomplete at the time of his study, and his emphasis on the loss of Conrad's mother while the family was in political exile, along with Meyer's own inability to distinguish between the novelist and his characters, resulted in consistent interpretation of women characters as threatening, monstrous and frightening. In an earlier study of Conrad from a feminist perspective, I quoted Meyer's summary statement linking Conrad to what Meyer took to be his early experience:

> Conrad's heroes are motherless wanderers, postponing through momentary bursts of action their long-awaited return to a mother, whose untimely death has sown the seeds of longing and remorse, and whose voice, whispered from beyond the grave, utters her insistent claim upon her son's return.[4]

---

3   Ruth L. Nadelhaft, *Joseph Conrad*, Atlantic Highlands, NJ: Humanities Press International, Inc., 1991, p. 2.
4   Nadelhaft, *Conrad*, p. 3.

Especially in the early novels, in which women regularly testify to the abuses and failures of colonialism, Meyer describes at length the ferocious and sexually devouring natures of major women characters. In the works based upon Conrad's East India explorations, especially, when Conrad as author was able to include articulate women characters who provide insight and critical perspectives on colonialism and patriarchy, Meyer recoils from the characters and attributes his own distaste to the author.

Since some of the major critics of Conrad framed their analyses, more biographical material has been made available, largely through the invaluable translations of letters of the Conrad family. From those letters and other documents and recollections, readers and critics can now construct a richer and far less reductive picture of Conrad's personal history and its possible relation to the development of character, both male and female, in his works from the earliest books. These works include, of course, *Heart of Darkness*, whose autobiographical elements made it particularly susceptible to the kind of incomplete and misleading psychological analysis fostered by Meyer's work.

Familial background, which figures in the early section of *Heart of Darkness*, includes Conrad's continued involvement with members of his Polish family. Through the materials made available in Zdzislaw Najder's two books published in 1983, *Joseph Conrad: A Chronicle* and *Conrad Under Familial Eyes*, it is now possible – indeed necessary – to reconsider the image of women which was fundamental to Conrad in his early life and which continues to illuminate his complex use of female figures in all his work, including, of course, *Heart of Darkness*. If in *Heart of Darkness* it is Marlow's contention that women know nothing of politics, or the 'real world', for that matter, that disjunction between women and the world belongs to Marlow, the created character, rather than to Conrad, the man and author. The most important women in the familial life in which Joseph Conrad came to maturity were his mother and his aunt. Conrad's aunt was his great support throughout his life and was far more complex than Marlow's aunt, for whom she served as a point of departure to be discussed later in this essay. Letters from Conrad's mother reveal her to have been far different from the austere, removed and simply tragic figure described by earlier Conrad biographers and scholars. Instead, she was a vibrant and courageous colleague and participant in her husband's generous and patriotic actions, displaying determination and deliberate optimism in her letters during his desperate time in prison before the exile during which she died. Images of such warm, devoted and politically committed women fill Conrad's later works: Natalie Haldin in *Under Western Eyes*, for one major example, Emilia Gould in *Nostromo*, for another. In the early works, the fierce and determined figure of Aissa, a woman generally described by critics in unflattering and dismissive terms, provides an opportunity for the author to criticize the workings of imperialism directly but without intellectual posturing or discursive passages of analysis. Aissa's arguments are not simply passionate rants but are developed in consultation with the pragmatic (and disregarded) elite of her tribal culture.

The use of women figures as commentators upon the major action, as revealing windows into the workings of political, cultural and economic colonialism, was well established in Conrad's work before he conceived of *Heart of Darkness*. Attentive readers of the two early novels, *Almayer's Folly* and *Outcast of the*

Islands, recognize the complex uses of native and half-caste women who capture the attention of self-important European men. Neither of the protagonists of the two early novels, Almayer or Willems, offers much in the way of self-knowledge or introspective capacity. They prefigure the self-absorption and moral hollowness of Kurtz who is the vacant heart of *Heart of Darkness*.

The two early novels ordinarily do not receive much attention in conjunction with the significant works which follow them: 'In the earliest novels, women characters served to criticize the dominant mode of political and moral thought; in their words and by their lives they offered alternative visions. In the novels and tales which follow, Conrad turns to a new narrative method which, in effect, compensates for the absence of fully developed and integrated female characters: the unnamed male narrator of *The Nigger of the 'Narcissus'* and Charlie Marlow of *Heart of Darkness* and *Lord Jim*.'[5] It is uncommon to see the arrival of Conrad's most famous narrative character as a development from or a replacement for the active commentary of female characters. But the scarcity of detail provided for Marlow, his enigmatic presence and distance from the story he both tells and embodies, allowed Conrad to develop the 'outsider' perspective provided earlier by women characters who might be only too easily dismissed or disregarded both within the text and by their reader-critics. Some feminist critics acknowledge the presence of women as observers and commentators in the text of *Heart of Darkness* while continuing to see the work as primarily excluding women readers and presenting a number of unappealing and difficult choices to such readers. Women, according to at least one feminist critic, cannot experience the 'horror' at the center of the work directly since it is withheld from the Intended. And the Intended is only one of the women declared categorically by Marlow to be entirely out of touch with the real, presumably, significant world only too available to Marlow.[6] Nina Pelikan Straus concluded that while women readers may find some way to appreciate the text (she offers a number of reading strategies), in the end the best that women readers can do is to remain detached from *Heart of Darkness* and refuse to grant the status of high art to the work. Perhaps it is worth making a distinction between feminist readers of *Heart of Darkness* who consider it in isolation from the rest of Conrad's body of work and those few feminist readers who come to *Heart of Darkness* in the dual context of Conrad's surrounding life and work and the world in which *Heart of Darkness* remains a deeply rewarding text for human readers.

Heart of Darkness is not without significant women characters, though they do not serve as protagonists. Enigmatic figures of women appear early in the text (the two silent but arresting women who guard the entrance to the Company office: one fat, one slim, seeming to ignore Marlow entirely, yet preternaturally aware of him as he soon discovers). 'The slim one got up and walked straight at me – still knitting with downcast eyes – and only just as I began to think of getting out of her way, as you would for a somnambulist, stood still and looked up.'[7]

5   Nadelhaft, *Conrad*, p. 37.
6   Pelikan Straus, 'The Exclusion of the Intended . . .', p. 125.
7   D.C.R.A Goonetilleke (ed.), *Heart of Darkness, Joseph Conrad*, Peterborough, Ontario, Canada: Broadview Press, 2003 edn, p. 75. Unless otherwise stated, all subsequent quotations from this novel are drawn from the same edition.

Unsurprisingly, the women have taken note of Marlow and 'the slim one' leads him precisely to the proper waiting room. Marlow, like many readers of Conrad, notes the presence of these women but takes for granted their knowledge about him. His lack of interest in the inscrutable women who sit at the entrance to his new career provides information to all readers: about Marlow and about the presence of women at thresholds. Marlow's generalizations about the role of women, his insistence that women are 'out of it', receives abundant contradiction early in the development of *Heart of Darkness*. These enigmatic women are in the work world. 'People were arriving, and the younger one was walking back and forth introducing them' (Ch. I, p. 76). As Marlow continues to remember the experience he says a bit more about the older woman as well.

> The old one sat on her chair. Her flat cloth slippers were propped up on a foot-warmer, and a cat reposed in her lap. She wore a starched white affair on her head, had a wart on one cheek, and silver-rimmed spectacles hung on the tip of her nose. She glanced at me above the glasses. The swift and indifferent placidity of that look troubled me.
>
> (Ch. I, p. 76)

However dismissive Marlow's tone may be, he reports that he was troubled by the air of knowledge the older woman projected. At least in the ante-room for those on the verge of committing themselves to the rapacious world of African plunder, the silent presence of two women, office functionaries, testifies to women's involvement in the bureaucratic nature of imperialism, its ability to turn individuals into silent participants. If one understands part of the import of feminist analysis to be its enquiry into the ways that existing social and cultural organization define the roles of men and women, an order which might perhaps be changed by exposure and analysis of the confining and sometimes destructive nature of those roles, then this brief passage emerges as critical in a feminist reading of *Heart of Darkness*. For these functionaries who keep the bodies moving along the path towards the Congo, and all the other centres of commercial exploitation, have themselves become part of the system that allows no one, certainly no woman, to be 'out of it'. One of the key insights of twentieth-century feminism, one which underpins even the most recondite academic analysis, is that the personal is the political. That primary assumption is often implicit in Conrad's works, and it is certainly exemplified in the development of *Heart of Darkness* in which every female figure demonstrates the political thrust of the work in the smallest of personal details. So the mysterious women in the ante-room function on several levels at once, obscure and portentous to Marlow, indicative of a mythical realm to some critics, and representative of vast numbers of under-class women in nineteenth-century Europe who made a meagre living serving the vast enterprises of far-flung empires.

Marlow's aunt, modelled at least to some extent upon Conrad's beloved aunt Marguerite Poradowska, is similarly vital to the underlying meaning of the story and recognizable as both an individual and a type in her appearance. Marlow's tone, as he describes his aunt and her machinations on his behalf, is little short of sardonic. It is in this context that he remarks women's lack of genuine contact with reality. 'It's queer how out of touch with truth women are.' His summing up comes just after his account of his 'long quiet chat' beside the fireplace in his aunt's charming (and charmingly typical) drawing room. During that chat, Marlow recounts that

> it became quite plain to me I had been represented to the wife of the high dignitary, and goodness knows to how many more people besides, as an exceptional and gifted creature – a piece of good fortune for the Company – a man you don't get hold of every day.... Something like an emissary of light, something like a lower sort of apostle.
>
> (Ch. I, pp. 78–9)

He goes on to note that this kind of talk (or 'rot' as he calls it) had been current in the newspapers and in conversation around that time. So, in fact, his aunt was not out of touch but was rather in the current of imperialistic thought, just as Kurtz, and Kurtz's Intended, and the rest of cultivated European society was. Indeed, the description Marlow gleans of himself that presumably gained for him the commission he was unable to gain by his own efforts, sounds remarkably like the description of Kurtz that was circulating in Africa when Marlow reached the first station on his journey towards his boat and the river. The only rebuttal Marlow offers to his aunt's 'bright' account is the feeble 'hint that the Company was run for profit'. This scene offers any discerning reader, but especially one reading from a feminist perspective, a remarkable parallel to the much-discussed final scene in which Marlow meets – and lies to – Kurtz's Intended. It is in that scene that Marlow reluctantly affirms his sense of closeness to Kurtz who, unlike any woman, has 'been there'. Perhaps to spare the Intended, perhaps to perform some act of fealty towards Kurtz, Marlow consciously lies to the Intended and offers her, as Kurtz's last words, not what he actually gasped but, instead, her name. ' "I knew it",' she exclaims, triumphantly. (Ch. III, p. 157)

Again, Marlow finds himself in a drawing room, furnished in the manner of its kind; though the furnishings are described in some detail, they are not inherently distinguishable from the furnishings of the aunt's drawing room. And the Marlow who mutters and grimaces and fails to speak the truth about Kurtz is the same Marlow who failed to speak the truth about himself to his aunt in her drawing room. Not being Marlow but writing Marlow, Conrad suggests through the prose and the structure of this complex tale that if women are out of it that is because they are *kept* out of it. Marlow's self-justifying sense of allegiance to Kurtz, thanks to the earlier scene with his aunt, emerges sharply as an indictment of Marlow himself, because the earlier scenes with women, without yet even considering the powerful figure of the woman on the banks of the river itself, have already shown readers the equivocation Marlow displays when it comes to speaking truth to women. A woman who reads the newspapers and mingles with those who wield power, like Marlow's aunt, is no different from the overwrought and deluded Intended.

As in the earlier scene with his aunt, Marlow adopts a tone that barely conceals his despair and distaste. Every utterance on his part is double-edged, contributing to the sense of exclusion as the lot of women. The Intended's halting utterances are choked with grief, love and misplaced admiration, while Marlow's mutterings and mumblings pass for shared grief but reflect rather his acute dislike for the scene in which he finds himself. He sees his own memories, not hers, his own experiences, not hers. And in this moment he yokes together the vivid image of 'another . . . [woman], tragic also, and bedecked with powerless charms, stretching bare brown arms over the glitter of the infernal stream, the stream of darkness' (Ch. III, pp. 156–7) to the dimly lit image of the woman before him. Not recognizing the affinity between his aunt and the Intended, an affinity created not only by their shared class and situation but by their lack of access to true depiction of the exploitation which provides their class and circumstances, Marlow seizes instead on a connection entirely of his own construction. While Marlow takes a sort of perverse pride in his solidarity with Kurtz, who has the dubious virtue of having explored the full consequences of kicking away the support of European moral tradition, he never acknowledges his own role in the brutalization of women. If it is true, as some feminist critics of *Heart of Darkness* claim, that women cannot have the same experience as men who enter this text, Marlow's consistent behaviour in the drawing rooms of women challenges male experience of the text as well.

There is, finally, one more significant female figure in *Heart of Darkness* who has inspired her own critical commentary: the native mistress whose image haunts Marlow in the drawing room of the Intended. Feminist critics, along with many others who are serious readers of *Heart of Darkness*, have struggled, and continue to struggle, with the image of the African mistress. Marianna Torgovnick, author of *Gone Primitive: Savage Intellects, Modern Lives* confesses at the beginning of her discussion of Conrad's novel that 'I have read *Heart of Darkness* many times and always been a bit repelled by it.'[8] Torgovnick feels the connection of universal sisterhood with the African mistress, while another cultural critic, Gayatri Spivack, cautions against precisely this assumption of 'a truth of global sisterhood'.[9] This sharp difference in approach between two women critics speaks to the ambiguity and lasting effectiveness of Conrad's choices as a writer, employing characterization and narrative techniques to embody what is essentially a feminist stance in regard to the imperial age. That stance is distinct from what Marlow experiences, what Marlow reports, what Marlow projects. And the distinction between the author and his narrator is never more telling than in the depiction of the African mistress:

> 'For Marlow, the sight is "a wild and gorgeous apparition of a woman . . . She was savage and superb, wild-eyed and magnificent; there was something ominous and stately in her deliberate progress." Like Baudelaire [whose poem, 'Le Cygne' concludes with an image of a nameless black woman] Conrad's narrator attempts to express his vision of female savagery and the core of Africa in one elaborate image. Spivack warns us . . . that we must neither accept the author's reduction of women's experience to the evocative image nor indulge our own fantasy of sisterhood with the source of the image.'[10]

8 Torgovnick, *Gone Primtive*, p. 145.
9 Spivack, 'Imperialism and sexual difference', *Oxford Literary Review*, 1986, Vol. 8, 226.
10 Nadelhaft, *Conrad*, p. 47.

In other words, the contemporary feminist reader must be conscious of the self-constructed boundaries of feminist readership. If feminist analysis provides us with the certain knowledge that there are no universals, that the personal is the political, and that every form of feminism is itself humbled by its awareness of partiality, such analysis makes us aware of our own limitations and the limitations of any interpretation based solely on reader response. For the reader – male or female – cannot penetrate 'any more than Marlow could . . . the reality and the selfhood of that apparition across the river . . . The contemporary reader who now wishes to stand on the other side of the river and look from the perspective of the native woman has a position of some narrow dignity from which to observe.'[11]

The narrative makes clear that none of the males in Marlow's rescue party comprehends the character of the African mistress. The comments of the Russian, 'the man of patches', are perfectly obtuse. ' "If she had offered to come aboard I really think I would have tried to shoot her," ' (III, p. 138) he offers after she turns away and disappears into the thickets beside the river. As he describes the last incident he remembers in which she figures, it is clear that Kurtz disregarded her as well. None of the men claim to understand her; one way of clarifying her impact is to recognize, as Conrad did in all his early works, the cultural and gender gulf at the heart of Western imperialism and colonialism. Her colour, her dress, her gestures, her very being remain inexplicable. Marlow's easy generality about women falters in the face of the African mistress, for she is not 'out of it'; she is, rather, at the very heart of the mystery that defeats Marlow in the end.

At the last, when the woman and members of her tribe shout their protest at Kurtz's departure, Marlow asks Kurtz: ' "Do you understand this" ' making it clear that he, for one, does not. And Kurtz answers enigmatically, ' "Do I not?" ' Their exchange presents us with a clear indication of the limits of European male knowledge. It prefigures, as well, Marlow's own reluctance to see the full consequence of Kurtz's foray into the jungle as the bearer of the best of European traditions. For as Kurtz faces death, and his features are transfigured by his understanding of himself and his deeds, Marlow blows out the candle and leaves the cabin. It is left to the contemptuous manager's boy to witness and report the death of Kurtz. Marlow, sitting at his dinner, knows that he must be perceived as 'brutally callous', but he believes himself to have been touched by destiny in the form of self-knowledge 'that comes too late'.

With such a reading of *Heart of Darkness*, informed by feminist analysis and close attention to the individual women of the text and the developing role that they play in the unfolding of the tale, it seems clear that neither men nor women may comfortably experience this text. To identify with Marlow is to experience his self-deception and limited understanding of his own narrative; yet to deny Marlow's particular narrative is to deny a central tenet of Conrad's impressionist method which inevitably overwhelms the observer who is truly in the moment. The women in the text, placed as they are at the margins, provide glimpses to contemporary readers willing to examine Marlow's version from those margins.

11 Nadelhaft, *Conrad*, p. 47.

It is telling that, according to Edward Garnett, Conrad left out of the finished narrative several incidents which he included in 'a very full synopsis of what he intended to write'. One key incident which does not appear is a scene 'which described the hero lying sick to death in a native hut, tended by an old negress who brought him water from day to day when he had been abandoned by all the Belgians. "She saved my life," Conrad said; "the white men never came near me." '[12] Garnett, recollecting the long conversation with Conrad, regretted the loss of such a key event. 'The effect of the written narrative was no less sombre than the spoken, and the end was more consummate; but I regretted the omission of various scenes . . .' Conrad's decision not to include the touching ministrations of the 'old negress' provides one of the clearest indications of the author's removal of himself from the centre of the narrative and his deliberate creation of Charlie Marlow to serve purposes far more complex than disguised autobiography.

The images of women in *Heart of Darkness* thus serve purposefully *not* to include a redeeming notion of care which might bridge the gulf between the white Europeans (men) and the black Africans (men and women). Rather, Conrad chose through Marlow to examine that gulf and to illustrate Marlow's inability to understand more than he was capable of understanding – which was, in turn, always less than the author who determined Marlow's limits and tested our own as readers.

Those women who were allowed into the narrative serve very specific and compelling purposes. They remind us, by their brief and unsettling presences, how limited Marlow's vision is, how dependent he is upon the presence of women throughout his journey. To some extent, they save the life of the narrative.

---

12 Garnett, 1928, in *G:HD*, p. 168.

J. Hillis Miller, 'Heart of Darkness Revisited' (1990)

> J. Hillis Miller has stated: 'Deconstruction is not a dismantling of the structure of a text, but a demonstration that it has already dismantled itself.'[1] Eschewing the context in which *Heart of Darkness* is set, he unravels a set of binary oppositions between kinds of texts: the apocalypse, the parable and Marlow's stories. Basing his view on a post-structuralist assumption, he argues that *Heart of Darkness* goes against the grain of normal logic and encompasses contradictions. He highlights the figurative nature of its language. After all, it is true that the writer subconsciously deals in related images – but not always consistently. Miller focuses on the indeterminacy of meaning in the novella, which he sees as a characteristic of an ironic text. It is perfectly true that Conrad is a self-conscious, ultra-careful writer, a disciple of Flaubert. But it seems to me possible to argue that, in *Heart of Darkness*, Conrad employs mystification as a strategy; he conducts us to the heart of an intimation as profound and awe-striking as the Greek mysteries which gave knowledge hidden to the uninitiated. Consequently, clarity and coherence may have been the least of his aims. See Critical history, **p. 62**).

From *Throes, Parables, Performatives* (1990)

I begin with three questions: Is it senseless accident, a result of the crude misinterpretation or gross transformation of the mass media that the cinematic version of *Heart of Darkness* is called *Apocalypse Now*, or is there already something apocalyptic about Conrad's novel in itself? What are the distinctive features of an apocalyptic text? How would we know when we had one in hand?

I shall approach an answer to these questions by the somewhat roundabout way of an assertion that if *Heart of Darkness* is perhaps only problematically apocalyptic, there can be no doubt that it is parabolic. The distinctive feature of a

---

1 Miller, 'Stevens' Rock and Criticism as Cure, II', in *The Georgia Review*, 30, 1976, p. 341.

parable, whether sacred or secular, is the use of a realistic story, a story in one way or another based firmly on what Marx calls man's 'real conditions of life, and his relations with his kind',[2] to express another reality or truth not otherwise expressible. When the disciples ask Jesus why he speaks to the multitudes in parables, he answers, 'Therefore speak I to them in parables: because they seeing see not; and hearing they hear not, neither do they understand' (Matthew 13:13). A little later Matthew tells the reader that 'without a parable spake he not unto them: That it might be fulfilled which was spoken by the prophet, saying, I will open my mouth in parables; I will utter things which have been kept secret from the foundation of the world' (13:34 –35). Those things which have been kept secret from the foundation of the world will not be revealed until they have been spoken in parable, that is, in terms which the multitude who lack spiritual seeing and hearing nevertheless see and hear, namely, the everyday details of their lives of fishing, farming and domestic economy.

Conrad's story is a parable, in part, because it is grounded firmly in the details of real experience. Biographers such as Ian Watt, Frederick Karl and Norman Sherry tell us all that is likely to be learned of Conrad's actual experience in the Congo, as well as of the historical originals of Kurtz, the parti-coloured harlequin-garbed Russian, and other characters in the novel. If parables are characteristically grounded in representations of realistic or historical truth, *Heart of Darkness* admirably fulfills this requirement of parable. But it fills another requirement, too. Conrad's novel is parable because, although it is based on what Marx called 'real conditions', its narrator attempts through his tale to reveal some as-yet-unseen reality.

Unlike allegory, which tries to shed light on the past or even on our origins, parable tends to be oriented toward the future, toward last things, toward the mysteries of the kingdom of heaven and how to get there. Parable tends to express what Paul at the end of Romans, in echo of Matthew, calls 'the revelation of the mystery, which was kept secret since the world began, but now is made manifest' (Romans16: 25–26). Parable, as we can now see, has at least one thing in common with apocalypse: it too is an act of unveiling that which has never been seen or known before. Apocalypse *means* unveiling; an apocalypse is a narrative unveiling or revelation. The last book of the Bible is the paradigmatic example of apocalypse in our tradition, though it is by no means the only example. The book of Revelation seeks to unveil a mystery of the future, namely, what will happen at time's ending.

My contention, then, is that *Heart of Darkness* fits, in its own way, the definitions of both parable and apocalypse, and that much illumination is shed on it by interpreting it in the light of the generic classifications. As Marlow says of his experience in the heart of darkness: 'It was sombre enough, too – . . . not very clear either. No, not very clear. And yet it seemed to throw a kind of light.'[3] A

2   Karl Marx, 'Manifesto of the Communist Party', in *The Marx-Engels Reader*, ed. Robert C. Tucker, New York: Norton, 1978 edn, p. 476.

3   *Joseph Conrad: Heart of Darkness* ed. D.C.R.A. Goonetilleke, Peterborough, Ontario, Canada & New York: Broadview Press, 2003 edn, I, p. 72. All subsequent quotations from this novel are drawn from the same edition.

narrative that sheds light, that penetrates darkness, that clarifies and illuminates – this is one definition of that mode of discourse called parabolic or apocalyptic, but it might also serve to define the work of criticism or interpretation. All criticism claims to be enlightenment or *Aufklarung*.

How, though, does a story enlighten or clarify: in what ways may narratives illuminate or unveil? Conrad's narrator distinguishes between two different ways in which a narrative may be related to its meaning:

> The yarns of seamen have a direct simplicity, the whole meaning of which lies within the shell of a cracked nut. But Marlow was not typical (if his propensity to spin yarns be excepted), and to him the meaning of an episode was not inside like a kernel but outside [Ms: outside in the unseen], enveloping the tale which brought it out only as a glow brings out a haze, in the likeness of one of these misty halos that sometimes are made visible by the spectral illumination of moonshine.
>
> (Ch. I, p. 70)

The narrator here employs two figures to describe two kinds of stories: simple tales and parables. Through the two figures, moreover, Conrad attempts to present the different ways in which these two kinds of narration relate to their meanings.

The meanings of the stories of most seamen, says the narrator, are inside the narration like the kernel of a cracked nut. I take it the narrator means the meanings of such stories are easily expressed, detachable from the stories and open to paraphrase in other terms, as when one draws an obvious moral: 'Crime doesn't pay', or 'Honesty is the best policy', or 'The truth will out', or 'Love conquers all'. The figure of the cracked nut suggests that the story itself, its characters and narrative details, are the inedible shell which must be removed and discarded so the meaning of the story may be assimilated. This relation of the story to its meaning is a particular version of the relation of container to thing contained. The substitution of contained for container, in this case meaning for story, is one version of that figure called in classical rhetoric synecdoche, but this is a metonymic rather than a metaphorical synecdoche.[4] The meaning is adjacent to the story, contained within it as nut within shell, but the meaning has no intrinsic similarity or kinship to the story. Its relation to the story that contains it is purely contingent. The one happens to touch the other, as shell surrounds nut, as bottle its liquid contents, or as shrine-case its iconic image.

It is far otherwise with Marlow's stories. Their meaning – like the meaning of a parable – is outside, not in. It envelops the tale rather than being enveloped by it. The relation of container and thing contained is reversed. The meaning now contains the tale. Moreover, perhaps because of that enveloping containment, or perhaps for more obscure reasons, the relation of the tale to its meaning is no longer that of dissimilarity and contingency. The tale is the necessary agency of

---

4 In metaphorical synecdoche, a part of something is used to signify the whole: 'I see a sail' means 'I see a ship'. A metonymic synecdoche is one in which the signifying part is really only something contiguous with the thing signified, not intrinsic to it: 'the bottle' is a metonymic synecdoche for liquor, since glass cannot really be part of liquor in the way a sail is part of a ship.

the bringing into the open or revelation of that particular meaning. It is not so much that the meaning is like the tale. It is not. But the tale is in preordained correspondence to or in resonance with the meaning. The tale magically brings the 'unseen' meaning out and makes it visible.

Conrad has the narrator express this subtle concept of parabolic narration according to the parabolic 'likeness' of a certain atmospheric phenomenon. 'Likeness' is a homonym of the German *Gleichnis*, which is itself a term for parable. The meaning of a parable appears in the 'spectral' likeness of the story that reveals it, or rather, it appears in the likeness of an exterior light surrounding the story, just as the narrator's theory of parable appears not as such but in the 'likeness' of the figure he proposes. Thus, the figure does double duty, both as a figure for the way Marlow's stories express their meaning and as a figure for itself, so to speak; that is, as a figure for its own mode of working. This is according to a mind-twisting torsion of the figure back on itself that is a regular feature of such figures of figuration, parables of parable, or stories about storytelling. The figure both illuminates its own working and at the same time obscures or undermines it, since a figure of a figure is an absurdity, or, as Wallace Stevens puts it, there is no such thing as a metaphor of a metaphor. What was the figurative vehicle of the first metaphor automatically becomes the literal tenor of the second metaphor.[5]

Let us look more closely at the exact term of the metaphor Conrad's narrator proposes. To Marlow, the narrator says, 'the meaning of an episode was not inside like a kernel but outside, enveloping the tale which brought it out only as a glow brings out haze, in the likeness of one of these spectral illuminations of moonshine.' The first simile here ('as a glow') is doubled by a second, similitude of a similitude ('in the likeness of . . .'). The 'haze' is there all around on a dark night, but, like the meaning of one of Marlow's tales, it is invisible, inaudible, intangible in itself, like the darkness, or like that 'something great and invincible' Marlow is aware of in the African wilderness, something 'like evil or truth, waiting patiently for the passing away of this fantastic invasion' (Ch. I, p. 92). The haze, too, is like the climactic name for that truth, the enveloping meaning of the tale: 'the horror', those last words of Kurtz that seem all around in the gathering darkness when Marlow makes his visit to Kurtz's Intended and tells his lie. 'The dusk,' Marlow says, 'was repeating them in a persistent whisper all around us, in a whisper that seemed to swell menacingly like the first whisper of a rising wind. "The horror! The horror!" '(Ch. III, p. 157)

The working of Conrad's figure is much more complex than perhaps it at first appears, both in itself and in the context of the fine grain of the texture of language in *Heart of Darkness* as a whole, as well as in the context of the traditional complex of figures, narrative motifs and concepts to which it somewhat obscurely alludes. The atmospheric phenomenon that Conrad uses as the vehicle of his parabolic metaphor is a perfectly real one, universally experienced. It is as referential and as widely known as the facts of farming Jesus uses in the parable of the

---

5   The 'vehicle' of a figurative expression is the term used to refer to something else; the 'tenor' is the person, thing or concept referred to by the vehicle. In the metaphorical synecdoche used as an example in footnote 4, 'sail' is the vehicle, 'ship' the tenor; in the metonymic synecdoche, 'bottle' is the vehicle, 'liquor' the tenor. If you say you feel blue to mean you feel sad, 'blue' is the vehicle, 'sadness' the tenor.

sower. If you sow your seed on stony ground it will not be likely to sprout. An otherwise invisible mist or haze at night will show up as a halo around the moon. As in the case of Jesus' parable of the sower, Conrad uses his realistic and almost universally known facts as the means of expressing indirectly another truth less visible and less widely known, just as the narrative of *Heart of Darkness* as a whole is based on the facts of history and on the facts of Conrad's life but uses these to express something transhistorical and transpersonal, the evasive and elusive 'truth' underlying both historical and personal experience.

Both Jesus' parable of the sower and Conrad's parable of the moonshine in the mist, curiously enough, have to do with their own efficacy – that is, with the efficacy of parable. Both are posited on their own necessary failure. Jesus' parable of the sower will give more only to those who already have and will take away from those who have not even what they have. If you can understand the parable you do not need it. If you need it you cannot possibly understand it. You are stony ground on which the seed of the word falls unavailing. Your eyes and ears are closed, even though the function of parables is to open the eyes and ears of the multitude to the mysteries of the kingdom of heaven. In the same way, Conrad, in a famous passage in the preface to *The Nigger of the 'Narcissus'*, tells his readers, 'My task which I am trying to achieve is, by the power of the written word, to make you hear, to make you feel – it is, before all, to make you *see*.' No reader of Conrad can doubt that he means to make the reader see not only the vivid facts of the story he tells but the evasive truth behind them, of which they are the obscure revelation, what Conrad calls, a bit beyond the famous phrase from the preface just quoted, 'that glimpse of truth for which you have forgotten to ask'. To see the facts, out there in the sunlight, is also to see the dark truth that lies behind them. All Conrad's work turns on this double paradox: first the paradox of the two senses of seeing, seeing as physical vision and seeing as seeing through, as penetrating to or unveiling the hidden invisible truth, and second the paradox of seeing the darkness in terms of the light. Nor can the careful reader of Conrad doubt that in Conrad's case too, as in the case of the Jesus of the parable of the sower, the goal of tearing the veil of familiarity from the world and making us *see* cannot be accomplished. If we see the darkness already, we do not need *Heart of Darkness*. If we do not see it, reading *Heart of Darkness* or even hearing Marlow tell it will not help us. We shall remain among those who 'seeing see not; and hearing they hear not, neither do they understand'. Marlow makes this clear in an extraordinary passage in *Heart of Darkness*, one of those places in which the reader is returned to the primary scene of narration on board the *Nellie*. Marlow is explaining the first lie he told for Kurtz, his prevarication misleading the bricklayer at the central station into believing that he [Marlow] has great power back home:

> 'I became in an instant as much of a pretence as the rest of the bewitched pilgrims. This simply because I had a notion it somehow would be of help to that Kurtz whom at the time I did not see – you understand. He was just a word for me. I did not see the man in the name any more than you do. Do you see him? Do you see the story? Do you see anything? It seems to me I am trying to tell you a dream – making a vain attempt, because no relation of a dream can convey the dream-sensation, that

commingling of absurdity, surprise, and bewilderment in a tremor of struggling revolt, that notion of being captured by the incredible which is of the very essence of dreams . . .'

He was silent for a while.

'. . . No, it is impossible; it is impossible to convey the life-sensation of any given epoch of one's existence – that which makes its truth, its meaning – its subtle and penetrating essence. It is impossible. We live, as we dream – alone . . .'

He paused again as if reflecting, then added:

'Of course in this you fellows see more than I could then. You see me, whom you know . . .'

It had become so pitch dark that we listeners could hardly see one another. For a long time already he, sitting apart, had been no more to us than a voice. There was not a word from anybody. The others might have been asleep, but I was awake. I listened, I listened on the watch for the sentence, for the word, that would give me the clue to the faint uneasiness inspired by this narrative that seemed to shape itself without human lips in the heavy night-air of the river.

(Ch. I, p. 97)

The denial of the possibility of making the reader see by means of literature is made here through a series of moves, each one ironically going beyond and undermining the one before. When this passage is set against the one about the moonshine, the two together bring out into the open, like a halo in the mist, the way *Heart of Darkness* is posited on the impossibility of achieving its goal of revelation, or, to put this another way, the way it is a revelation of the impossibility of revelation.

In Conrad's parable of the moonshine, the moon shines already with reflected and secondary light. Its light is reflected from the primary light of that sun which is almost never mentioned as such in *Heart of Darkness*. The sun is only present in the glitter of its reflection from this or that object, for example, the surface of that river which, like the white place of the unexplored Congo on the map, fascinates Marlow like a snake. In one passage it is moonlight, already reflected light, which is reflected again from the river: 'The moon had spread over everything a thin layer of silver – over the rank grass, over the mud, upon the wall of matted vegetation standing higher than the wall of a temple, over the great river I could see through a sombre gap glittering, glittering, as it flowed broadly by without a murmur' (Ch. I, p. 96). In the case of the parable of the moonshine too that halo brought out in the mist is twice-reflected light. The story, according to Conrad's analogy, the facts that may be named and seen, is the moonlight, while the halo brought out around the moon by the reflection of the moonlight from the dif-fused, otherwise invisible droplets of the mist, is the meaning of the tale, or rather, the meaning of the tale is the darkness which is made visible by that halo of twice reflected light. But of course the halo does nothing of the sort. It only makes visible more light. What can be seen is only what can be seen. In the end this is always only more light, direct or reflected. The darkness is in principle invisible and remains invisible. All that can be said is that the halo gives the spectator indirect knowledge that the darkness is there. The glow brings out the haze, the story brings out its meaning, by magically generating knowledge that something is there, the haze in one case, the meaning of the story, inarticulate and impossible to be articulated, in any direct way at least, in the other. The expression of the meaning of the story is never the plain statement of that meaning but is always no more than a parabolic 'likeness' of the meaning, as the haze is brought out 'in the likeness of one of those misty halos that sometimes are made visible by the spectral illumination of moonshine'.

In the passage in which Marlow makes explicit his sense of the impossibility of his enterprise, he says to his auditors on the *Nellie* first that he did not see Kurtz in his name any more than they do. The auditors of any story are forced to see everything of the story 'in its name', since a story is made of nothing but names and their adjacent words. There is nothing to see literally in any story except the words on the page, the movement of the lips of the teller. Unlike Marlow, his listeners never have a chance to see or experience directly the man behind the name. The reader, if he happens at this moment to think of it (and the passage is clearly an invitation to such thinking, an invocation of it), is in exactly the same situation as that of Marlow's auditor, only worse. When Marlow appeals to his auditors, Conrad is by a kind of ventriloquism appealing to his readers: 'Do you see him? Do you see the story? Do you see anything? It seems to me I am trying to tell you a dream – making a vain attempt.' Conrad speaks through Marlow to us. The reader too can reach the truth behind the story only through names, never through any direct perception or experience. In the reader's case it is not even names proffered by a living man before him, only names coldly and impersonally printed on the pages of the pages of the book he holds in his hand. Even if the reader goes behind the fiction to the historical reality on which it is based, as Ian Watt and others have done, he or she will only confront more words on more pages – Conrad's letters or the historical records of the conquest and exploitation of the Congo. The situation of the auditors even of a living speaker, Marlow says, is scarcely better, since what a story must convey through names and other words is not the fact but the 'life-sensation' behind the fact, 'which makes its truth, its meaning – its subtle and penetrating essence'. This is once more the halo around the moon, the meaning enveloping the tale. This meaning is as impossible to convey by way of the life-facts that may be named as the 'dream-sensation' is able to be conveyed through a relation of the bare facts of the dream. Anyone knows this who has ever tried to tell another person his dream and has found how lame and flat, or how laughable, it sounds, since 'no relation of a dream can convey the dream-sensation'. According to Marlow's metaphor or proportional analogy: as the facts of a dream are to the dream-sensation, so the facts of a life are to the life-sensation. Conrad makes an absolute distinction between experience and the interpretation of written or spoken sign. The sensation may only be experienced directly and may by no means, oral or written, be communicated to another: 'We live, as we dream, alone.'

Nevertheless, Marlow tells his auditors, they have one direct or experimental access to the truth enveloping the story: 'You fellows see more than I could then. You see me, whom you know.' There is a double irony in this. To see the man who has had the experience is to have an avenue to the experience for which the man speaks, to which he bears witness. Marlow's auditors see more than he could then – that is, before his actual encounter with Kurtz. Ironically, the witness cannot bear witness for himself. He cannot see himself or cannot see through himself or by means of himself, in spite of, or in contradiction of, Conrad's (or Marlow's) assertion a few paragraph later that work is 'the chance to find yourself. Your own reality – for yourself, not for others – what no other man can ever know. They can only see the mere show, and never can tell what it really means' (Ch. I, p. 99). Though each man can only experience his own reality, his own truth, the paradox involved here seems to run, he can only experience it through another or by means of another as witness to a truth deeper in, behind the other. Marlow's auditors can only learn indirectly, through Marlow, whom they see. They therefore know more than he did. Marlow could only learn through Kurtz, when he finally encountered him face to face. The reader of *Heart of Darkness* learns through the relation of the primary narrator, who learned through Marlow, who learned through Kurtz. This proliferating relay of witnesses, one behind another, each revealing another truth further in which turns out to be only another witness corresponds to the narrative form of *Heart of Darkness*. The novel is a sequence of episodes, each structured according to the model of appearances, signs, which are also obstacles or veils. Each veil must be lifted to reveal a truth behind which always turns out to be another episode, another witness, another veil to be lifted in its turn. Each such episode is a 'fact dazzling, to be seen, like the foam on the depths of the sea, like a ripple on an unfathomable enigma' (Ch. II, p. 115), the fact for example that though the cannibal Africans on Marlow's steamer were starving, they did not eat the white men. But behind each enigmatic fact is only another fact. The relay of witness behind witness behind witness, voice behind voice behind voice, each speaking in ventriloquism through the one next farther out, is a characteristic of the genre of the apocalypse. In the book of Revelation, God speaks through Jesus, who speaks through a messenger angel, who speaks through John of Patmos, who speaks to us.

There is another reason beyond the necessities of revelation for this structure. The truth behind the last witness, behind Kurtz for example in *Heart of Darkness*, is, no one can doubt it, death, 'the horror', or, to put this another way, 'death' is another name for what Kurtz names 'the horror'. No man can confront that truth face to face and survive. Death or the horror can only be experienced indirectly, by the way of the face and voice of another. The relay of witnesses both reveals death and, luckily, hides it. As Marlow says, 'the inner truth is hidden – luckily, luckily' (Ch. II, p. 105). This is another regular feature of the genre of the apocalypse. The word 'apocalypse' means 'unveiling', 'revelation', but what the apocalypse unveils is not the truth of the end of the world which it announces, but the act of unveiling. The unveiling unveils unveiling. It leaves its readers, auditors, witnesses, as far as ever from the always 'not quite yet' of the imminent revelation – luckily. Marlow says it was not his own near-death on the way home down the river, 'not my own extremity I remember best', but Kurtz's 'extremity that I seem to have lived through'. Then he adds, 'True, he had made that last stride, he had stepped over the edge, while I had been permitted to draw back my hesitating foot. And perhaps in this is the whole difference; perhaps all the wisdom, and all truth, and all sincerity, are just compressed into that inappreciable moment of time in which we step over the threshold of the invisible. Perhaps!' (Ch. III, pp. 149–50) Marlow, like Orpheus returning without Eurydice from the land of the dead, comes back to civilization with nothing, nothing to bear witness to, nothing to reveal but the process of unveiling that makes up the whole of the narration of *Heart of Darkness*. Marlow did not go far enough into the darkness, but if he had, like Kurtz he could not have come back. All the reader gets is Marlow's report of Kurtz's face: 'It was as though a veil had been rent. I saw on that ivory face the expression of sombre pride, of ruthless power, of craven terror – of an intense and hopeless despair' (Ch. III, p. 148).

I have suggested that there are two ironies in what Marlow says when he breaks his narration to address his auditors directly. The first irony is the fact that the auditors see more than Marlow did because they see Marlow, whom they know; the second is that we readers of the novel see no living witness. (By Marlow's own account that is not enough. Seeing only happens by direct experience, and no act of reading is direct experience. The book's claim to give the reader access to the dark truth behind appearance is withdrawn by the terms in which it is proffered.) But there is, in fact, a third irony in this relay of ironies behind ironies in that Marlow's auditors of course do not see Marlow either. It is too dark. They hear only his disembodied voice. 'It had become so pitch dark,' says the narrator, 'that we listeners could hardly see one another. For a long time already he, sitting apart, had been no more to us than a voice.' Marlow's narrative does not seem to be spoken by a living incarnate witness, there before his auditors in the flesh. It is a 'narrative that seemed to shape itself without human lips in the heavy night-air of the river'. This voice can be linked to no individual speaker or writer as the ultimate source of its messages, not to Marlow, nor to Kurtz, nor to the first narrator, nor even to Conrad himself. The voice is spoken by no one to no one. It always comes from another, from the other of any identifiable speaker or writer. It traverses all these voices as what speaks through them. It gives them authority and at the same time dispossesses them, deprives them of authority, since they only speak with the delegated authority of another. As Marlow says of the voice of Kurtz and of all the other voices, they are what remain as a dying unanimous and anonymous drone or clang that exceeds any single identifiable voice and in the end is spoken by no one:

> A voice. He was very little more than a voice. And I heard – him – it – this voice – other voices – all of them were so little more than voices – and the memory of that time itself lingers around me, impalpable, like a dying vibration of one immense jabber, silly, atrocious, sordid, savage, or simply mean, without any kind of sense. Voices, voices – . . .
>
> (Ch. II, p. 122)

For the reader, too, *Heart of Darkness* lingers in the mind or memory chiefly as a cacophony of dissonant voices. It is as though the story were spoken or written not by an identifiable narrator but directly by the darkness itself, just as Kurtz's last words seem whispered by the circumambient dusky air when Marlow makes his visit to Kurtz's Intended, and just as Kurtz himself presents himself to Marlow as a voice, a voice which exceeds Kurtz and seems to speak from beyond him: 'Kurtz discoursed. A voice! a voice! It rang deep to the very last. It survived its strength to hide in the magnificent folds of eloquence the barren darkness of his heart' (Ch. III, p. 146). Kurtz has 'the gift of expression, the bewildering, the illuminating, the most exalted and the most contemptible, the pulsating stream of light, or the deceitful flow from the heart of an impenetrable darkness' (Ch. II, p. 121). Kurtz has intended to use his eloquence as a means of 'wringing the heart of the wilderness', but 'the wilderness had found him out early, and had taken on him a terrible vengeance for the fantastic invasion' (Ch. III, p. 134). The direction of the flow of language reverses. It flows from the darkness instead of toward it. Kurtz is 'hollow at the core' (Ch. III, p. 134), and so the wilderness can speak through him, use him so to speak as a ventriloquist's dummy through which its terrible messages may be broadcast to the world: 'Exterminate all the brutes!' 'The horror!' (Ch. II, p. 125; Ch. III, p. 148) The speaker to is spoken through. Kurtz's disembodied voice, or the voice behind voice behind voice of the narrators, or that 'roaring chorus of articulated, rapid, breathless utterance' (Ch. III, p. 145) shouted by the natives on the bank, when Kurtz is taken on board the steamer – these are in the end no more direct a testimony of the truth than the words on the page as Conrad wrote them. The absence of a visible speaker of Marlow's words and the emphasis on the way Kurtz is a disembodied voice function as indirect expressions of the fact that *Heart of Darkness* itself is words without person, words which cannot be traced back to any single personality. This is once more confirmation of my claim that *Heart of Darkness* belongs to the genre of the parabolic apocalypse. The apocalypse is after all a written not an oral genre, and, as Jacques Derrida has pointed out, one characteristic of an apocalypse is that it turns on the invitation or 'Come' spoken or written always by someone other than the one who seems to utter or write it.[6]

A full exploration of the way *Heart of Darkness* is an apocalypse would need to be put under the multiple aegis of the converging figures of irony, antithesis, catachresis, synecdoche, *aletheia* and personification. Irony is a name for the pervasive tone of Marlow's narration, which undercuts as it affirms. Antithesis identifies the division of what is presented in the story in terms of seemingly firm oppositions that always ultimately break down. Catachresis is the proper name for a parabolic revelation of the darkness by means of visible figures that do not substitute for any possible literal expression of that darkness. Synecdoche is the name for the questionable relation of similarity between the visible sign, the skin of the surface, the foam on the sea, and what lies behind it, the pulsating heart of darkness, the black depths of the sea. Unveiling or *aletheia* labels that endless process of apocalyptic revelation that never quite comes off. The revelation is always future. Personification, finally, is a name for the consistent presentation of the darkness as some kind of living creature with a heart, ultimately as a woman who unmans all those male questors who try to dominate her. This pervasive personification is most dramatically embodied in the native woman, Kurtz's mistress: 'the immense wilderness, the colossal body of the fecund and mysterious life seemed to look at her, pensive, as though it had been looking at the image of its own tenebrous and passionate soul' (Ch. III, pp. 137–8).

Heart of Darkness is perhaps most explicitly apocalyptic in announcing the end, the end of Western civilization, or of Western imperialism, the reversal of

6 See Jacques Derrida, 'D'un ton apocalyptique adopte naguere en philosophie', in *Les Fins de l'homme*, ed. Phillippe Lacoue-Labarthe and Jean-Luc Nancy, Paris: Flammarion, 1981, pp. 445–79, especially p. 468ff. The essay has been translated by John P. Learey, Jr., and published in the 1982 number of *Semeia* (pp. 62–97).

idealism into savagery. As is always the case with apocalypses, the end is announced as something always imminent, never quite yet. Apocalypse is never now. The novel sets women, who are out of it, against men, who can live with the facts and have a belief to protect them against the darkness. Men can breathe dead hippo and not be contaminated. Male practicality and idealism reverse, however. They turn into their opposites because they are hollow at the core. They are vulnerable to the horror. They *are* the horror. The idealistic suppression of savage customs becomes, 'Exterminate all the brutes!' Male idealism is the same thing as the extermination of the brutes. The suppression of savage customs is the extermination of the brutes. This is not just word play but actual fact, as the history of the white man's conquest of the world has abundantly demonstrated. This conquest means the end of the brutes, but it means also, in Conrad's view of history, the end of Western civilization, with its ideals of progress, enlightenment and reason, its goal of carrying the torch of civilization into the wilderness and wringing the heart of the darkness. Or it is the imminence of that end which has never quite come as long as there is someone to speak or write of it.

I claim to have demonstrated that *Heart of Darkness* is not only parabolic but also apocalyptic. It fits that strange genre of the apocalyptic text, the sort of text that promises an ultimate revelation without giving it, and says always 'Come' and 'Wait'. But there is an extra twist given to the paradigmatic form of the apocalypse in *Heart of Darkness*. The *Aufklärung* or enlightenment in this case is of the fact that the darkness can never be enlightened. The darkness enters into every gesture of enlightenment to enfeeble it, to hollow it out, to corrupt it and thereby to turn its reason into unreason, its pretence of shedding light into more darkness. Marlow as narrator is in complicity with this reversal in the act of identifying it in others. He too claims, like the characteristic writer of an apocalypse, to know something no one else knows and to be qualified on that basis to judge and enlighten them. 'I found myself back in the sepulchral city,' says Marlow of his return from the Congo,

> resenting the sight of people hurrying through the street to filch a little money from each other, to devour their infamous cookery, to gulp their unwholesome beer, to dream their insignificant and silly dreams. They trespassed upon my thoughts. They were intruders whose knowledge of life was to me an irritating pretence, because I felt so sure they could not possibly know the things I knew.
>
> (Ch. III, p. 150)

The consistent tone of Marlow's narration is ironical. Irony is truth-telling or a means of truth-telling, of unveiling. At the same time it is a defence against the truth. This doubleness makes it, though it seems so coolly reasonable, another mode of unreason, the unreason of a fundamental undecidability. If irony is a defence, it is also inadvertently a means of participation. Though Marlow says, 'I have a voice too, and for good or evil mine is a speech that cannot be silenced' (Ch. II, p. 108), as though his speaking were a cloak against the darkness, he too, in speaking ironically, becomes, like Kurtz, one of those speaking tubes or relay stations through whom the darkness speaks. As theorists of irony from Friedrich Schlegel and Soren Kierkegaard to Paul de Man have argued, irony is the one trope that cannot be mastered or used as an instrument of mastery. An ironic statement is essentially indeterminate or undecidable in meaning. The man who attempts to say one thing while clearly meaning another ends up by saying the first thing too, in spite of himself. One irony leads to another. The ironies proliferate into a great crowd of little conflicting ironies. It is impossible to know in just what tone of voice one should read one of Marlow's sardonic ironies. Each is uttered simultaneously in innumerable conflicting tones going all the way from the lightest and most comical to the darkest, most sombre and tragic. It is impossible to decide exactly which quality of voice should be allowed to predominate over the others. Try reading aloud the passage cited above and you will see this. Marlow's tone and meaning are indeterminate; his description of the clamour of native voices on the shore or of the murmur of all those voices he remembers from that time in his life also functions as an appropriate displaced description of his own discourse. Marlow's irony makes his speech in its own way another version of that multiple cacophonous and deceitful voice flowing from the heart of darkness, 'a complaining clamour, modulated in savage discords', or a 'tumultuous and mournful uproar', another version of that 'one immense jabber, silly, atrocious, sordid, savage, or simply mean, without any kind of sense', not a voice, but voices (Ch. II, p. 112; II, p. 122). In this inextricable tangle of voices and voices speaking within voices, Marlow's narration fulfils, no doubt without deliberate intent on Conrad's part, one of the primary laws of the genre of the apocalypse.

The final fold in this folding in of complicities in these ambiguous acts of unveiling is my own complicity as demystifying commentator. Behind or before Marlow is Conrad, and before or behind him stands the reader or critic. My commentary unveils a lack of decisive unveiling in *Heart of Darkness*. I have attempted to perform an act of generic classification, with all the covert violence and unreason of that act, since no work is wholly commensurate with the boundaries of any genre. By unveiling the lack of unveiling in *Heart of Darkness*, I have become another witness in my turn, as much guilty as any other in the line of witnesses of covering over while claiming to illuminate. My *Aufklärung* too has been of the continuing impenetrability of Conrad's *Heart of Darkness*.

Peter Brooks, 'An Unreadable Report: Conrad's *Heart of Darkness*' (1984)

In *Reading for the Plot*, Peter Brooks combines structuralism, psychoanalysis and narratology in talking 'of the dynamics of temporality and reading, of the motor forces that drive the text forward, of the desires that connect narrative ends and beginnings, and make of the textual middle a highly charged field of force'.[1] Several terms Brooks employs may need clarification. *Fabula* and *sjužet* were used by the Russian Formalists, active in the early twentieth century but not making an impact on European critical discourse until the 1960s and 1970s. The *fabula* is the sequence of events if these were related chronologically. The *sjužet* is the order in which the events are actually told which may depart more or less from the chronological order. In English, *fabula* is often translated as 'story' and *sjužet* as 'plot', a translation which Brooks partly accepts but to which he adds a dimension: for him, 'plot' is, in a sense, the interpretative activity that is elicited by the distinction between *fabula* and *sjužet*; it is an aspect of the *sjužet* in that it is the 'active shaping force' of the *sjužet* (p. 13), but as it fashions the *sjužet*, shaping a particular ordering of events, it also makes us attempt to grasp and understand the *fabula*, to reorder the events in chronological sequence. In French narratology, the *fabula* is the equivalent of *histoire* (story) and *sjužet* of *récit* (account) or *discourse* (discourse). As Brooks points out, the French narratologist Gérard Genette adds a third category which he calls *narration* ('narrating'): this means, in Brooks' paraphrase, 'the level at which narratives sometimes dramatize the means and agency (real or fictive) of their telling' (p. 328). This third category is relevant to a consideration of *Heart of Darkness*. Brooks' essay on the narrative of *Heart of Darkness* is powerful, though his presentation of the detective story as exemplary of narrative logic seems to me debatable in the case of *Heart of Darkness*. See Critical history, **p. 63**.

---

1   Brooks, *Reading for the Plot: Design and Intention in Narrative*, Cambridge, Massachusetts: Harvard UP, 1984, 1992, pp. xiii–xiv.

From *Reading for the Plot: Design and Intention in Narrative* (1984, 1992)

Joseph Conrad's *Heart of Darkness* – published in the last year of the nineteenth century – poses in an exemplary way central questions about the shape and epistemology of narrative. It displays an acute self-consciousness about the organizing features of traditional narrative, working with them still, but suspiciously, with constant reference to the inadequacy of the inherited orders of meaning. It suggests affinities to that preeminently nineteenth-century genre, the detective story, but a detective story gone modernist: a tale of inconclusive solutions to crimes of problematic status. In its representation of an effort to reach endings that would retrospectively illuminate beginnings and middles, it pursues a reflection on the formal limits of narrative, but within a frame of discourse that appears to subvert finalities of form. Most of all, it engages the very motive of narrative in its tale of a complexly motivated attempt to recover the story of another within one's own, and to retell both in a context that further complicates relations of actors, tellers and listeners. Ultimately, all these questions, and everything one says about the tale, must be reconceived within the context of Marlow's act of narration aboard the *Nellie* at the moment of the turning of the tide on the Thames, in the relation of this narrator to his narratees and the relation of the narrative situation to the stories enacted within it.

Heart of Darkness is a framed tale, in which a first narrator introduces Marlow and has the last word after Marlow has fallen silent; and embedded within Marlow's tale is apparently another, Kurtz's, which never quite gets told – as perhaps Marlow's does not quite either, for the frame structure here is characterized by notable uncertainties. Referring to Gérard Genette's tripartite distinction of narrative levels, it is evident that in *Heart of Darkness* everything must eventually be recovered on the plane of narrating, in the act of telling which itself attempts to recover the problematic relations of Marlow's narrative plot to his story, and of his plot and story to Kurtz's story, which in turn entertains doubtful relations with Kurtz's narrative plot and its narrating. Marlow's narrative plot will more and more as it proceeds take as its story what Marlow understands to be Kurtz's story. Yet Kurtz's story has other plots, ways in which he would like to have it told: for instance, in his *Report to the Society for the Suppression of Savage Customs* (a plot subverted by the scribbled and forgotten footnote 'Exterminate all the brutes!'); or else the manner in which posthumously he commands Marlow's 'loyalty' in retelling it – as lie – to his Intended. Ultimately, we must ask what motivates Marlow's retellings – of his own and Kurtz's mortal adventures – in the gathering dusk on the Thames estuary.

One way to begin to unpack the dense narrative layerings of *Heart of Darkness* may be through the various orders of signification and belief – ready-made life plots – that the text casts up along the way: orders that marshal reality and might explain it if only one could believe them, if only there did not always seem to be something subverting them. One such order, for instance, is the Company, its door flanked by the two knitters of black wool, one of whom – or is it by now a third, to complete the suggestion of the Parcae? – obtrudes herself upon Marlow's memory at the moment of maximum blackness 'as a most improper person to be sitting at the other end of such an affair'.[2] In the knitted web – shroud, pall, or is it rather Ariadne's thread into a dark labyrinth? – the Company's design reaches to the depths of the dark continent. The company as ordering is related to the 'idea': 'The conquest of the earth . . . is not a pretty thing when you look into it too much. What redeems it is the idea only' (Ch. I, pp. 50–1). The 'idea' is the fiction of the mission, which upon inspection is seen to cover up the most rapacious and vicious of imperialisms. Here surely is one relation of order as ready-made plot to story in *Heart of Darkness*: a relation of cover-up, concealment, lie. Yet one should note a certain admiration in Marlow for the idea in itself: a recognition of the necessity for plot, for signifying system, even in the absence of its correspondence to reality (which may, for instance, suggest a reason for his effacing Kurtz's scribbled footnote before passing on the *Report to the Society for the Suppression of Savage Customs* to the press). The juxtaposition of ready-made order to reality, and Marlow's capacity to see both the admirable and the absurd in such attempted applications of order, is well suggested by the Company's chief accountant in the lower station, in high starched collar and cuffs, 'bent over his books . . . making perfectly correct entries of perfectly correct transactions; and fifty feet below I could see the still tree-tops of the grove of death' (Ch. I, p. 70). The building of the railroad, with its objectless blasting of a path to nowhere, would be another example; even more compelling is perhaps the picture of the French warship shelling an incomprehensible coast:

> Once, I remember, we came upon a man-of-war anchored off the coast.
> There wasn't even a shed there, and she was shelling the bush. It appears
> the French had one of their wars going on thereabouts. Her ensign
> dropped limp like a rag; the muzzles of the long six-inch guns stuck out
> all over the low hull; the greasy, slimy swell swung her up lazily and let
> her down, swaying her thin masts. In the empty immensity of earth, sky
> and water, there she was, incomprehensible, firing into a continent.
> Pop, would go one of the six-inch guns; a small flame would dart and
> vanish, a little white smoke would disappear, a tiny projectile would
> give a feeble screech – and nothing happened. Nothing could happen.
> There was a touch of insanity in the proceeding, a sense of lugubrious
> drollery in the sight; and it was not dissipated by somebody on board
> assuring me earnestly there was a camp of natives – he called them
> enemies! – hidden out of sight somewhere.
>
> (Ch. I, pp. 61–2)

The traditional ordering systems – war, camp, enemies – lead to the logical consequences – men-of-war, cannonades – which are wholly incongruous to the situation requiring mastery. There is an absurd disproportion between the ordering systems deployed and the triviality of their effect, as if someone had designed a machine to produce work far smaller than the energy put into it. And there are many other examples that conform to such laws of incongruous effect.

---

2   Conrad, *Heart of Darkness*, in *Youth and Two Other Stories*, Garden City, NY, 1924, II, p. 124.
    Subsequent references are to this edition and are incorporated in the text.

The question of orderings comes to be articulated within the very heart of darkness in an exchange between Marlow and the manager on the question of Kurtz's 'method' in the acquisition of ivory, which, we have already learned from the Russian – Kurtz's admirer, and the chief teller of his tale – Kurtz mainly obtained by raiding the country. The manager's rhetoric is punctuated by Marlow's dissents:

> 'I don't deny there is a remarkable quantity of ivory – mostly fossil. We must save it, at all events – but look how precarious the position is – and why? Because the method is unsound.' 'Do you,' said I, looking at the shore, 'call it "unsound method"?' 'Without doubt,' he exclaimed hotly. 'Don't you?' . . . 'No method at all,' I murmured after a while. 'Exactly,' he exulted. 'I anticipated this. Shows a complete want of judgment. It is my duty to point it out in the in the proper quarter.' 'Oh,' said I, 'that fellow – what's his name? – the brickmaker, will make a readable report for you.' He appeared confounded for a moment. It seemed to me I had never breathed an atmosphere so vile, and I turned mentally to Kurtz for relief – positively for relief.
>
> (Ch. II, pp. 137–8)

The result of this exchange is that Marlow finds himself classified with those of 'unsound method', which, of course, is a way of moralizing as lapse from order any recognition of the absence of order, using the concept of disorder to conceal the radical condition of orderlessness. The manager's language – 'unsound method', 'want of judgment', 'duty to point it out in the proper quarter' – refers to ordering systems and in so doing finds a way to mask perception of what Kurtz's experience really signifies. The 'readable report', which Marlow notes to be the usual order for dealing with such deviations as Kurtz's, would represent the ultimate system of false ordering, ready-made discourse. What we really need, Marlow seems to suggest, is an *unreadable* report – something like Kurtz's *Report*, perhaps, with its utterly contradictory messages, or perhaps Marlow's eventual retelling of the whole affair.

The text, then, appears to speak of a repeated 'trying out' of orders, all of which distort what they claim to organize, all of which may indeed cover up a very lack of possibility of order. This may suggest one relationship between story and narrative plot in the text: a relationship of disquieting uncertainty, where story never appears to be quite matched to the narrative plot that is responsible for it. Yet the orders tried out in *Heart of Darkness* may in their very tenuousness be necessary to the process of striving toward meaning: as if to say that the plotting of stories remains necessary even where we have ceased to believe in the plots we use. Certain minimum canons of readability remain necessary if we are to be able to discern the locus of the necessarily unreadable.

Marlow's own initial relationship to the matter of orderings is curious, and recognized by himself as such. Marlow is eminently the man of work, proud of his seamanship, concerned with what he calls the 'surface-truth' (Ch. II, p. 97) of steering, mechanics, repairs, devoted to the values of the master mariner codified in Towson's (or Towser's) *An Inquiry into Some Points of Seamanship*: 'Not a very enthralling book; but at the first glance you could see there a singleness of intention, an honest concern for the right way of going to work, which made these pages . . . luminous with another than a professional light' (Ch. II, p. 97). Yet as he presents his decision to undertake his African journey, it appears capricious, irrational, unmotivated. The decision reaches back to his boyhood passion for maps – which are another external ordering of reality – yet particularly his attraction to the unmapped within them, to their blank spaces. The space to which he will journey in the story recounted in *Heart of Darkness* – for convenience, we may call it the Congo, though it is never so named, never named at all, in the text – appeared 'the biggest, the most blank, so to speak' (Ch. I, p. 52). By the time of his journey, the blank has been filled in, 'with rivers and lakes and names'; indeed, possibly it has been filled overfull with 'ideas', for 'It had become a place of blackness' (p. 52). But blackness appears to motivate as strongly as blankness. Marlow in fact appears to recognize that his explanation lacks coherence, when he goes on to describe the 'mighty big river . . . resembling an immense snake uncoiled', and himself as the 'silly little bird' that is 'fascinated' by the snake – so fascinated that he began to have recourse, as he never had before, to women relatives on the Continent, in order to have a captaincy in the Company trading on the river. The desire for the journey is childish, absolute, persistent through contradictions; the journey itself appears compulsive, gratuitous, unmotivated. In the manner of Marlow himself, the reader must, in the absence of clear purpose or goal to the journey, be content with a general 'fascination'. The point bears some insistence, for Marlow's description of his trip up the river will in fact be also a description of how the journey came to be motivated: of the precipitation of a motivating plot within the originally unmotivated journey, and narrative.

'Going up that river was like travelling back to the earliest beginnings of the world . . .' (II, p. 92). The way up is the way back: Marlow's individual journey repeats, ontogenetically, a kind of reverse phylogeny,[3] and unravelling of the threads of civilization. His quest, we might say, is also an inquest, an investigation leading toward beginnings and origins; and the traditional story line of the journey comes to be doubled by the more specifically goal-oriented plot line of the inquest. What makes it so is his discovery that he has been preceded in his journey by the 'remarkable' Mr Kurtz, who becomes the object of inquest, providing a motive for the previously gratuitous voyage. Kurtz in fact provides a magnetizing goal of quest and inquest since he not only has led the way up the river, he has also returned upriver instead of coming back to the Central Station as he was supposed to do: Marlow indeed is able to 'see Kurtz for the first time', in his imagination, in this return upriver, 'setting his face towards the depths of the wilderness'. It can in fact be pieced together from various remarks of the Company officials that the very reason for Marlow's being sent on his journey upriver is to detect the meaning and the consequences of Kurtz's return upriver – a presiding intention to his voyage of which Marlow becomes aware only in its midst, at the Central Station. It is thus gradually impressed upon Marlow, and the reader, that Marlow

---

3 'Ontogenetically' and 'phylogeny' recalled a commonplace of nineteenth-century evolutionary science, that 'ontogeny recapitulates phylogeny': the development of an individual being (ontogeny) was supposed to repeat the evolutionary stages of the species (phylogeny), with the implication that both can always progress a little further. Marlow's journey, the 'furthest point' of his experience, could be interpreted as reversing the development of the human race.

is in a state of belatedness or secondariness in relation to the forerunner; his journey is a repetition, which gains its meaning from its attachment to the prior journey. Marlow's plot (*sjužet*) repeats Kurtz's story (*fabula*), takes this as its motivating force – and then will seek also to know and to incorporate Kurtz's own plot for his story.

So it is that Marlow's inquest, in the manner of the detective's, becomes the retracing of the track of a precursor. The detective story in its classic form is built on the overlay or superimposition of two temporal orders, the time of the crime (events and motives leading up to the crime) and the time of the inquest (events and motives leading away from the crime, but aimed at reconstructing it), the former sequence *in absentia*, lost to representation except insofar as it can be reconstructed in the time of the inquest, the latter *in praesentia* but existing merely to actualize the absent sequence of the crime. Tzvetan Todorov identified the relation of these two orders as the relation of *fabula* to *sjužet* that one finds in any narrative: a story postulated as prior gone over by a narrative plot that claims thereby to realize it.[4] The detective story may in this manner lay bare the structure of any narrative, particularly its claim to be a retracing of events that have already occurred. The detective retracing the trace of his predecessor and thus uncovering and constructing the meaning and the authority of the narrative represents the very process of narrative representation. This couple, the criminal precursor and the latecomer detective, has special relevance to the situation of Marlow and Kurtz. No more than the detective's, Marlow's narrative is not primary: it attaches itself to another's story, seeking there its authority; it retraces another's path, repeats a journey already undertaken.

In Marlow's narrative, then, we witness the formation of motivation in the middle of the journey, though in his act of narration this motivation may stand at its very inception, as part of the very motive of telling, since his own story has become narratable only in relation to Kurtz's. In a phrase that marks his first explicit recognition of a goal to his journey, and hence of a plot to his story, Marlow states, 'Where the pilgrims imagined it [the steamboat] crawled to I don't know. To some place they expected to get something, I bet! For me it crawled toward Kurtz – exclusively' (Ch. II, p. 95). The reason for Marlow's choice of this 'exclusive' and seemingly arbitrary motivation is made more specific following the attack on the steamboat, in a manner that helps us to understand the uses of plot. Thinking that the attack may betoken the death of Kurtz (later we learn that Kurtz himself ordered the attack), Marlow feels an 'extreme disappointment', as if 'I had travelled all this way for the sole purpose of talking with Mr Kurtz. Talking with . . .' (Ch. II, p. 113). His choice of terms to image his anticipated meeting with Kurtz now leads him to recognition that it was indeed Kurtz as talker that he sought:

> I . . . became aware that this was exactly what I had been looking for-
> ward to – a talk with Kurtz. I made the strange discovery that I had
> never imagined him as doing, you know, but as discoursing . . . The man

4   See Tzvetan Todorov, 'Typologie du roman policier', in *Poétique de la prose*, Paris, 1971, pp. 55–65; English trans. Richard Howard, *The Poetics of Prose*, Ithaca, NY, 1977.

presented himself as a voice … The point was in his being a gifted creature, and that of all his gifts the one that stood out preeminently, that carried with it a sense of real presence, was his ability to talk, his words – the gift of expression, the bewildering, the illuminating, the most exalted and the most contemptible, the pulsating stream of light, or the deceitful flow from the heart of an impenetrable darkness.

(II, pp. 113–14)

The definition of Kurtz through his 'gift of expression' and as 'a voice', and Marlow's postulation of this definition of Kurtz as the motivating goal of his own journey, serve to conceptualize the narrative end as expression, voice, articulation, or what Walter Benjamin termed simply 'wisdom': the goal of all storytelling which, with the decline of traditional oral transmission, has in the 'privatized' genre of the novel come to be defined exclusively as the meaning of an individual life. And we have seen that in Benjamin's argument, the meaning of a life cannot be known until the moment of death: it is at death that a life first assumes transmissible form – becomes a completed and significant statement – so that it is death that provides the authority or 'sanction' of narrative. The deathbed scene of the nineteenth-century novel eminently represents the moment of summing-up of a life's meaning and a transmission of accumulated wisdom to succeeding generations. Paternal figures within novels write their own obituaries, transmitting to the younger protagonists something of the authority necessary to view the meaning of their own lives retrospectively, in terms of the significance that will be brought by the as yet unwritten end.

To Marlow, Kurtz is doubly such a deathbed figure and writer of obituary. In the first place, he has reached his journey's end, he is lodged in the heart of darkness and it is from that 'farthest point of navigation' that he offers his discourse, the 'pulsating stream of light' or 'deceitful flow'. Kurtz has reached further, deeper than anyone else, and his gift for expression means that he should be able to give articulate shape to his terminus. 'Kurtz discoursed. A voice! a voice!' Marlow will later report. But by that point Kurtz's report on the meaning of his navigation into the heart of the jungle will be compounded with his journey to his life's end, and his terminal report on his inner descent into darkness. So that Kurtz's discourse stands to make sense of Marlow's voyage and his life, his journey and his inquest: to offer that final articulation that will give a meaning to journey and experience here at what Marlow has doubly identified as 'the farthest point of navigation and the culminating point of my experience' (Ch. I, p. 51). Kurtz is he who has already turned experience into Benjamin's 'wisdom', turned story into well-formed narrative plot, matter into pure voice, and who stands ready to narrate life's story in significant form. Marlow's own narrative can make sense only when his inquest has reached a 'solution' that is not a simple detection but the finding of a message written at and by the death of another. The meaning of his narrative plot has indeed come to depend on Kurtz's articulation of the meaning of *his* plot: Marlow's structuring of his own *fabula* as *sjužet* has attached itself to Kurtz's *fabula*, and can find its significant outcome only in finding Kurtz's *sjužet*.

For Kurtz, in the heart of darkness and at life's end, has 'stepped over the edge' and has 'summed up'. Since it is a 'summing up' that Marlow has discovered to be what most he has been seeking – that summary illumination that retrospectively makes sense of all that has gone before – his insistence that Kurtz has summed up is vitally important. At the end of the journey lies, not ivory, gold, or a fountain of youth, but the capacity to turn experience into language: a voice. But here we are forced to give closer scrutiny to Marlow's affirmations and their curious self-cancellations. Noting that after Kurtz's death he almost died himself, Marlow continues in reflection on ultimate articulations:

> I was within a hair's breadth of the last opportunity for pronouncement, and I found with humiliation that probably I would have nothing to say. This is the reason why I affirm that Kurtz was a remarkable man. He had something to say. He said it. Since I had peeped over the edge myself, I understand better the meaning of his stare that could not see the flame of the candle but was wide enough to embrace the whole universe, piercing enough to penetrate all the hearts that beat in the darkness. He had summed up – he had judged. 'The horror!' He was a remarkable man. After all, this was the expression of some sort of belief; it had candour, it had conviction, it had a vibrating note of revolt in its whisper, it had the appalling face of a glimpsed truth – the strange commingling of desire and hate. And it is not my own extremity I remember best – a vision of grayness without form filled with physical pain, and a careless contempt for the evanescence of all things – even of this pain itself. No! It is his extremity that I seem to have lived through. True, he had made that last stride, he had stepped over the edge, while I had been permitted to draw back my hesitating foot. And perhaps in this is the whole difference; perhaps all the wisdom, and all truth, and all sincerity, are just compressed into that inappreciable moment of time in which we step over the threshold of the invisible. Perhaps! I like to think my summing-up would not have been a word of careless contempt. Better his cry – much better. It was an affirmation, a moral victory paid for by innumerable defeats, by abominable terrors, by abominable satisfactions. But it was a victory! That is why I have remained loyal to Kurtz to the last, and even beyond, when a long time after I heard once more not his own voice, but the echo of his magnificent eloquence thrown to me from a soul as translucently pure as a cliff of crystal.
>
> (Ch. III, pp. 151–2)

The passage is one that epitomizes all our difficulties with Marlow as narrator, for the resonance of its ethical pronouncements seems somehow to get in the way of the designation of a starker and possibly contradictory truth: the moral rhetoric appears in some measure a cover-up. Marlow explicitly confirms Benjamin's argument concerning storytelling and wisdom, and confirms his need for Kurtz as the paternal figure whose final articulation transmits wisdom. Kurtz 'had summed up'. And this summary articulation, which concerns not only Kurtz's individual experience but also penetrates 'all the hearts that beat in the darkness', comes from 'over the edge', on the other side, *beyond* life, or more accurately, on the threshold of the beyond, with one foot on either side; whereas Marlow has only 'peeped' over the edge. In his hypothesis that 'all the wisdom, and all truth' are compressed into this moment of termination and threshold, Marlow evokes the tradition of the 'panoramic vision of the dying': as he says just before the passage I quoted at length, 'Did he [Kurtz] live his life again in every detail of desire, temptation, and surrender during that supreme moment of complete knowledge?' (III, p. 149). The supremacy of the moment should inform Kurtz's *ultima verba*, his summing-up: in his discourse is wrought his 'victory'.

And yet, when after considering that 'all the wisdom, and all truth' may lie compacted in that last moment, that 'last opportunity for pronouncement', Marlow states: 'I like to think my summing-up would not have been a word of careless contempt', he may subvert the rhetorical system of the passage quoted by inculcating a major doubt concerning the proper characterization of Kurtz's 'word'. The uncertainties of Marlow's argument here are suggested by other curiosities of diction and rhetoric. 'Better his cry' is a curious comparative to use in regard to a word that Marlow claims was *not* spoken (the word of careless contempt). 'But it was a victory' appears somewhat strange in that one doesn't ordinarily introduce a clause by a concessive when the previous clause is ostensibly making the same affirmation. Marlow's discourse seems to shape itself in opposition to the anticipated objections of an imagined interlocutor. By protesting too much, he builds those putative objections dialogically into his own discourse, making it (in Mikhail Bakhtin's terms) 'double voiced'.[5] Double voicing indeed is suggested by the evocation of the 'echo' of Kurtz's voice. This 'echo of his magnificent eloquence' becomes the most highly problematic element of the passage when, later, we understand that the 'soul as translucently pure as a cliff of crystal' is Kurtz's Intended, and that the 'echo' which she hears is a pure fiction in blatant contradiction to that which Marlow hears in the same room with her: a lie which Marlow is obliged to confirm as conscious cover-up of the continuing reverberation of Kurtz's last words: 'The horror! The horror!'

This is no doubt the point at issue: that Kurtz's final words answer so poorly to all of Marlow's insistence on summing-up as a moment of final articulation of wisdom, truth and sincerity, as affirmation and as moral victory. Marlow affirms that it is Kurtz's ultimate capacity to judge, to use human language in its communicative and its normative dimensions to transmit an evaluation of his soul's adventures on this earth, that constitutes his victory: the victory of articulation itself. And yet, 'The horror! The horror!' is more accurately characterized when Marlow calls it a 'cry'. It comes about as close as articulated speech can come to the primal cry, to a blurted emotional reaction of uncertain reference and context. To present 'The horror!' as articulation of that wisdom lying in wait at the end of the tale, at journey's end and life's end, is to make a mockery of storytelling and ethics, or to gull one's listeners – as Marlow himself seems to realize when he finds that he cannot repeat Kurtz's last words to the Intended, but must rather cover them up by a conventional ending: 'The last word he pronounced was – your name' (Ch. III p. 161). The contrast of this fictive act of naming – 'proper' naming – with Kurtz's actual cry may suggest how poorly Kurtz's summing-up fits

5 On the 'dialogic' and 'double-voicedness' see in particular Mikhail Bakhtin, 'Discourse in the Novel', in *The Dialogic Imagination*, ed. Michael Holquist, trans. Holquist and Caryl Emerson, Austin, Texas, 1981, pp. 259–422; and *Problems of Dostoevsky's Poetics*, trans. R.W. Rotsel, Ann Arbor, Michigan, 1973.

Marlow's description of it. Indeed, his cry so resembles the 'word of careless contempt' that when we find this phrase in Marlow's account, we tend to take it as applying to Kurtz's last utterance, only to find that it is given as the very contrary thereof. Something is amiss.

We can concede to Marlow his reading of the ethical signified of Kurtz's last words, his 'judgment upon the adventures of his soul on this earth' (Ch. III p. 150) – though we may find the reference of this signified somewhat ambiguous: is the horror within Kurtz or without? Is it experience or reaction to experience? But we have a problem conceiving the signifier as fulfilling the conditions of the wisdom-and-truth-articulating function of the end. More than a masterful, summary, victorious articulation, 'The horror!' appears as minimal language, language on the verge of reversion to savagery, on the verge of a fall from language. That Kurtz's experience in the heart of darkness should represent and be represented by a fall from language does not surprise us: this belongs to the very logic of the heart of darkness, which is consistently characterized as 'unspeakable'. There are the 'unspeakable rites' (Ch. II, p. 118) at which Kurtz presides, the 'unspeakable secrets' of his 'method' (Ch. III, p. 138), and, at the very heart of the darkness – at the moment when Marlow pursues Kurtz into the jungle at night, to struggle with his soul and carry him back to the steamer – we have only this characterization of the dark ceremony unfolding by the campfire: 'It was very awful' (Ch. III, p. 143). Critics have most often been content to point to the moral signified of such phrases – or to criticize them, and Conrad, for a lack of referential and ethical specificity – but we should feel obliged to read them in their literal statement.[6] What stands at the heart of darkness – at the journey's end and at the core of this tale – is unsayable, extralinguistic.

It cannot be otherwise, for the heart of darkness – and Kurtz himself in the heart – is beyond the system of human social structures which makes language possible and is itself made possible by language: which is unthinkable except through and as language, as that which demarcates culture from nature. The issue is most directly addressed by Marlow when he contrasts Kurtz's position within the unspeakable and unimaginable darkness to that of his solidly 'moored' listeners aboard the *Nellie*:

> It was impossible – it was not good for one either – trying to imagine. He had taken a high seat amongst the devils of the land – I mean literally. You can't understand. How could you? – with solid pavement under your feet, surrounded by kind neighbours ready to cheer you or to fall on you, stepping delicately between the butcher and the policeman, in the holy terror of scandal and gallows and lunatic asylums – how can you imagine what particular region of the first ages a man's untrammelled feet may take him into by the way of solitude – utter solitude without a policeman – by the way of silence – utter silence, where no

---

6 F.R. Leavis succinctly states a common critical position when, in reference to another passage from *Heart of Darkness*, he says: 'He [Conrad] is intent on making a virtue out of not knowing what he means.' – *The Great Tradition*, Garden City, NY, 1954, p. 219. Among other failures of perception, this remark fails to take account of the fact that it is Marlow, not Conrad, who is speaking.

warning voice of a kind neighbour can be heard whispering of public opinion? These little things make all the great difference.

(Ch. II, p. 116)

Language is here presented, accurately enough, as a system of police. Incorporate with the *polis*, language forms the basis of social organization (which itself functions as a language) as a system of difference, hence of distinction and restraint, which polices individually by making it part of a transindividual, intersubjective system: precisely what we call society. To policing is contrasted the utter silence of utter solitude: the realm beyond interlocution, beyond dialogue, hence beyond language. As Marlow puts it when he struggles to return Kurtz from the jungle to the steamboat, 'I had to deal with a being to whom I could not appeal in the name of anything high or low . . . He had kicked himself loose of the earth.' (Ch. III, p. 144)

If Kurtz's summing-up may represent ethically a return to the earth and its names (though the ethical reference of his last pronouncement is at least ambiguous) as an act of language, 'The horror! The horror!' stands on the verge of non-language, of non-sense. This is not to characterize 'The horror!' as the Romantic ineffable: if Marlow appears to affirm an ineffable behind Kurtz's words, his whole narrative rather demonstrates the nothingness of that behind. Marlow continually seems to promise a penetration into the heart of darkness, along with a concurrent recognition that he is confined to the 'surface truth'. There is no reconciliation of this standoff, but there may be the suggestion that language as interlocutionary and thus as social system, simply can have no dealings with an ineffable. For language, nothing will come of nothing.[7]

Certainly the summing-up provided by Kurtz cannot represent the kind of terminal wisdom that Marlow seeks, to make sense of both Kurtz's story and his own story and hence to bring his narrative to a coherent and significant end. Kurtz's final articulation should perhaps be typed as more than anything else anaphoric, pointing to the unsayable dumbness of the heart of darkness and to the impossible end of the perfect narrative plot. In this sense, Kurtz's narrative never fully exists, never fully gets itself told. And for the same reason, Marlow's narrative can never speak the end that it has sought so hard to find, and that it has postulated as the very premise and guarantee of its meaning. Marlow's search for meaning appears ever to be suspended, rather in the manner of his description of his encounter with death: 'My destiny! Droll thing life is – that mysterious arrangement of merciless logic for a futile purpose. The most you can hope from it is some knowledge of yourself – that comes too late – a crop of unextinguishable regrets' (Ch. III, p. 150). The logic of life's plot is never vouchsafed knowledge of that end which might make its purpose significant. Such knowledge as there is always is caught in a process of suspension and deferral, so that it comes too late. Marlow as the belated follower of Kurtz the predecessor is too late, as, the tale implies, he who seeks to know the end, rather than simply live it, must always be. Ends are not – are no longer? – available.

---

7 See James Guetti: 'But *Heart of Darkness* goes beyond *Moby-Dick*, for the suggestion that the ineffable may simply be an emptiness is present throughout the story.' – *The Limits of Metaphor*, Ithaca, NY, 1967, p. 66.

The necessary syntactic incompletion of the life story is referred to by the Marlow who is one of the narrators of *Lord Jim*, a novel contemporaneous with *Heart of Darkness*:

> And besides, the last word is not said, – probably shall never be said. Are not our lives too short for that full utterance which through all our stammerings is of course our only and abiding intention? I have given up expecting whose last words, whose ring, if they could only be pronounced, would shake both heaven and earth. There is never time to say our last word – the last word of our love, of our desire, faith, remorse, submission, revolt.[8]

Marlow here defines the 'intention' of life as 'utterance', as the articulation of Benjamin's 'wisdom', and as the completion of that fully predicated sentence which to Barthes constitutes the classical narrative. Does this Marlow give up the other Marlow's search for the 'summing-up', or does he rather reaffirm that since it is unknowable in one's own life it must be sought in the voice of another, as in Kurtz's? The word 'stammerings' may imply that the search for utterance will always encounter a crossing of voices, creating a dialogic discourse of more complex reference and truth than the heaven-and-earth-shaking last word.

Returning to *Heart of Darkness*, we must ask what we are to make of Marlow's puzzling continued affirmation of Kurtz's 'victory', and his proclamation of continued 'loyalty' to Kurtz because of this victory. Is it that Marlow recognizes his own continuing need for the terminal articulation by which everything else makes sense, and thus in the face of all evidence to the contrary continues to affirm the articulate significance of Kurtz's final cry? In order to make sense of his own story, Marlow needs an ending 'borrowed' from another's story. In the lack of finality of the promised end, Marlow must continue to attach his story to Kurtz's, since to detach it would be to admit that his narrative on board the *Nellie* is radically unmotivated, arbitrary, perhaps meaningless. As he has conceded at the start of his narrative, the story was 'sombre' and 'not very clear. And yet it seemed to throw a kind of light' (Ch. I, p. 51). His loyalty to Kurtz is perhaps ultimately the loyalty of *sjužet* to *fabula*: the loyalty of telling to told, of detective to criminal, follower to forerunner, repetition to recollection. It is only through the postulation of a repetition that narrative plot gains motivation and the implication of meaning, as if, in the absence of any definable meaning in either *fabula* or *sjužet*, it were in the fact of repetition of one by the other that meaning could be made to inhere.

Marlow's 'loyalty' to Kurtz is overtly tested in the last episode recounted in his narrative, the meeting with Kurtz's Intended. She insists that there must be a traditional pattern of transmission from person to person, from one story to another, from precursor to those left behind: ' "Something must remain. His words, at least, have not died." "His words will remain," I said.' (Ch. III, p. 156)

8   Conrad, *Lord Jim*, Garden City, NY, 1924, p. 255. Conrad broke off work on *Lord Jim* to write *Heart of Darkness*, returning to the former when the latter was finished. There is thus a particularly close relation between these two Marlows, though one does not want to call them the same.

Since she believes that the meaning of Kurtz's life story lies in the words he has left behind, the Intended naturally demands to know Kurtz's last words, those which, capping the utterance expressing his life, should fix him semantically for posterity, endow his story with authority. If up to now Marlow has insisted that Kurtz's last words constitute a victory, here he discovers that as an official conclusion to Kurtz's story they will not do. The Intended asks that he repeat Kurtz's last words:

> I was on the point of crying at her, 'Don't you hear them?' The dusk was repeating them in a persistent whisper all around us, in a whisper that seemed to swell menacingly like the first whisper of a rising wind. 'The horror! The horror!'
> 'His last word – to live with,' she insisted. 'Don't you understand I loved him – I loved him – I loved him!'
> I pulled myself together and spoke slowly.
> 'The last word he pronounced was – your name.'

(Ch. III, p. 161)

Marlow's retreat here into a conventional ending to Kurtz's story, his telling of a lie – and Marlow hates lies because they have 'a flavour of mortality' (Ch. I, p. 82) – marks a decision that Kurtz's last words belong to the category of the unspeakable. Language as a system of social communication and transmission, as the medium of official biographies and readable reports, has no place for the unspeakable; it is used rather to cover up the unnameable, to reweave the seamless web of signification. The cover-up accomplished by Marlow's substituting 'your name' – the name of the Intended, which we are never in fact given – for the nameless, as if to say that any proper name can be used, according to the circumstance, to ward off the threat of a fall from language. This substitutability of names, of course, marks a notable alterability of stories: the narrative of Kurtz composed by Marlow for the Intended is different from that told to the other narratees, those on board the *Nellie*. The way stories are told, and what they mean, seems to depend as much on narratees and narrative situation as on narrator.

That Marlow's narration on board the *Nellie* concludes – or more accurately, breaks off – just after he has told of his lie to the Intended suggests the link between his lie and his narrative. Having once presented a lying version of Kurtz's story, he apparently needs to retell it, restituting its darkness this time, and in particular showing its place in Marlow's own story. Marlow's lie on behalf of Kurtz's official story, alluded to early in his narrative, prior to the account of his meeting with Kurtz, has been from the start implicitly the most powerful motive to Marlow's act of narration, which comes to break the silence of dusk on the Thames without explicit raison d'être. By its end, Marlow's narrative has revealed the central motive that compelled his act of narration. He is not simply a teller of tales, but a reteller. He must retell a story, that of Kurtz, mistold the first time. And in doing so, he must complicate it by telling how he came to know it, thus adding another layer of plot and eventually transforming the relation of telling to told, so that it is finally less Kurtz's story that he tells than his own story inhabited, as it were, by Kurtz's story. The question may then be whether Marlow can tell the story 'right' the second time around: whether the story that needs telling can properly be told at all, since proper telling may imply a conventional semantics and syntax that are unfaithful to Marlow's experience of Kurtz's experience of the heart of darkness.

This brings us back to the final issue we need to address, that of Marlow as storyteller, retelling his story on the deck of the *Nellie* to a certain group of listeners. Marlow's tale is proffered at a moment of suspension: the moment of the turning of the tide, as the mariners wait for the outbound tide in the Thames estuary in order to begin a new voyage. By the time Marlow falls silent, they will have missed the 'first of the ebb'. Marlow's tale inserts itself, then, in a moment of indefinable suspension between the flood and the ebb of the tide, at a decisive turning point that passes undiscerned to those who depend on it. This suspended temporality finds a counterpart in the first narrator's description of Marlow's tales as reversals or negative images of those usually spoken by seamen, in that they do not frame their wisdom in the conventional manner:

> The yarns of seamen have a direct simplicity, the whole meaning of which lies within the shell of a cracked nut. But Marlow was not typical (if his propensity to spin yarns be excepted), and to him the meaning of an episode was not inside like a kernel but outside, enveloping the tale which brought it out only as a glow brings out a haze, in the likeness of one of these misty halos that sometimes are made visible by the spectral illumination of moonshine.
>
> (Ch. I, p. 48)

This way of characterizing Marlow's narratives first of all puts us on warning that the structure of 'framed narration' used in *Heart of Darkness* will not in this instance give a neat pattern of nested boxes, bracketed core structures, nuts within shells. If we consider how each of the inner frames opens and closes, we realize that in a traditional patterning we should have a structure in which the first narrator presents Marlow as the second narrator, who presents Kurtz as the third narrator; then Kurtz would tell his tale to its end and fall silent; Marlow would then finish his own tale, framing Kurtz's; and the first narrator would reappear to close the outer frame.[9] In fact, Kurtz never fulfills the promise of a coherent inner frame, a core structure, for although we are told repeatedly that 'he discoursed', we get very little report of what he said. Kurtz never assumes the narration of his own story, which comes to us in a curiously lateral and indeed non-narrated form, from the Russian: 'this amazing tale that was not so much told as suggested to me in desolate exclamations, completed by shrugs, in interrupted phrases, in hints ending in deep sighs' (Ch. III, p. 129). And since Kurtz's story in its telling becomes bound up with Marlow's, it never is clearly demarcated from its frames. Then, at the close of Marlow's narration, where we might expect the first narrator to step in with a closing comment – a final 'summing up' – we have an apparent avoidance of explicit reaction to Marlow's narrative. There is simply citation of the director's remark that they have missed the first of the ebb (ambiguous indication

---

9   That is, a classic framed tale would present a set of nested boxes, a set of brackets within brackets.

of either inattentiveness or else absorption, pensivity) and the first narrator's final descriptive sentence: 'I raised my head. The offing was barred by a black bank of clouds, and the tranquil waterway leading to the uttermost ends of the earth flowed sombre under an overcast sky – seemed to lead into the heart of an immense darkness' (Ch. III, p. 162). Thus there is a generalization of the darkness at the heart of Marlow's (and Kurtz's) stories, rather than any defining illumination. The Thames which initially was presented as leading up to a place of darkness – a place of gloom, and once itself a heart of darkness – now leads out to darkness as well. Darkness is everywhere visible. The encompassing darkness offers one realization of the image the first narrator has used to describe Marlow's tales, where meaning is not within but 'enveloping'. The tale, that image tells us, does not contain meaning, but rather brings it out as a surrounding medium, acting itself as a virtual source of illumination which must be perceived in that which, outside itself, it illuminates: 'as a glow brings out a haze', in the manner of a misty halo made visible 'by the spectral illumination of moonshine'. Marlow's tale makes the darkness visible.

4

ADAPTATIONS

Adaptations

As from John Powell's visit to Conrad in 1910, the novella has generated creative efforts in different media. The American composer and pianist offered to adapt it for an opera libretto. Following Conrad's advice, he chose instead to compose *Rhapsodie negre* (1917) for piano and orchestra.

Nine films have been inspired by the novella but only three are available now, on videotape/DVD, and I will discuss these.[1] The most famous is Francis Ford Coppola's *Apocalypse Now* (1979). Coppola consciously used the novella as an intertext in making his film and firmly indicates this by the fact that the central figures in both are similar in character and both named Kurtz. Conrad's name originally appeared in the screen credits but was deleted after one of the listed writers protested through the Screen Writers' Guild. In *Apocalypse Now*, the equivalent to the frame narrator in the novella, is the camera. It is a truism that the camera gives a point of view and comments. During the opening scene in Willard's darkened hotel room in Saigon, the camera enters his mind and sees through his eyes as it gives shots of the greenness of palm trees streaming into war's poisonous gases, the green fronds of palm trees, helicopter rotors and blades of the fan, all in clever montage, and establishes him as the film's vantage point. Yet, just as the novella is narrated through Marlow's eyes but Conrad goes beyond this by presenting a view of the teller and his idiosyncrasies, *Apocalypse Now* is narrated through Willard but the camera is free to move beyond Willard's viewpoint. Unlike Marlow who has absorbed his Congo experience and is now calm in his acquired wisdom, Willard is still in the grip of his nightmarish experience.

Phrases in the film echo those in *Heart of Darkness* as when the American managerial powers summon Willard and commission him to 'terminate [Kurtz] with extreme prejudice'. They admit that Kurtz was 'one of the most outstanding officers this country has ever produced, a good man too, a humanitarian man', but then 'his ideas, methods become unsound'. They charge him with murder and insanity, and play a recording of Kurtz's voice as evidence. Willard 'wanted a

---

1   The other films are: 1955 Camera Three WCBS-TV production, 1958 CBS-TV Playhouse 90 show with Boris Karloff as Kurtz, 1968 Italian Documento Film adaptation, 1977 French *Le Crabe-Tambour* based on Pierre Schoendoerffer's novel inspired by Conrad, 1978 Spanish-Arando Films version, 1995 BBC-TV reading of the story with background footage.

mission' and accepts the one given him. He, however, finds it problematic from the beginning. He could not connect up the voice on the tape with the man. He later wonders 'what they had against Kurtz. It wasn't just insanity and murder. There was enough of that to go around for everybody.' He 'recognizes, like Marlow, that Kurtz merely externalizes and makes visible the far greater barbarism, cruelty, and hypocrisy of the invading "civilized" nation.'[2] It later becomes clear that the real reason for the resentment of the high command against Kurtz was that he was not following their programme, stepping out of line and still being successful, a fact that amounted to a criticism of them.

From 1955 to 1975, South Vietnam and the United States made a protracted and unsuccessful effort to prevent the communists of North Vietnam from uniting South Vietnam with North Vietnam under their leadership. Coppola focuses on the American military involvement. E.N. Dorall argues that the 'film is about war, not colonization'.[3] If we use the term 'imperialism' rather than 'colonization', it becomes clear that the film is about a form of imperialism. The war is an expression of imperialistic aspirations. Vietnam is the hot tip of the Cold War. Imperialism with acquisitiveness, brutality and violence, is common to both the film and the novella, atrocities in Vietnam parallel those in the Congo – though the types of imperialism are different. ' "Defending democracy" was the American equivalent of the "civilizing work" ' of the European imperialists in the age of Empire.[4]

To begin his Marlow-like journey up the river [Nung] to confront Kurtz, Willard has to depend on the U.S. Air Cavalry and its Captain, Kil[l]gore, presented satirically, his name emblematic of his character and of certain trends in American expansionism and militarism on distant battlegrounds. Kilgore has two options to enter the river, 'both hot', and he chooses Charlie's Point because it is good for surfing, revealing self-indulgence. He says: 'I love the smell of napalam in the morning. That gasoline smell . . . Smells like victory.' Yet Kilgore is not merely destructive, he inspires his men. He has to launch a successful assault and uses air power. The projection in terms of visual and sound effects is spectacular. The camera captures the menacing grace of the planes. Wagner's 'Ride of the Valkyries' is employed not just for sound effects but to demoralize the Vietcong. Like the use of the ivory piano keys of the Intended, the use of Wagner implicates high culture in imperialism and also adds a further critical note when we realize that Wagner inspired the Nazis. [*Apocalypse Now* presents such scintillating and complex aural – and visual – montages (aeroplane noises, music, silence, echoes etc.) that Coppola coined a new title, 'sound designer' to describe Walter Murch's contribution.] On the Vietcong side, the camera focuses on unarmed natives, women, children and straw huts. The American military machine seems absurdly formidable and the Americans guilty of murderous irresponsibility.

Heart of Darkness and *Apocalypse Now* have much in common, but they are set in different times and different locations. Coppola's film mirrors a period

2   Margot Norris, 'A Choice of Nightmares: Reading "Heart of Darkness" through *Apocalypse Now*', in *Approaches to Teaching Conrad's 'Heart of Darkness' and 'The Secret Sharer'*, p. 120.
3   Dorall, 'Conrad and Coppola: Different Centers of Darkness', in *Joseph Conrad: Heart of Darkness*, ed. Robert Kimdrough, NY: Norton, 1988 edn, p. 306.
4   Seymour Chatman, '2 ½ film versions of *Heart of Darkness*', in *Conrad on Film*, ed. Gene M. Moore, Cambridge UP, 1997, p. 215.

which no longer even posits a polarity between what is morally permissible and what is not. 'Good' and 'evil' were distinct enough in Conrad's and Nietzsche's time for it to be an immense step (a transgression, perhaps) to go beyond both. Now, or rather even as far back as Vietnam, where there was not only killing but the destruction of growth and fertility, surely, it is the Agent Orange that spreads through the foliage. Nothing but destruction exists. In the 1890s, Marlow can be a morally better man, saner, more controlled, more benevolent that Kurtz; now society/the Establishment itself empowers Willard's brutal sacrifice of Kurtz. Indeed, the natives' sacrificial slaying of the ox has more reverent attitude to this source of sustenance than the killing of the renegade Kurtz or the beast hoisted skyward by the helicopter, a source of rare steaks consumed in a consumerist society in its militaristic aspect (for Willard and his companions in the Mess scene and for Kilgore's men). Beef is the staff of life to Americans; the film gives prominence to the ox and brings to the surface that beef involves slaughter.

Just as *Heart of Darkness* alludes to imperialisms beyond the Congo, *Apocalypse Now* widens its scope beyond Vietnam. Margot Norris points out how it alludes to both the American genocide of native Indians (in Kilgore's cowboy hat and the Playboy girls' costumes and 'Cowboys and Indians' number during the USO show) and slavery (by the references to Abraham Lincoln during Willard's briefing and by the presence of African Americans among the boat's crew).[5] As Willard travels up the Nung in the boat, he reads Kurtz's dossier given him at the army headquarters. His personality, like Marlow's, is invaded by Kurtz, a sense of unwilling and forceful intrusion. Willard moves over to Kurtz's side: 'The more I read and began to understand, the more I admired him.' Like *Heart of Darkness*, *Apocalypse Now* is a journey into the interior, deeper into war, man growing increasingly bestial, showing the dark underside of civilization, as well as an interior journey, a journey into the self of both Willard and Kurtz.

Willard's last stop is at the Do Lung Bridge. The visual and sound effects make the scene surreal. There is complete confusion there; no commanding officer is to be found. In order to advance, the Americans build the bridge by day; it is destroyed in the night by the Vietcong. The whole sequence communicates the futility of the American enterprise. The approach to Kurtz, in the novella and in the film, is through a white fog. Like Marlow's steamer, Willard's boat is attacked by natives – to prevent Kurtz being taken away. Like Marlow's helmsman, Willard's helmsman is killed. Willard's crew want to return home and, ironically, they are attacked while reading their letters and listening to their tapes from home; the young African American Clean dies while his mother's voice speaks of her family's affection for him, pleading with him to return home in one piece.

When Marlow approaches Kurtz's compound, he sees the heads on the posts around it through a telescope, and Conrad *conveys* the shock via miniaturizing the scene. Coppola, on the other hand, shows a profusion of bodies hanging from trees and heads protruding from the ground to create a visual shock, the profusion compelling the audience to *share* the shock. The equivalent of the Harlequin is the photo-journalist whom Willard meets before Kurtz. The Harlequin is a 'holy fool' but the photo-journalist is far more knowledgeable and cynical, as is

---

5   Norris, 'A Choice of Nightmares', p. 121.

suited to his profession and period, a sort of hippie radical; both are alike in their admiration of Kurtz. Linda Costanzo Cahir describes the photo-journalist as 'crazed'[6] but he is really not so. He is under Kurtz's spell, yet he can say: 'The man is clear in his mind but his soul is mad.'

The climactic sequence between Kurtz and Willard is slow and muted to underline the film's final wisdom. Kurtz, like Conrad's Kurtz, is murderous but impressive. He explains his life. Its turning-point was the episode when the Americans inoculated Vietnamese children against polio and the Vietcong then hacked off every inoculated arm. He drew a lesson: 'You had to have men who are moral and, at the same time, are able to utilize their amoral instincts to kill without feeling, without passion, without judgment, because it is judgment that defeats us.' The camera focuses and lays stress on Frazer's *The Golden Bough* and Jessie L. Weston's *From Ritual to Romance* which shows that Coppola is addressing himself not just to the general audience but to an intellectual audience. Kurtz's mind has been working on these books, judging by his words. He wants to die, not as a sordid renegade, but 'standing up, like a soldier'. In fact, these books have induced in him a conception of himself as becoming a God by dying for his people. The killing of Kurtz and the killing of the ox by his 'children' are parallel sacrificial acts. This anthropological element does not originate from *Heart of Darkness* but from T.S. Eliot's use of these two books in *The Waste Land* and his use of phrases from the novella for the epigraph and title of 'The Hollow Men' which Coppola, evidently finding Eliot's vision apposite, makes Kurtz read. Kurtz is aware that he is deteriorating and, when the King is past his prime, he must die to promote the fertility of the fields. Kurtz, then, consents to his death. Willard kills him but does not complete the corollary of accepting Kurtz's mantle. Kurtz describes Willard who first arrives at his camp as 'an errand boy sent by grocery clerks to collect a bill', but Willard, shaken by his experience, not interested in reward, returns to his own world a wiser man. The conclusion of the film has no equivalent to the scene with the Intended (nor an equivalent to Kurtz's African woman), but Kurtz wants Willard to go to his home and tell his son 'everything', revealing an affection and honesty as a saving grace.

The film strikes a deeper note of negation than the novella. Marlow is guilty in so far as he is implicated in the imperial system. Willard is more culpable in a different era. Marlow subscribes to a code of conduct, a code of decencies, and shows fellow-feeling for the Africans, whereas Willard, a hired assassin, does not subscribe to any such codes and does/says nothing to contradict the references to the Vietnamese as 'savages'. Marlow has defences against darkness – work, restraint, standards, unshaken values in the Victorian age. Coppola deals with an era when all values are questioned.

Apocalypse Now is a fascinating, involving and also very demanding film, a cinematic masterpiece that has grown from a literary masterpiece.

Nicolas Roeg's *Heart of Darkness* (1994) is closer to the externals of the novella. His postcolonial Marlow is sensitive, but less complex than Conrad's Marlow conditioned by Victorian values of patriotism, duty and restraint which

---

6   Cahir, *'Narratological Parallels in Joseph Conrad's "Heart of Darkness" and Francis Ford Coppola's "Apocalypse Now"'*, in *Joseph Conrad's Heart of Darkness: A Casebook*, ed. Gene M. Moore, Oxford & New York: Oxford UP, 2004, p. 192.

conflict with his empathic visions of atavistic liberation. Roeg simply condemns imperialism; Conrad, in his time, though bound by its imperatives, cuts deeper. As the film opens, Marlow on his boat docked at the wharf addresses the director, accountant and lawyer of the Company which sent him out: 'It was one of the dark places of the earth – the vilest scramble for loot that ever disfigured the history of human conscience and geographical exploration.' The camera visually stresses the inequity/iniquity of a colonial economy by showing Europeans trading beads for ivory, the brutality of the colonizers by showing the lashing of an African alleged to have burnt a shed full of European goods, and the fact that the colony is Belgian by focusing on a photograph of King Leopold. The film, like the novella, presents the two knitting women in the Company office as Fates, brooding figures which haunt Marlow's dreams.

Reflecting current concerns regarding racism and feminism, Roeg gives space to Africans and women. The Africans bulk larger than in the novella. The easy relationship between European and African, between boy and master, seem hardly Victorian or in keeping with a colonial milieu. Moreover, Roeg unwittingly divests the Africans of a dignity which Conrad projects: Mfumu's 'Eat him' sounds ferocious, ogre-like in contrast to the curt, matter-of-factness of Conrad's cannibal, just as Marlow pushing an African away from Mfumu's corpse and saying 'Don't touch him' implies that the crew would greedily (since their starvation is elided) consume their mate then and there. Though Roeg develops Marlow's friendship with the helmsman, Marlow's 'Goodbye, my friend' to the dying man comes across as less significant than Conrad's rendering of Marlow's recognition of the final look of kinship/intimacy. Similarly, Roeg's multiplicity of women (the accountant's invisible laundress becomes obtrusive and flirtatious; an additional black matron at the Central Station casts knowing glances) reduces the impact of Kurtz's woman – who is further robbed of the majesty and power Conrad gives her, as she is shown slinking around Kurtz's quarters, or petulantly hurling some object.

Even Africa is scaled down: the Congo is a nondescript little stream; the jungle seedy, no massive obsessive presence. It is merely background, not a metaphor for an interior journey: thus, the metaphor is stated but not shown. Kurtz says: 'The jungle, you see, has . . . designs on everything. It is an immeasurable assault on ordinary human understanding. It blooms in mischief. It invites you to dig down into yourself. But it is dangerous to tear away the layers from our thoughts and look into the abyss.' Living in a jungle and losing touch with society and its rules, Kurtz, looking impressive and weary, thinks over darkness. Marlow shares Kurtz's vision. He blocks the director's 'But *you* returned' with 'Did I?' He is still at the heart of darkness, having seen the depths to which a man (civilized, intellectual and an inspired artist) can sink as well as the absurdity of life tied to death. He tells the director that the import of Kurtz's 'documents' is 'not scientific' but 'philosophic'. There is more stress on Kurtz as an artist than in the novella – the paintings are visual equivalents of Kurtz's manifold skills, as journalist, demagogue, painter, etc. In the accountant's quarters there is a portrait of the Intended, austerely clothed in black, while one in Kurtz's dwelling is nude, indicating his increasing sensuality/sensual rapacity. The Harlequin (a good cinematic equivalent to the character in the novella) has stayed in Kurtz's area only because he is under Kurtz's spell. His loud laughter expresses not only his simplicity and eccentricity but his instinctive joy at having white company, yet he leaves them because 'I will not see that man again'.

The film also reveals the 1990s interest in ecology. The credits are shot against a dead elephant's hide, suggesting the slaughter of elephants necessitated by the ivory trade. The camera focuses on the masses of tusks at Kurtz's station. Kurtz, confronted with the prospect of death, accustomed to dealing it, having gone beyond human limits, kills his pet monkey, perhaps Roeg's condemnation of the deprivation of freedom and security from abuse suffered by domesticated animals, underlining the issue of animal rights. Marlow's shock and concern are shared by the audience.

Roeg's film attempts to strike a compromise between Conrad and recent concerns/attitudes and suffers as a consequence, yet remains an interesting, albeit simplistic, version of the novella.

The wide appeal of Conrad's novella is shown by popular versions where connections with the original are tenuous. It is a launching pad for *Cannibal Women in the Avocado Jungle of Death* (1988), directed by J.F. Lawton. It is a spoof of the novella, *Apocalypse Now*, adventure films, and also a social and political satire on the gender debate and governmental pressures on academia – campy at a higher level. 'California is the last secure supply of avocados in the free world', but the Piranha women – 'an ancient commune of feminists, so radical, so militant, so left of centre, they . . . eat their men' – now led by a feminist writer, Dr Francine Kurtz, 'a renegade ethnographer' (like Colonel Kurtz, the renegade officer), are preventing the harvest of avocados. Dr Margo Hunt, a feminist professor, is sent by National Security to negotiate. Accompanied by Bunny, her dumb adoring student, and equally dumb Jim, hired as guide, Margo goes up river into the deadly jungle (like Marlow and Willard). They are attacked (like Marlow and Willard) – with potholders by a group of feminized men who, converted to macho men via beer by Jim, attempt to gang-rape Bunny, and encounter the Barracuda women who are at war with the Piranha because 'men should be eaten with clam sauce, not guacamole', since women fight about trivial matters! Margo, finally, confronts Kurtz (like Marlow and Willard). Kurtz explains why she had gone over the edge and joined the Piranha: 'the horror', her reaction to a talk show about her feminist book. The spoof appears frivolous but the underlying satire is smart, and the film, despite its low budget, is a competent take-off of *King Solomon's Mines* (see Text and contexts, p. 9f.).

In 1995, the Sixties' trouper Marianne Faithful teamed up with hippie poet Heathcote William to compose a pop song based on the novella.

The novella's basic convention, the first person narrator, is ideal for a radio rendering, as Orson Welles realized. He directed and starred in two half-hour dramatizations: the first for *Mercury Theatre on the Air* on 6 November 1938 and the second on 13 March 1945 to launch a series titled *This Is My Best*. In between he tried to produce a film version, but it ran over the budget and was abandoned. He made *Citizen Kane* instead.

These offshoots/outgrowths, profound, frivolous or mediocre, testify to the inescapable impact on the contemporary consciousness of *Heart of Darkness*/the original.

5

Further reading and web resources

Further reading

Recommended edition of *Heart of Darkness*:

D.C.R.A. Goonetilleke (ed.), *Joseph Conrad: Heart of Darkness*, Peterborough, Ontario, Canada & New York, Broadview Press, 2nd edn 1999, reprinted 2003.

This edition includes a reliable text, an introduction and explanatory notes as well as a fascinating variety of contemporary documents and photographs that help to set this extraordinary work in the context of the period from which it emerged.

General Reference

Owen Knowles and Gene M. Moore, *Oxford Reader's Companion to Conrad*, Oxford: Oxford UP, 2000. – Conrad encyclopedia.

Imperialism and literature – in general

D.C.R.A. Goonetilleke, *Developing Countries in British Fiction*, London: Macmillan, New Jersey: Rowman & Littlefield, 1977 – studies the British reactions to the developing countries (mainly of Conrad, Kipling, Forster, D.H. Lawrence, Joyce Cary) in the age of Empire.

Patrick Brantlinger, *Rule of Darkness: British Literature and Imperialism, 1830–1914*, Ithaca, NY, & London: Cornell UP, 1988.

Edward Said, *Culture and Imperialism*, London: Chatto, 1993 (see Critical history, p. 66).

Joseph Conrad – biography

Jocelyn Baines, *Joseph Conrad: A Critical Biography*, London: Weidenfeld, 1993 edn (see Critical history, p. 54).

Zdzislaw Najder, *Joseph Conrad: A Chronicle*, Cambridge: Cambridge UP, 1983; rev. edn *Joseph Conrad: A Life*, Camden House, 2007 (see Critical history, **pp. 58–9**).

Sources/background

Norman Sherry, *Conrad's Western World*, Cambridge: Cambridge UP, 1971 (see Critical history, **p. 56**).

Peter Edgerly Firchow, *Envisioning Africa: Racism and Imperialism in Conrad's Heart of Darkness*, Kentucky: Kentucky UP, 2000 (see Critical history, **p. 66**).

Literary/cultural contexts

Ian Watt, *Conrad in the Nineteenth Century*, London: Chatto & Windus, 1980 (see Critical History, **pp. 57–8**).

Andrea White, *Joseph Conrad and the Adventure Tradition*, Cambridge: Cambridge UP, 1993 (see Critical history, **pp. 66–7**).

Peter Childs, *Modernism*, London: Routledge, 2005 edn – introduction to this literary and cultural revolution in the late nineteenth and early twentieth centuries.

H. Rider Haggard, *King Solomon's Mines*, 1885, any edition, (see Literary context, **pp. 9–11**).

Joseph Conrad, 'An Outpost of Progress', 1898, any edition – if compared with *Heart of Darkness*, this shows expansion of Conrad's interests and technique.

Historical context

Adam Hochschild, *King Leopold's Ghost: A Story of Greed, Terror and Heroism in Colonial Africa*, London: Pan, 2002 edn – a comprehensive history of the Congo under Leopold.

Georges Nzongola-Ntalaja, *The Congo from Leopold to Kabila: A People's History*, London & New York: Zed Books, 2002 – for developments after Leopold to the present.

Studies of Conrad

Edward Said, *Joseph Conrad and the Fiction of Autobiography*, Cambridge, MA: Harvard UP, 1966 (see Critical history, **pp. 65–6**).

Benita Parry, *Conrad and Imperialism*, London: Macmillan, 1983 (see Critical history, **p. 62**).

Jakob Lothe, *Conrad's Narrative Method*, Oxford: Clarendon, 1989 – an important book on its subject.

D.C.R.A. Goonetilleke, *Joseph Conrad: Beyond Culture and Background*, London: Macmillan, New York: St. Martin's, 1990 – invokes culture and background and, at the same time, shows how incompletely these account for Conrad's achievement.

Robert Hampson, *Joseph Conrad: Betrayal and Identity*, London: Macmillan, 1992 (see Critical history, **p. 65**).

A.M. Roberts, *Conrad and Masculinity*, Basingstoke & New York: Palgrave, 2000 (see Critical history, **pp. 67–8**).

J.H. Stape (ed.), *The Cambridge Companion to Joseph Conrad*, Cambridge: Cambridge UP, 1996 – essays on general topics as well as specific texts.

Casebooks/editions of *Heart of Darkness*

Harold Bloom (ed.), *Joseph Conrad's Heart of Darkness: Modern Critical Interpretations*, New York: Chelsea House, 1987 – selected interpretations 1966–85.

Ross C. Murfin (ed.), *Joseph Conrad, Heart of Darkness: A Case Study in Contemporary Criticism*, New York: St. Martin, 1996 edn – offers a view of recent critical trends – the psychoanalytic, reader-response, feminist, deconstructive, new historicist – in five essays.

Hunt Hawkins & Brian W. Shaffer (ed.), *Approaches to Teaching Conrad's 'Heart of Darkness' and 'The Secret Sharer'*, New York: Modern Language Association of America, 2002 – addressed to teachers, it would benefit students too, especially its discussions of social contexts, literary issues and controversies.

John Armstrong (ed.), *Joseph Conrad: Heart of Darkness*, New York: Norton, 2005 – for alternative interpretations and background material.

Critical history

Nicholas Tredell (ed.), *Joseph Conrad: Heart of Darkness*, New York: Columbia UP, 1998 – a critical guide from 1899 to the early 1990s with generous extracts.

Adaptations

Gene M. Moore (ed.), *Conrad on Film*, Cambridge: Cambridge UP, 1997 – the best book on the subject.

Gene D. Phillips, *Conrad and Cinema: The Art of Adaptation*, New York: Peter Lang, 1997 – elementary but the only other book-length study of the subject.

Journals

Conradiana: A Journal of Joseph Conrad Studies (USA)
The Conradian: Journal of the Joseph Conrad Society (UK)
– these journals often carry articles on *Heart of Darkness*.

Web resources

http://books.guardian.co.uk/review/story/0,12084,900102,00.html – 'Out of Africa': Caryl Phillips interviews Chinua Achebe, 2003; Achebe restates his view of *Heart of Darkness*.

http://www.postcolonialweb.org – for background regarding postcolonial perspectives, theories of colonialism and postcolonialism.

http://www.victorianweb.org – for background information regarding Victorian culture, the initial publication context of *Heart of Darkness*.

http://social.chass.ncsu.edu/wyrick/debclass/Ssmith.htm – an analysis of *Heart of Darkness* from the Marxist perspective.

http://www.lawrence.edu/dept/FRESHMAN_STUDIES/YATZECK_HEART.HTML – a freshman's lecture on *Heart of Darkness*.

University of Virginia online library – see also Electronic Text Center at UVa Library.

http://www.sparknotes.com/lit/heart – a useful, if simple, introduction to *Heart of Darkness*.

http://web.cocc.edu/cagatucci/classes/eng109/HeartSG.htm – itemized questions about the text, a reading guide.

http://school.discovery.com//lessonplans/programs/heartofdarkness – introduction to the text at high school level.

http://pinkmonkey.com/booknotes/monkeynotes/pmHeartDarkness01.asp – introduction to the text at high school level.

http://www.imdb.com – for comments on adaptations.

Index